Allergy-free
COOKBOOK

Allergy-free COOKBOOK

Alice Sherwood

DK

DK

LONDON, NEW YORK, MELBOURNE, MUNICH, DELHI

Project editor Helen Murray   **Senior editor** Esther Ripley
US editor Jane Perlmutter   **US senior editor** Jill Hamilton
Project designer Vicky Read   **Senior art editor** Anne Fisher
DTP designer Sonia Charbonnier   **Jacket designer** Nicola Powling
Production controller Luca Frassinetti   **Managing editor** Penny Warren
Managing art editor Marianne Markham   **Art director** Peter Luff
Creative publisher Mary-Clare Jerram   **Medical advisor** Adam Fox
Home economist Carolyn Humphries   **Food styling** Sarah Tildesley
Photographer Kate Whitaker   **Photography art direction** Luis Peral

Every effort has been made to ensure that the information
contained in this book is complete and accurate. However, neither
the publisher nor the author is engaged in rendering professional
advice or services to the individual reader. Professional medical
advice should be obtained on personal health matters. Neither the
publisher nor the author accept any legal responsibility for any
personal injury or other damage or loss arising from the use or
misuse of the information and advice in this book.

First American Edition, 2007
This paperback edition, 2009
Published in the United States by
DK Publishing, 375 Hudson Street, New York, New York 10014
09 10 11 10 9 8 7 6 5 4 3 2 1
175215—09/2009

DK books are available at special discounts when purchased in bulk for
sales promotions, premiums, fund-raising, or educational use. For details,
contact: DK Publishing Special Markets, 375 Hudson Street, New York,
New York 10014 or SpecialSales@dk.com.

A catalog record for this book is available from the Library of
Congress. ISBN 978-0-7566-5440-5

Printed and bound in Singapore by Star Standard Singapore

Discover more at
www.dk.com

Once a medical curiosity, food allergy has increased dramatically over the past 30 years, even being referred to as an epidemic. When I make a diagnosis of food allergy, I have become increasingly aware that this has implications not just for the patient attending my clinic but also for their extended family and friends, both present and future. With so much of our lives revolving around food, the impact of needing to avoid just a single food can be huge. Invitations to dinner parties and social gatherings become a source of embarrassment and anxiety rather than enjoyment. A simple trip to the supermarket can become a lengthy series of food label examinations and a family trip abroad, if even considered, a delicate military operation.

Some families respond to the allergy of one of its members by severely restricting the foods that the whole family eats. This fear of contact with certain foods leads to a reliance on a small group of bland ingredients. As a result, the diet may be safe but also very boring and repetitive, not to mention resented by those who do not actually have the allergy themselves. Other families try to limit only the diet of the affected person but this can lead to feelings of isolation at mealtimes as well as the extra effort of trying to provide two different meals for one sitting.

Alice Sherwood has taken an altogether more positive approach. Instead of focusing on restrictions, she has found ways to sidestep them in her own favorite dishes, as well as exploring the cuisine of other cultures. Her imaginative approach to replacing common allergenic ingredients has paid dividends—a collection of recipes that allow the whole family to enjoy delicious creations without anybody feeling left out. However, this book is far more than just a collection of recipes. Alice's positive attitude toward the challenges faced by a family with a food allergic child reveals an insight that could be offered only by somebody with first hand experience. You have probably picked up this book with the hope of finding some inspiration for the kitchen. You will certainly find that here—as well as a lot more besides.

Bon Appetit!

Adam Fox

Dr. Adam Fox
MA(Hons), MB, BS, MRCPCH
Consultant Paediatric Allergist,
Guy's and St Thomas' Hospitals NHS Foundation Trust, London

5   Foreword
8   Introduction
11 How to use this book

Living with allergies

14 What are food allergies?
22 Staying positive
24 Allergy etiquette
26 Your allergic child
29 Eating out
30 Special occasions
31 Traveling hopefully
32 Worldwide cuisine
36 Shopping
40 What not to eat
43 So much food to enjoy
45 Your pantry
48 Substituting ingredients

The recipes

BREAKFASTS
52 Honey granola
54 Croissants
57 Pancakes
58 Corned beef hash
59 Smoothies
62 Cinnamon, raisin, & apple muffins
63 Blueberry muffins
65 Chocolate croissants
67 Kedgeree

SIDE DISHES, APPETIZERS, & LIGHT MEALS
68 Tortillas
70 Tortilla chips
71 Herb dip
72 Crostini & toppings
74 California temaki sushi
76 Blini with smoked salmon
77 Chicken fajitas
79 Chicken drumsticks
80 Soy-honey glazed sausages
81 Grilled polenta
83 Seven-layer dip
84 Bacon & onion quiche
85 Gazpacho
86 Leek & butternut squash soup
89 Crispy squid
90 Fresh spring rolls
91 Tabbouleh
    Cucumber & wakame salad
92 Middle Eastern salad
94 Gratin gallois
95 Roast potatoes with garlic & sea salt

FISH, MEAT, & POULTRY
96   Fish pie
98   Tandoori fish
99   Marinated swordfish
101 Miso marinated salmon
102 Potato-crusted halibut
103 Shrimp dumplings
105 Scallops & shrimp with lentils
106 Chicken pie
108 Chicken, olive, & chickpea stew
109 Lemon thyme grilled chicken

Contents

111 Thai green chicken curry
114 Chicken roasted in olive oil
115 Duck with apples & celeriac
116 Fegato alla Veneziana
117 Ragu Bolognese
118 Osso buco
120 Vitello tonnato
121 Meatloaf
122 Chili con carne
124 Vietnamese beef stew
126 Chinese-style spare ribs
127 Roast pork with fennel
128 Moussaka
130 Classic shepherd's pie
131 Spinach & yogurt lamb curry
132 Honeyed Welsh lamb
135 Lamb tagine

PASTA, NOODLES, & RICE
136 Lasagne al forno
139 Haddock & spinach pasta bake
141 Pasta with arugula
142 Noodles in hot ginger broth
144 Basmati & wild rice pilaf
145 Risotto alla Milanese

DESSERTS
146 Plum crumble
149 Apple tart
150 Classic rice pudding
151 Fragrant poached peaches
154 Petits pots au chocolat
155 Sweet chestnut terrine
156 Green tea ice cream
158 Mango yogurt ice
159 Coconut sorbet
     Rhubarb sorbet
161 Panna cotta
162 Crêpes

BREADS & BAKING
164 Brown bread
167 Quick soda bread
168 White farmhouse loaf
170 French-style bread
173 Focaccia
174 Southern skillet cornbread

176 Northern cornbread
177 Spiced yogurt raisin bread
179 Pizza Margherita
180 Piecrust
183 Shortbread
184 Raisin scones
186 Giant chocolate chip cookies
187 Gingerbread
188 Fruity oatmeal squares
189 Chocolate crinkle cookies
192 Vanilla cupcakes
193 Chocolate brownies
194 Raspberry mallow crispies
195 Lemon syrup polenta cake
196 Chocolate layer cake
199 Rich fruit cake
200 Dark chocolate torte
201 Peach-topped cheesecake
203 Carrot cake
204 Fresh fruit & cream gâteau
207 Chocolate truffles

SAUCES, DRESSINGS, & ACCOMPANIMENTS
208 Béchamel sauce
209 Roast garlic tofu aïoli
210 Mayonnaise
     Vietnamese dipping sauce
211 Pesto
     Red pepper dip
212 Asian slaw
213 Raita
     Tarragon dressing
214 Chestnut stuffing
215 Vegetable gravy
216 Chantilly topping
     Cashew cream

218 Resources
221 Index
224 Acknowledgments

Introduction

There are many good reasons for writing a cookbook. Mine are love of good food and cooking and a desire to share the food I love with friends and family. However, I had a very important extra reason: I wanted to produce a fantastic cookbook that would also work for people who can't eat certain foods because I have a child who is allergic to two foods: eggs and nuts. Later, as it turned out, I found quite a few friends were avoiding dairy and wheat, but Archie's allergies were the starting point.

I was also spurred on to write *The Allergy-free Cookbook* for the simplest and most classic of reasons: it is the book that I couldn't find when I needed it. I was looking for a cookbook that was as full of beautiful, mouth-watering recipes and enticing pictures as any of the glossy books that already graced my bookshelf. But I wanted one that empathized with people with food hypersensitivities and the difficulties they encounter, while not treating them either as marginal medical cases or as hypochondriacs. There should be dishes, I felt, that people could eat together without even realizing they were dairy free or egg free.

"Dining with one's friends and beloved family is certainly one of life's primal and most innocent delights, one that is both soul-satisfying and eternal," Julia Child wrote. I wanted an allergy-friendly cookbook that kept that notion at its core. Lastly, I wanted to concentrate on freshly prepared food made of healthy ingredients, using the vegetables from my garden as well as the haul from my local supermarket.

Our world turned upside down

My own path to understanding how allergy and intolerance affect your life, and what you can do to make the best of living with them, is similar to many. My elder son, Archie, was diagnosed as allergic to eggs, nuts, and peanuts, although his younger brother, Ben, is not. It turned our world upside down. It was frankly scary to accept that normally harmless foods can be lethal to my child. I needed a helping hand to learn to deal with the problems of never being able to go out to dine or to a party without carrying a packed meal. Favorite foods were suddenly out of bounds and simple things like eating at other people's houses became a minefield. People, it transpired, were actually scared to invite us for dinner. It took me a long time to find out what I needed to know and how to explain it to other people.

However, as I talked to other people I realized that Archie and I weren't alone. I found friends whose children had been diagnosed as celiac; lactose intolerance among both colleagues at work and parents at my son's school; neighbors' children who couldn't touch nuts or peanuts; and adults who had given up dairy or wheat for a variety of health, diet, and lifestyle reasons. We shared experiences and found similar problems, not least the difficulty of explaining to other people what the problems are and how to ask them for help.

Eat everything you can

As I began to plan and develop my recipes I became increasingly wary of the "one size fits all" allergen-free concoctions (recipes that are simultaneously dairy free, egg free, nut free, and gluten free, and quite often free of sesame, soy, fish and seafood, too) that I found in most allergy cookbooks. I couldn't see why not being able to eat one or two thing meant having no choice about the rest. My philosophy is—why avoid all those things if you don't need to? You will be missing out—not just on taste and enjoyment but quite possibly on nutrients, too. The health implications of that worried me, especially for anyone feeding young children.

▲ Alice passes on tips and techniques for allergy-safe cooking to her nine-year-old son, Archie.

The major food allergens

The US has a list of foods that are responsible for 90 percent of food allergies and must therefore be included on any package labeling. In the US, there are eight groups of these allergens: milk, eggs, fish, crustacean shellfish (such as shrimp), peanuts, tree nuts, wheat, and soy. In Canada, this list also includes sesame seeds and sulfites.

For the cook, four of these food groups are particularly difficult to avoid because they are used in so many different dishes, so in this cookbook I've chosen to focus on gluten (found in most grains, especially wheat); eggs; nuts (both tree nuts and peanuts); and dairy (by this, I mean milk and all products containing milk, such as cheese and yogurt).

Research shows that most people with food problems are actually allergic to, or intolerant of, only one or two foods. So it made sense to develop alternative versions to cater for each of my four food allergens in the recipes of this book. The premise and indeed the promise of this book is that every recipe has individually a gluten-free, a dairy-free, an egg-free, and a nut-free version. This means some recipes may have up to three versions, though others need only one.

Obviously you should avoid fish or seafood recipes if that's your problem. Although shellfish is the most common food allergy for adults in the US, I didn't want to leave it out of the book because, for people not allergic to seafood, it is delicious, nutritious, and adds variety to the diet. Sesame seeds are sprinkled on a few dishes but are easy to omit or replace. Soy appears only as a dairy substitute or as soy sauce. If soy is your allergy, you know that the problem is not the loss of a major nutrient or cooking ingredient, which soy isn't, but the fact that it is a key ingredient in so many processed foods.

People with multiple food allergies find life especially difficult and although this book cannot cater comprehensively for them, there are recipes that they will find immediately usable and others that can be adapted easily. More than a quarter of the recipes are free of all four groups; three-quarters are egg and nut free; and a fair proportion of these recipes are dairy or gluten free as well. "Watch out for" appears on some recipes to flag up other potential allergens, such as pine nuts, that may need to be omitted or replaced if you, or the person you are cooking for, is unable to tolerate them. These alerts also highlight hidden pitfalls for people who may not be attuned to the fine details of food sensitivity but want to cook for friends and family who have an allergy or intolerance. They should be encouraged!

forbidden foods. Some were general—toppings to use instead of nuts and which dairy-free milks taste best in which dishes—but some had to be precise, especially for baking; an egg substitute has to replace the same amount of liquid as one egg, and have a similar binding or raising power, too.

If the versions look different from each other or need a slightly different treatment, I've made a point of telling you. Where something is non-intuitive, like a cake batter that seems too liquid but works well when cooked, or gluten-free pastry that has a dryish feel that might tempt you to add more water (don't!), I've noted that. Every version

To make a chocolate birthday cake for a child who has to turn down treats at every party, and to see his face light up with pleasure, is my greatest triumph

My cooking
We live in London and spend vacations at my husband's family farm in rural mid-Wales, but my own culinary influences range from French and Mediterranean to Middle Eastern and Vietnamese. My recipes reflect this and range from pastas, risottos, tagines, and rice paper rolls to *panna cotta*, plum crumble, and apple tart. Some are inspired by my French mother's home cookery, some by the exceptional fresh produce we have in Wales. One of the joys of writing this book has been going deeper into new cuisines and discovering, for example, that many Thai and Japanese dishes are dairy free while Mexican tortillas, chili, and cornbread are usually naturally gluten free.

Authentic food is important to me. Classic recipes can sometimes be improved upon but why play around with them just for the sake of novelty? To make many of the recipes in egg-, dairy- and gluten-free forms involves innovative substitutions and unfamiliar ingredients, so I've adapted the classics only as much as I need to.

A new kind of cooking calls for a new confidence. I've built up a file of alternatives to

of every recipe has been tested by me, by home economist Carolyn Humphries, and also friends and family—people in real homes with unreliable ovens and drafty kitchens.

Celebrating food
This book celebrates food, whether it's fine dining for grown-ups or special treats for children's parties; home-cooked classics like shepherd's pie or exotics like hand-rolled sushi; decadent creamy desserts, chocolate-lovers' indulgences, or light tangy fruit sorbets. Whatever their food issues, people want to cook and eat wonderful food without any feeling of missing out. To make a chocolate birthday cake for my nut- and egg-allergic child, who has to turn down treats at every party he goes to, and to see his face light up with pleasure, is my greatest triumph.

For me, proving to Archie that a whole world of delicious food is open to him has been one of the most rewarding parts of producing this book. Whether you are using this book for yourself, your children, for friends, or family, I hope you enjoy cooking and eating these recipes as much as I do.

How to use this book

Every recipe in this book has been adapted and tested to create up to four different versions for each of the four major food sensitivities—eggs, gluten, nuts, and dairy. Use the symbols and text at the top of each recipe to guide you to the right version. Some recipes are naturally free of all four allergens so if you need a safe dish for guests with mixed allergies and intolerances, choose a recipe with all four symbols, such as Vietnamese beef stew (p.124) or Coconut sorbet (p.159). Alternatively, adapt a version to make it both dairy and gluten free, for example, by combining the gluten-free and dairy-free substitutions.

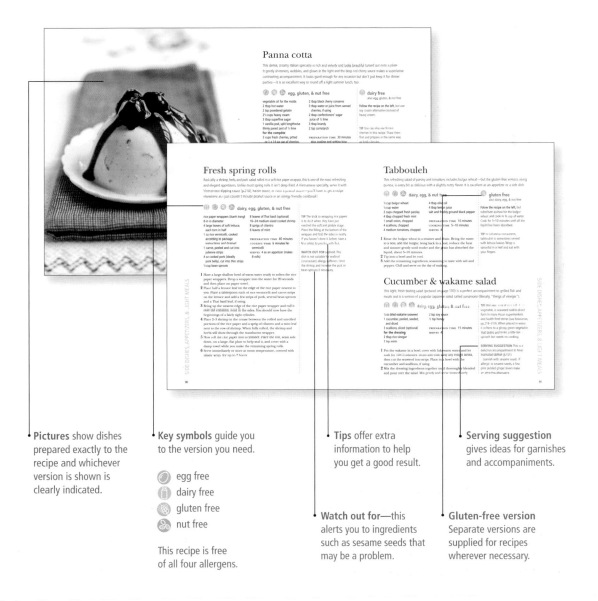

• **Pictures** show dishes prepared exactly to the recipe and whichever version is shown is clearly indicated.

• **Key symbols** guide you to the version you need.

  (◎) egg free
  (◎) dairy free
  (◎) gluten free
  (◎) nut free

  This recipe is free of all four allergens.

• **Tips** offer extra information to help you get a good result.

• **Watch out for**—this alerts you to ingredients such as sesame seeds that may be a problem.

• **Serving suggestion** gives ideas for garnishes and accompaniments.

• **Gluten-free version** Separate versions are supplied for recipes wherever necessary.

Living with allergies

What are food allergies?

There are many more allergies and food sensitivities around today and almost as many explanations why. Those who regard them as a "disease of modern society" cite factors such as environmental chemicals and pollution. Perversely, better diagnosis has also increased the numbers reported. Some specialists adhere to the theory that improvements in hygiene and medical science have helped weaken our immune systems. A further explanation is that we've evolved at a different and slower rate than our diets and that we are eating so many new foods that our bodies can no longer cope.

Whatever the causes, allergies and intolerances are now part of our collective experience and, although they're not contagious illnesses, they do affect the way people live. You will find multiple sources of information and advice on the subject and much of it is confusing, conflicting, and incorrect. My aim here is not to diagnose your allergy or intolerance, which should obviously be done only by a physician, but to highlight the essentials to help you get the best from this cookbook. If you don't suffer from a food problem yourself but want to cook for someone who does, what you read here should help you better understand what might be needed.

▼ Party food—olives, caperberries, rice crackers, and root vegetable crisps steer clear of most major food allergens.

What does it mean?

Rather confusingly, people use the words allergy, intolerance, and sensitivity interchangeably and to refer to a multitude of different things. Allergy specialists refer to allergies as "true" or "classical" allergies, in contrast to intolerances and sensitivities, which are harder to pinpoint. In everyday speech, people use "I'm allergic to it" to mean anything from "it gives me a rash" to "I just don't like it."

Hypersensitivity is an umbrella term used to cover all types of allergy and intolerance but you need to be more precise and clear when you are trying to pinpoint, treat, plan for, or tell someone about a food sensitivity, especially where children and/or a life-threatening risk may be involved. You may find yourself discussing food issues with many different people from physicians, dietitians, and nurses to family, friends, schools, colleagues, airlines, and restaurants. There are some basic distinctions:
• **Classical food allergies** such as those to milk, eggs, and nuts are caused by the immune system. Reactions to them can be immediate as in anaphylaxis (see right) or delayed, for example eczema may get worse.
• **Food intolerances** are also reactions to foods but they don't involve the immune system and are not so clear-cut in either their symptoms or causes.
• **Celiac disease** is an auto-immune condition that causes chronic severe symptoms and has a specific diagnosis and treatment.

Classical or "true" allergies

All allergies, including food allergies, are the result of the body's immune system overreacting to a substance that is normally harmless. The immune system is a complex and sophisticated defense system that protects us from bacteria, viruses, parasites, some chemicals, and sometimes even cancer by identifying harmful proteins (antigens) and creating specific defenses to them (antibodies). Killer cells are produced to destroy invaders and protect the body.

Problems occur when the immune system wrongly interprets an otherwise harmless substance, such as a food, as an allergen, and the body's defenses kick in. Histamine is released, causing effects that range from troubling to life-threatening.

Reactions and symptoms

Many allergic reactions occur within a few minutes of exposure to the food in question. Reactions include itchy rashes that look a bit like hives and swelling of lips, tongue, face, and throat, which can be dangerous if they block the airway. Abdominal cramps, nausea, and vomiting may occur. The most serious reactions, known as anaphylaxis, are much rarer and are most frequently found in peanut and nut allergy sufferers. They have symptoms that are widespread within the body and occur frighteningly fast.

For an allergic reaction to occur, the body has to have had previous exposure to an allergen: This can be before birth if the food is eaten during pregnancy or after birth through breast milk, or through exposure to food products in the environment. After "sensitization"—the time it takes the body to build up a dislike for the allergen—the first reaction may be from the smallest amount. From then onward, unless a child grows out of an allergy, there will always be a reaction but it may vary in strength and severity.

Diagnosis and testing

Classical allergies can be diagnosed using several reliable medical tests but since hypersensitivity reactions to food can be caused by a number of things other than allergies, a certain amount of detective work may be needed. Your doctor will also carry out a physical examination, ask about your family's medical history and your own "food history," and may ask you to keep a food and symptom diary for a period of time.

ANAPHYLAXIS

Anaphylaxis is an extreme allergic reaction that is potentially life-threatening. Food triggers differ in adults and children but include peanuts, tree nuts (such as almonds, walnuts, cashews, and Brazils), fish, shellfish, dairy products, and eggs. Other causes include wasp or bee stings, natural latex (rubber), penicillin, or any other drug.

Initial signs of anaphylaxis usually start within seconds of contact with the allergen and may begin with a tingling sensation, itching, or a metallic taste in the mouth. Other symptoms can include:

- hives (urticaria) anywhere on the body
- a sensation of warmth
- severe asthma
- swelling of the mouth and throat area
- difficulty breathing
- vomiting and diarrhea
- cramping
- a drop in blood pressure
- loss of consciousness

Anaphylaxis is always an emergency so if you or someone else is having an attack, dial 911 for emergency help or get someone else to do it for you. If you have anaphylactic reactions, you will always need to be on the lookout for whatever triggers them and carry preloaded epinephrine (adrenaline) injection kits. These are used at the first sign of an attack. Even if you then recover, you still need to go to the hospital in an ambulance.

▼ An emergency kit for a person at risk of serious allergic reactions may include prescribed medicine, an inhaler, and an epinephrine injection pen. A MedicAlert® bracelet should be worn at all times.

Further specific tests to reach final diagnosis of food allergy and to identify which food(s) and other substances you react to include:

• **A clear history** of your allergic response to food, which can be enough to diagnose an allergy.

• **Skin prick tests,** which can diagnose allergies to foods, pollens, and house-dust mites among others. They help establish what you might be allergic to, as well as rule out substances.

• **A blood specific IgE (RAST) test,** which involves taking a blood sample for laboratory analysis. The antibodies produced in the blood are measured to establish the likelihood of an allergic reaction. Like any laboratory test, it has false positives and negatives.

• **Patch tests**—these involve applying test substances to the skin under adhesive tape, which is left in place for 48 hours. These tests are used to diagnose allergic contact dermatitis (inflammation of the skin) and some delayed allergic reactions to food. They need to be interpreted by an experienced allergist.

• **A food challenge** may be done to confirm or diagnose an allergy or to test if someone has grown out of it. The suspected allergen is given to the patient in controlled dosages in the hospital under medical supervision.

Because people grow out of some allergies, typically milk and egg, children should be tested regularly to see whether they are still allergic. By age five, about 80 percent grow out of milk allergies; about 50 percent out of egg allergies; and about 20 percent out of peanut allergies.

Tests to be cautious about

Many advertised tests are not scientifically proven and may not be valid. These include any tests, such as hair analysis, that are carried out by mail with no doctor present to do a physical examination or take your medical history. Also be wary of cytotoxic blood tests (because the rationale has been questioned and results can be inconsistent), pulse tests, pendulum tests, dowsing, and any tests that measure "energy fields or flows" either by physical or electrical means. Even IgE tests offered on the open market should be avoided because the results need to be interpreted by a clinician. If you take these seriously you run the

risk of failing to diagnose an allergy or conversely eliminating whole food groups containing valuable nutrients if falsely diagnosed. This is particularly serious in the case of children because a balanced diet is essential for healthy growth. No one should cut out whole food groups without medical advice and consultation with a registered dietitian.

Who has food allergies?

Some causes of food sensitivities tend to run in families; this predisposition to allergies is known as "atopy" and sufferers are described as "atopic." If asthma, eczema, hay fever (seasonal rhinitis), or hives (urticaria) run in your family, you are more likely to develop a food allergy, although it is not inevitable. If you have one child with an allergy, get other children in the family checked out too.

At present the only cure for a food allergy is to avoid the food you are allergic to, but doctors are investigating ways of preventing allergies in the next generation using, for example, probiotics (the "friendly" bacteria that live in a healthy gut) during pregnancy. Other developments for the future include immunotherapy using "allergy vaccines." Forms of immunotherapy exist for pollen-induced hay fever and bee stings and some non-food allergies but as yet there are no proven, tested desensitization techniques available.

Cross reactions

Cross reactivity means that being allergic to one food can make you more likely to be allergic to another one. Surprisingly, these are not always foods that are closely related. Peanuts, for example, are part of the legume family, which includes black-eyed peas, kidney and lima beans, and soybeans, yet most people who have a peanut allergy are fine with all of these other legumes, but do have a problem with tree nuts. The standard advice is if you are allergic to nuts or peanuts, you should avoid both.

If you have an allergy and are unsure about what else is unsafe to eat, consult your physician or allergist, who will use your food history and symptom diary to help them establish which other foods you should avoid.

Cross reactivity between nuts and seeds is less common; for example, most people who have to avoid nuts can eat sesame seeds (although about 15 percent cannot). Pine nuts are seeds and tolerated by many people with nut allergies. Similarly cross reactivity between animal products is unusual; people who are allergic to eggs can usually eat chicken—so roasts and stews are unlikely to be out of bounds.

Within the shellfish group, crustaceans (shrimp, crab, and lobster) are most likely to cause a reaction, but allergy to mollusks (clam, oysters, and abalone, for example) is becoming more common. Some people are allergic to both types.

Food intolerances

Often self-diagnosed, food intolerance is a more general and diffuse term. It is used by the medical profession when a person's history and tests show that a particular food is causing symptoms but the immune system is not involved or is unlikely to be the major factor producing the symptoms.

Food intolerances tend to have multiple causes and multiple symptoms. They can be temporary or fluctuate because tolerance levels vary and typically occur after eating a suspect food over a

▼ Trouble-free treats can be made without problem ingredients such as eggs, gluten, and dairy products.

longer period of time and in larger amounts than the trace needed to trigger an allergic response. They do not cause severe anaphylactic reactions.

Intolerances are more difficult to diagnose than allergies but should by no means be regarded as a modern myth. Doctors diagnose food intolerance by taking a medical, family, and food history and combining it with selective elimination of various possible causes to arrive at the most likely suspect.

If you have symptoms that disappear when you eliminate a food under medical supervision and then reappear when the food is reintroduced, that is proof enough of a food intolerance. Common food intolerances include:

• **Lactose intolerance,** which is the inability to tolerate milk and dairy products (see p.19).

• **Food additives**—these are controversial but some that may cause problems include tartrazine (orange food dye) and azo dyes; food flavorings such as monosodium glutamate (MSG), frequently found in Chinese restaurant food; and some sugar substitutes used in low-calorie sweeteners, soft drinks, and foods. Preservatives such as sulfites, used to preserve dried fruits (typically apricots), and benzoates and some food antioxidants have also been implicated. The easiest way to avoid these is to eat freshly prepared food and avoid heavily processed ingredients.

• **Histamines,** found naturally in foods such as cheese, some fish, and alcoholic drinks, can cause reactions resembling allergy.

• **Idiopathic food intolerances** is the term used to describe food-related problems with no established mechanism. Foods that trigger them are often those eaten frequently, such as milk or wheat. These intolerances are widely reported, with symptoms ranging from migraines to diarrhea, joint pain, and general fatigue.

Every recipe has versions that are free of gluten, dairy (milk), eggs, and nuts

Major food problems

Among the many food allergies and intolerances, a handful cause problems because they are used in so many different products, often added for texture or flavor where you wouldn't even expect them. These are gluten (contained in grains such as wheat); dairy products (milk and all products containing milk); tree nuts and peanuts; and eggs, and these are the focus of my recipe variations. Every recipe has a version that is free of each of these four allergens, with some recipes naturally free of them all.

Although shellfish (the most common food allergy in adults), fish, and soy are serious food allergens, I have used them in some recipes, albeit with cautions, because they are easier to avoid. Anyone with serious or multiple food allergies and intolerances should be particularly careful to eat a balanced diet.

Egg allergy

An egg allergy is common in children, although many grow out if it. Here are some points to bear in mind when cooking for children and adults with egg allergy:

• **Proteins in both egg yolk and white** can cause reactions. People may be allergic to raw eggs or cooked eggs or both. Only rarely is a person

sensitive to only the white or the yolk.

• **Varying amounts of egg are needed** to trigger a reaction in different people. A severely allergic person at risk of anaphylactic shock will not risk eating even a crumb of cake; a mildly allergic person may chance a slice, but there is always a risk because reactions can vary in severity.

How to compensate

Eggs contain useful nutrients, most importantly proteins, and are a good source of vitamin D. To replace protein found in eggs, choose from meat, poultry, fish, milk and cheese, soy products, whole grains, nuts, and seeds. Vitamin D is found in oily fish (salmon, sardines, herring, mackerel, and pilchards) and dairy products.

Tree nuts and peanuts

Peanuts (a legume) and tree nuts (all other "true" nuts including almonds, Brazil nuts, cashews, hazelnuts, macadamias, pecans, pistachios, and walnuts) are often grouped together by allergy specialists because cross reactivity between these food groups occurs frequently.

Here are some points to bear in mind when catering for nut and peanut allergies:

• **A person may not be allergic to all nuts** but it is safest to avoid them all. As with other allergies, proteins cause the reaction. Cooking nuts or peanuts will not reduce any allergic reaction to them; in fact roasting peanuts makes it worse.

• **Reactions should never be ignored** even if they are mild because future reactions may be more severe. A person may have a mild reaction, such as localized tingling, itching, or a rash, to a small or significant amount of peanuts or tree nuts. Breathing or swallowing difficulties or fainting calls for immediate medical attention.

• **Some people may react to a tiny trace** of nuts or peanuts, hence "trace" warnings on packaging. For this type of allergy, take no chances with ingredients or cross contamination.

• **Skin contact with nuts or peanuts** may cause rashes and swelling of the lips if someone has a severe nut allergy. Handling the nuts may transfer the allergen to the inside of the mouth. Even airborne proteins may cause a reaction.

▲ Pancakes (p.57) has versions free of each allergen and Thai green chicken curry (p.111) is naturally free of them all.

How to compensate

Although nuts are not a diet essential, they are a valuable source of protein for vegetarians. Those with nut allergies should eat protein-rich legumes, and, if not vegan, eggs, dairy, and cheese.

Dairy sensitivity

There are two main causes of dairy sensitivity: lactose intolerance and milk allergy. It's important to distinguish between them because milk allergy can cause much more severe reactions.

Milk allergy

This problem is frequent in babies but most grow out of it by the age of five years. If you are cooking for children with a milk allergy, you need to be aware of the following:

• **Proteins in milk,** commonly casein and whey, trigger allergic reactions. These proteins are found in cows' and other mammals' milk; sheep and goats' milk are likely to cause similar reactions.

• **Reactions are often mild** and symptoms can affect many parts of the body. They include skin rashes, runny nose, and itchy eyes, gastrointestinal symptoms such as cramps, diarrhea, and vomiting, and breathing problems.

• **In mild allergies,** small amounts of processed dairy products such as cheese can be tolerated but not milk, cream, or yogurt.

• **In severe cases of milk allergy,** an anaphylactic reaction can develop within minutes and follow from a minute quantity of milk. All dairy products and traces of products must be avoided. Skin contact and, more rarely, inhaling milk proteins may also cause a reaction.

Lactose intolerance

Most of the populations of South East Asia, Japan, and many people of African origin are lactose intolerant. Their diets are traditionally dairy free and they become intolerant when introduced to dairy.

The condition is much more common than milk allergy and causes milder symptoms and discomfort. It sometimes follows on from a stomach bug, especially in young children, but this type is usually transient.

Here are some points to keep in mind when cooking for people with lactose intolerance:

• **Lactose is a sugar** found naturally in milk from mammals, including cow, sheep, goats, buffalo, and human milk. People who are intolerant of lactose do not produce enough of the enzyme lactase, which breaks down milk in the gut so it can be properly absorbed. This produces symptoms such as bloating, stomach pain, and diarrhea.

• **The amount of lactose needed** to cause the symptoms may vary with age. Babies are more sensitive; adults with lactose intolerance can sometimes take small quantities of milk without experiencing any symptoms.

How to compensate

Dairy foods are a valuable source of protein, fat, carbohydrate, and vitamin D as well as being rich in calcium, which is essential for strong, healthy bones and teeth. If you don't eat dairy foods, choose calcium-enriched soy or other dairy-free milks and include leafy vegetables, whole-grain bread, legumes, dried fruit, nuts and seeds, sardines or salmon, and calcium- and vitamin D-fortified bread and orange juice in your diet.

Gluten and wheat

Gluten is the cause of celiac disease, a serious and lifelong autoimmune condition. Other wheat

▼ Delicious dairy-free smoothies (p.59) can be made from a variety of milk and yogurt substitutes.

proteins can cause classical allergies, while intolerances to wheat, although widely reported, do not have clear-cut causes.

Celiac disease

Celiac disease is a serious permanent condition caused by a reaction to gluten in food, which affects up to 1 in 133 people in the US. The disease is genetic and the risk is increased if other family members are sufferers, but it is not inevitable.

Celiac is an autoimmune disease, which means that the body produces antibodies that attack its own tissues. The villi that line the gut are attacked and damaged, which leads to problems in absorbing essential nutrients in food. Symptoms can be mild, moderate, or serious and include stomach pain, bloating, diarrhea, and nausea. Although a reaction may follow soon after eating even a little gluten, it does not cause rapid or extreme symptoms, although severely affected sufferers may suffer from violent symptoms known as "celiac shock."

Because the symptoms can be vague although severe (and can be confused with irritable bowel

syndrome, wheat intolerance, or symptoms of stress), recognizing and diagnosing the problem can be a drawn-out and sometimes distressing process. The problem may go undiagnosed for years, leading to long-term complications such as anemia, weight loss, hair loss, osteoporosis, infertility, joint/bone pain, and malnutrition. The only reliable method of diagnosis is a gut biopsy.

Some useful information when cooking for people with celiac disease includes the following:
• **Attacks are triggered by gluten,** a protein found in many cereals including wheat (and grains related to wheat, such as spelt, triticale, and kamut), barley, rye, and oats. Products that contain gluten find their way into a great many processed foods, so understanding the composition of foods is essential. A few "borderline" grains such as oats may be tolerated.
• **Even a small amount of gluten may trigger** the return of symptoms that had ceased when gluten was excluded from their diet. As a general rule, celiacs need to avoid grains containing gluten.
• **A child may find it especially hard** to resist temptations like cookies and cakes so it is important to find safe, gluten-free alternatives to favorite foods. On a positive note, there are many naturally gluten-free grains out there—more than enough to make a gluten-free granola and provide substitutes for everything from pastry flour to couscous.

Wheat allergies
These are relatively rare and are caused by wheat proteins, typically albumin and globulin.
• **If wheat is eaten or even in some cases inhaled,** the allergic reaction can affect skin, stomach, and breathing. Reactions range from mild to life-threatening, and may come on very quickly.
• **Severe allergic reactions** can be triggered by a minute quantity of wheat so all wheat-based products must be avoided.

Wheat intolerances
Foods that cause intolerance are often those eaten frequently and regularly such as wheat. Diagnosis should be carried out by a physician and confirmed by an elimination diet.
• **Symptoms can be present** most of the time

and sufferers feel almost constantly unwell.
• **Many people are able to tolerate** the problem food if it is reintroduced after a suitable break.

How to compensate
If you have celiac disease or are gluten- or wheat-intolerant, you need to make sure you have enough fiber and iron (usually found in wholegrain bread and cereals) in your diet. Choose from fiber-rich legumes, brown rice, and rice bran, and fresh fruit and vegetables. Eating seeds, nuts, and dried fruits is also recommended. Good sources of iron are red meat, oily fish (salmon, sardines, herring, and mackerel), and shellfish. Green vegetables are good, too.

Healthy eaters
Finally, I hope this cookbook will be useful to those of you who are simply choosing to eat more healthily. While the most important factors in any diet are that it should be balanced, varied, and tasty, many of you may be cutting down on refined carbohydrates and fats and eating more wholegrains. Since dairy- and gluten-free alternatives often play a part, I hope my recipes inspire you to try new tastes and cooking experiences.

▼ Southern cornbread (p.174), cooked in a skillet and served with Chili con carne (p.122), is naturally gluten free.

Staying positive

My story is probably similar to yours. When you first discover you or someone very close to you has an allergy you are in a state of shock, even disbelief. You can see that life is going to change but you're not quite sure how, and it takes a while to learn how to cope with it on an emotional and a practical level—this is especially hard if you are dealing with a severe allergy where the need to set plans in place is vital.

Coping with emotions

There's no denying it's very upsetting to be told you or your child is going to have to live with a condition that's going to make life incredibly difficult. Yes, some children do grow out of some allergies, and who knows, one day there may be a cure. But for now you're stuck with it, and you need to allow yourself time to deal with the fact.

There's a grieving stage complete with unexpected cravings for the foods you'll miss. There's the "why me?" stage, which will recur periodically. If you have a close friend to rant to, so much the better, just be sure to make it up to them later. For genuine concerns, seek out reliable medical information and avoid the well-meaning amateurs.

One of the hardest things is to accept what you can't change, but this is the first step

Don't blame yourself for your or your child's allergy. It's no one's fault; you're just a victim of genes, environment, and bad luck. Dwelling on things that can't be changed is never a good strategy, especially if they are in the past or beyond your control. Similarly, don't waste time wading through competing theories on the cause of allergies in the press or on the internet; your focus now is on making the best of life.

One of the hardest things is to accept what you cannot change, but this is the first step toward planning a future without certain foods. I guarantee you won't have to miss out on the foods you love, but first you'll need a cool head

to identify all the risky situations you're going to find yourself in. Normal activities, like a meal out, are now a dangerous obstacle course. You'll have to learn to communicate about a topic fraught with emotions and scepticism effectively and respond to enquiries with convincing medical detail—and don't worry, you will. How you communicate is important, too. The key is to explain rather than complain, and that's a lot easier once you've been through the emotional stage.

You will need negotiation skills, too. I've never found it particularly easy to ask for things and would rather walk over hot coals than send wine or food back in a restaurant, but now I can walk into any kitchen, ask to discuss the menu or see the chef, and tell them just what I need.

Getting positive and practical

As always, follow this advice depending on the severity of your allergy or intolerance.
- **First of all,** if you or your child are at risk of a severe reaction to a food (see Anaphylaxis, p.15) put your emergency plans in place. If everyone knows what to do, where the emergency kit is kept, and where to contact you, you have the worst case scenario covered.
- **Set aside time** to plan for the changes that food hypersensitivities bring with them. It won't be a one-time effort, you'll have to plan for the long term. Prepare yourself and accept your family and friends' offers of help—this is no time to be a hero.
- **Make a detailed** list of all the eating situations you encounter and the risks and temptations involved. This is essential if a lapse will have serious consequences. With anaphylaxis, particularly for a child, there is NO room for error. Keeping a food diary can help pinpoint risky situations such as eating at other people's

houses, traveling, school meals, and restaurants, and help you steer a path through occasions when you are faced with sceptical relatives and helpful but ill-informed friends.

• **Build a support network.** Find out as much as you can about your condition from books, websites, and allergy organizations (see p.218–219). Make use of your physician and health center. To find special foods, visit and talk to supermarkets, health food stores, even pharmacies. Befriend owners and chefs in your local restaurants. Recruit friends and fellow sufferers so you can cook and cope together.

• **Ask for what you need.** There will be new situations where you have to ask for information or for different service. Be clear about what you need: a hamburger served without the bun; reassurance that the spoon serving your ice cream has not just been in the one with the nuts in it; to see the label on the package. People won't volunteer this information—you have to ask for it.

• **Be realistic** about what you can expect from others. People are basically well intentioned but busy. Catch them at the right time and you'll get a lot more assistance.

• **Never stop checking.** Don't make any assumptions; the chocolate bar you buy regularly because it is nut free may now be produced on a nut-contaminated production line. A restaurant may have a different chef tonight who puts cream in everything. The price of health is eternal vigilance. Take heart; soon it will become second nature.

▼ Egg-free world—Archie is discovering that the simple pleasures of baking don't need to be out of bounds.

Allergy etiquette

Awareness of allergies and food intolerances is fortunately on the increase and the shift in attitudes and behavior has clearly begun. Not so long ago vegetarianism was regarded by many as a peripheral food fad that didn't need to be catered for. Now, it's hard to find a place that doesn't offer meat-free options. The number of people who describe themselves as having food sensitivities is now greater than the number who call themselves vegetarian, so we can hope for a new code of good manners that involves thoughtfulness and consideration from both the allergy sufferer and those who cater for them.

If you have the food allergy or intolerance…

Tell other people as much as they need to know about your food sensitivity—and no more. Be clear about what you would like and realistic in your expectations. What you need to tell your child's school or an airline will be different from what your friends or dinner hosts need to know. Give timely information with the right level of detail.

Match your expectations to their expertise. Are you expecting a friend to suddenly become a medical expert or an incredibly gifted and flexible chef? Empathize with their situation and you will save yourself and others a lot of anguish. If you know your host finds it a strain making the simplest meal, eat before you set off to avoid disappointment. Conversely, if you know it would give someone pleasure to cook something special for you, then give them all the information they need and then relax and accept it with a smile.

Thank people effusively when they make an extra effort and tip generously

If you don't know what's in it, don't eat it. Ask what's in it and keep asking until you have the needed information. If it does not have a label, find out what the ingredients are. The more extreme your allergic reaction, the more important this is.

Bring your own food with you. This may seem like the reverse of conventional good manners but in fact it shows consideration. It means that as far as possible you plan to join in with what others are eating, but where you can't you are not putting an extra burden on your hosts. In restaurants, try as much as possible to eat when everyone else is served. If you haven't brought your own utensils with you and cross contamination is an issue, then it's perfectly in order to ask to wash some utensils or, in extreme circumstances, to use your fingers.

Avoid making a scene. Don't loudly refuse food or adopt an offended tone when offered something you can't eat. Nothing is gained by upsetting people. Just do what generations of guests and children have done before you and leave it on the side of the dish or hide it under your spoon.

Thank people effusively and tip generously. This is not difficult to do when someone has made the extra effort to accommodate your needs and it encourages good service in the future.

Don't go into the gory details. Who really needs to hear a detailed medical account of your condition except your physician? Having a food allergy or intolerance doesn't make you more interesting or socially desirable. Similarly…

Avoid militant activism. This may come naturally to those with a campaigning spirit, but your efforts should be directed toward manufacturers, retailers, and organizations, not the waitress, your friends, or anyone who will listen.

If someone else has the food allergy or intolerance…

Always ask for information. Follow the Essential Checklist (below) if you are dealing with food sensitivities. The people with the allergy or intolerance are the experts—especially if they are severely allergic. If they are children, ask them and confirm with a parent or caregiver.

It may sound obvious but you'd be surprised how many people try to guess even though they may be putting a person's health at risk by doing so. Make sure you ask these questions in advance or discreetly—don't embarrass the person and fellow guests by enquiring loudly or publicly about their food sensitivities.

Take it seriously. Give people the benefit of the doubt. Unless you are a specialist, you are unlikely to be able to assess the condition or what it's like to live with it. Food sensitivities range from potentially life-threatening, chronic illnesses to ones with mildly uncomfortable consequences.

ESSENTIAL CHECKLIST

- **Find out exactly what** the person is allergic to or intolerant of. This must be specific, for example, is it wheat in general or specifically gluten? Egg—cooked or raw? The notes on cross reactivity on page 16 may help.

- **Find out what happens** when the person ingests (eats, or in a very few cases, breathes) the substance. You need to ascertain the speed and severity of the reaction. Are they at risk of anaphylactic shock? If so, you will need to be extremely careful about possible cross contamination as well. Are they mildly or severely celiac? Even if they have a low-risk reaction such as "wheat makes me feel bloated and uncomfortable" or "it gives me a rash," it's still something you'd rather not be responsible for.

- **Find out how much** of the substance it takes to cause the reaction. For some people, even the smallest trace of nuts, for example, will be enough to cause anaphylactic shock. Others with a delayed allergic response may react only to larger doses of the food over a longer period of time.

I'm always surprised when people say something like "In my day we didn't have these new-fangled allergies." I always want to retort "In your day they probably didn't have mobile phones but that doesn't mean they don't exist now."

Put yourself in their place. How would you feel if someone decided not to ask your child for a play date because it's too much of a fuss to cater for her? Or, imagine you are the one child at the birthday party who can't eat the birthday cake.

Celebrate rather than commiserate. This may sound perverse, but negative attention is unhelpful. It keeps the sufferer in the "poor me" phase instead of celebrating all the foods that can be eaten and the creative culinary solutions that have been necessary. It is far better to make the factual enquiries and find out what they can eat.

Decide how much effort you are prepared to make to accommodate someone with special dietary needs. With the information you have garnered from following the Essential Checklist (see box, left), you can balance your desire to help against the likely amount of extra work and any risks involved. You may decide you want to make a great deal of effort for a relative or close friend, but less so for a business acquaintance, or that someone with a severe condition is just too scary to cater for—all of which is fine as long as you communicate back to them what you are doing.

Don't promise more than you can deliver. People shouldn't be offended if you suggest that they bring their own food, but they will be upset if you offer to provide for them and then let them down. Respond to inquiries about ingredients, but if you don't know or you're not completely sure, say so. Never guess. My bugbear is the well-intentioned but ill-informed host at children's parties who takes my son by the elbow and says "Darling, I'm sure there are lots of things you can eat here," offers him cake, cookies, and peanut butter sandwiches, all of which have a sporting chance of killing him, and then asks vaguely "Was it dairy or wheat you can't have?"

Your allergic child

Finding out that they have a food allergy is a lot for young children to cope with. It is especially hard for a shy child because it may set her apart from her friends. Children with allergies are often required to mature more quickly than their peers by learning self-reliance, empowerment, and responsibility at a young age so that they can assess the hazards and go out and enjoy what life has to offer.

Teach the basics

Explain the allergy to your child—the foods to be avoided, the symptoms, the treatment, and how to use the emergency kit, if relevant (see p.5).

Tell her not to accept food from other than a small group of known and trusted adults, unless she is sure she knows what's in it.

Encourage her to speak up about her allergy whenever it might be important and support her when she does, for example, at other people's houses and at restaurants. She should learn to automatically and confidently ask questions about any food offered such as how it was cooked and the ingredients.

Teach her to always read the ingredients lists and labels on products so that she becomes familiar with the names of problem ingredients and the different terms used for them. She needs to be aware that manufacturing processes, familiar menus, and recipes can change overnight and something that was safe last week may not be now.

Expose her to many different eating occasions—from picnics, barbecues, and fast food outlets to restaurants, weddings, and casual meals at friends' houses so that she becomes more confident about approaching and evaluating the relative risk of new eating situations.

If she has been prescribed epinephrine, make sure she is aware of the nominated adult at school and on school trips who will administer her injector pen. Around the age of 10 or 11, she should learn to use her own injector pen (although she will still need a nominated adult in case of emergency).

School life

Managing your child's allergy while she is at school relies on good teamwork and regular communication between you and the staff. The school and parents should work together to ensure that the child is not stigmatized but is able to join in all school activities, able to behave in any other way as a "normal" child would.

You should play the key role in assembling the team by fully informing the school, other parents, and children of the allowed foods and foods to be avoided. Supply the school with a management plan (see p.28) to make sure that the staff know what to do in an emergency, how to recognize the symptoms of an allergic reaction, and what to do if it happens. Make sure the school nurse and any teachers have copies. In most countries, school staff have the duty to safeguard the health of pupils but do not have to administer medicines—although many may volunteer to. Provide the school nurse or nominated staff member with any medicines and equipment, as well as permission to administer them, and arrange training sessions for the staff with you and your child.

It really helps if teachers take the lead in teaching your child's classmates about her allergy because the most important role for your allergic

Keep a box of allergy-free treats at houses of close friends to help your child feel welcome and relaxed around food

child's close friends may be to speak up for her. They should avoid food trading but your child still needs to feel included. Involve other parents so that close friends keep a box of allergy-safe treats at their houses for when she visits. This helps your child feel welcome and relaxed around food. Also, keep allergy-free treats at school or send in a tray of safe cakes or cookies so that your child can be involved in birthdays and other celebrations. Arrange with the school to make sure that there is a safe food shelf—an area where your child's foods, lunchbox, snacks, and treats can be stored in a marked and, if necessary, lockable container.

School meals and trips

Decide whether your child should eat school meals or packed lunches and remember to make special arrangements for school trips or summer camps. School caterers should be aware of food preparation issues as well as the ingredients to be avoided. The caterers need to set up a clear and consistent warning system to notify of allergens in school meals and they should receive regular updates from suppliers on changes in ingredients. They should keep the foods together with their labels. Caterers need to be aware of cross contamination risks and introduce procedures to minimize this.

MANAGEMENT PLAN

Before school begins discuss your child's needs with the pediatrician or allergy specialist and set up a management plan with their help. This needs to be individualized and modified as your child's needs change, and should include all the essential information for avoiding and dealing with emergency situations. Arrange for the school to have as many copies as necessary. Here is a sample plan.

Child's details

Name: Rebecca Lin   **Date of Birth:** November 4, 1997

Teacher's name: Mrs. Cavendish

Emergency contact details: Mary Lin (mother) Home: 516-324-0219; Work: 212-836-6523; Cell: 917-656-5938. Jon Lin (father) Work: 212-988-1149; Cell: 617-235-0320.

Allergic to: Nuts and peanuts, raw or cooked, and all foods containing nuts. NONE must be eaten. Any skin contact with nuts or peanuts must be avoided, too. Asthma sufferer.

Emergency procedures

• **Mild symptoms:** Tingling lips/skin rash. Do not ignore—continue to monitor.

• **Recognizing a serious reaction:** This follows immediately after nuts or traces of nuts are eaten: flushing, rash on body, swelling of mouth and throat, difficulty breathing and swallowing, vomiting, and fainting.

• **Treatment—Mild:** Administer 5 puffs of her inhaler and 2 tablespoons of antihistamine.
Serious: If a serious reaction is suspected, administer the first epinephrine injector pen immediately (following the instructions) and call an ambulance. Administer the second epinephrine pen after 5 minutes unless there is a marked improvement.

• **Epinephrine injector pen holder and location:** Mrs. Cavendish. Location: Bottom left-hand drawer of Mrs. Cavendish's desk in room 5B.

• **Trained staff members:** Mrs. Cavendish, Mr. Hammond, Miss Collins (school nurse).

• **Emergency calls and what to say:** Dial 911. Tell them Rebecca is allergic to nuts but has eaten some, describe her symptoms, and say what medication has been given. An adult is to accompany her in an ambulance to the hospital. Further details are available by phoning MedicALert (1-800-625-3780) and quoting Rebecca's membership number (US2939747).

Medication in emergency kit: Salbutamol inhaler (100mg); Piriton liquid (2mg); Junior epinephrine injector pen x 2

Consent & Agreement   M. Lin

Eating out

Although many restaurants are beginning to be aware of food allergies and intolerances, when you are eating out get as much information as possible ahead of your visit. If you are severely allergic it's a high-risk strategy to turn up and expect them to give you and your allergy their undivided attention. As always, follow the advice according to the severity of your allergy or intolerance.

Make friends and influence people

You don't want to have to explain your condition every time. Befriend the helpful people—at the coffee shop, cafeteria, wherever you find them—it will pay dividends. Our local butcher called me while on vacation to tell me that they'd changed the shepherds' pie topping and that it now included egg. A life-saving call for my son because I was just about to cook one for lunch.

> Don't take the waiter's word for how food is prepared; waiters collect food from the kitchen—they don't make it

Visit the venue

If you are organizing a celebration, business dinner, or a meal for a group, don't just do it over the phone, arrange a short visit at a quiet time. Don't be reticent: hairdressers are happy to give consultation appointments to prospective customers—there's no reason why restaurants shouldn't do so, too. Explain your needs and any requests to the manager and you will avoid embarrassing encounters during your meal.

Talk to the relevant person

Don't take the waiter's word for how food is prepared and cooked; waiters collect food from the kitchen—they don't make it. Talk to the people who prepare the food and explain what is at stake if they get it wrong. If you have celiac disease or may have an anaphylactic reaction to a substance, tell them exactly how serious the consequences can be if you eat even the smallest quantity of the substance. However, don't overstate a relatively mild allergy or intolerance; it does a disservice to those who really need to be taken seriously. If buying homemade food, make sure you talk to the person who cooked it.

Notify in advance

If you need to customize a meal, find out whether the food is freshly made and what packaged ingredients it contains. Ask to see labels on any processed ingredients. Give details of the allergen in question. If they are willing to adapt some of the dishes, discuss the process, ingredients, and risk factors. If you react to extremely small quantities of the allergen, point out that they will not be able to pick out the offending ingredient from already created dishes because traces of it will remain.

Check for cross contamination

This is only essential if a trace of the allergen will cause a reaction. It's not just plates and serving implements that can transfer traces of foods; hands can, too. Check whether the chef uses his hands to sprinkle nuts or cheese or to roll dough. Barbecues, grills, toasters, and griddles also carry fragments of what was cooked on them before.

Be open minded

Food intolerance is a great excuse to explore and experiment with new cuisines. It will be the silver lining to the cloud if your food sensitivity leads you to new culinary discoveries and dishes that become favorites. On pages 32–35 you can delve into a world of different cuisines to explore.

Special occasions

You don't have to give up visiting friends, staying with family, or going to parties, any more than you have to give up good food. But be aware, although your friends want to see you, and really good hosts will stock your favorite foods, they won't want to wait on you hand and foot. Be alert to the sensitivities of individuals and occasions since people can take offense if you don't eat their food. Family holidays, Christmas, and Thanksgiving already have their fair share of emotional trigger points and don't need more.

If you don't want your food issues to hijack a special occasion, keep the following points in mind. As always, use the advice according to the level of your allergy or intolerance.

Always call ahead and find out as much as you can about the menus and events. Will there be picnics, barbecues, formal events, or snacks? If it's a wedding, it will probably be catered—ask for the caterer's details and then call them yourself; the bride will have too much on her mind to worry about your food.

How long will you be there? If it's just for a meal, a snack ahead of time will see you through. If it's overnight you'll need breakfast provisions; any longer and you'll need to pack a box, bag, or even a suitcase full of food. If you know the refrigerator is likely to be full, take a cooler.

Keep your hosts happy by preplanning the time you'll need to spend in their kitchen and discussing it in advance. If all you need is to unwrap some gluten-free bread or stash your soy milk in the refrigerator, you'll be no trouble. If you want 20 minutes to boil some pasta or need a safe area for food preparation, prearrange a convenient time and space. Remember to label your food clearly so that others don't eat your food.

Don't endanger your health by eating something you shouldn't just to be polite. Rediscover those childhood skills and hide food you can't eat under a potato or in your napkin. And be fussy about serving spoons if you think cross contamination is an issue—you're worth it!

▲ Happy ever after—Archie's birthdays sometimes take a bit of extra planning.

BIRTHDAY SURPRISE

However meticulous your planning, there will always be the unexpected setback. For Archie's seventh birthday party we booked a table for 20 children in a local Chinese restaurant. Hand-drawn invitations had already been sent out, when the restaurant changed their mind about our booking—they were not prepared to allow Archie to bring in his own egg- and nut-free version of their egg-fried noodles meal, despite the fact that the 19 other children would be eating their food.

All my appeals for a little flexibility fell on deaf ears and I had to break the news to a baffled and almost tearful little boy. We relocated the party to a friendly (and cooperative) pizza parlor, everybody had a wonderful time, and we learned how valuable an ally a restaurant with a sympathetic manager can be—gradually adding to our list of places where we know people are friendly and helpful. The Chinese restaurant may have discovered too late the importance of good customer service—they had to close down a year later.

Traveling hopefully

Whether it's a family vacation or traveling on business, if you want a pleasant, productive, calm, and enjoyable trip with no crises or emergencies, advance planning and preparation is essential. Airlines, travel companies, and hotels are slowly becoming more helpful and responsive to people who have dietary requirements but don't just assume that they can help you—always check first. The responsibility lies with you to inform everyone as necessary. Once you've done the groundwork, you can relax and enjoy yourself.

Before you go

Last-minute travel may not be an option since most travel companies ask for weeks' or even months' notice to accommodate special dietary requirements. You also need time to do your research. This is a good time to make use of allergy and celiac associations (see p.218–219), since most have travel advice packs, information leaflets, and dietary alert cards (see below). Contact associations in the country you're visiting and ask them to recommend allergy-friendly travel companies, hotels, restaurants, and food stores. Find out how much you can buy at your destination and what you need to take. Pack enough safe food to get you to your destination and include some allowance for delays.

Make a checklist with two headings—"what" and "who." The "what" are the essentials you mustn't forget to take with you on your trip. These may include medical and travel insurance; safe snacks for the journey; MedicAlert® bracelets; emergency kits; and dietary alert cards. The "who" is the person responsible for bringing them.

Dietary alert cards

These are ideal if you are not fluent in the language of the country you are traveling to. Either make the cards yourself or get them from allergy or celiac organizations. The cards explain the risks and requirements of your condition, as well as what you can eat, in the local language, establishing you as a genuine medical case rather than a fussy eater. They take the stress out of ordering food because important details are unlikely to get lost in translation between you and the waiter, and the waiter and the chef.

Travel tips

Include essentials in your cabin baggage and carry any medication or equipment with you at all times. If you use an epinephrine injector pen, take extras, in their containers, with instructions on taking them and obtaining refills, to show customs officials that they are bona fide medicines.

If you are under medical supervision, get the details of a specialist at the nearest hospital to the place you are traveling to. Bring details of your condition with you in the local language.

In a train you're trapped for the duration of the journey, so take your own supplies. On bus and car trips, don't assume that the roadside stops will sell "safe" foods. Take soup and sandwiches to eat on the move, or stop for a picnic.

Most airlines, if notified ahead of time, will offer gluten-free meals and vegan meals, which are free of any animal products so are essentially meat, dairy, and egg free; some serve non-lactose meals. However, it is always safest to bring some food of your own, too. If you have a severe food allergy, do not take any risks—eat only food that you have prepared yourself, but be sure to check the latest security regulations from the Transportation Security Administration (TSA) regarding the packaging rules before you leave home.

Peanut products are no longer served on many airlines but there is still the risk that passengers may bring their own. Some airlines will announce that they have a severely allergic person on board, and ask passengers to leave peanuts in their bags.

Worldwide cuisine

When you have to cut out certain food, it's all too easy to focus on what you can't eat, yet broadening food horizons is a good antidote to allergies. If you don't limit yourself to one cuisine, a whole world of possibilities opens up. Travel provides plenty of opportunities to sample a different cuisine but you may prefer to try new dishes in restaurants at home first or cook them yourself. Don't rule out any cuisine even if it seems unsuitable. Italy may be the home of wheat-based pasta but for carbohydrate-loving gluten-avoiders there are also deliciously satisfying risottos, polenta, and potato gnocchi.

Being the product of many countries myself, there is no national bias to the culinary regions chosen in this book. I picked popular cuisines as well as great culinary traditions and grouped together those with advantages for a particular allergy group, for example Chinese and Southeast Asian, which are great for dairy-avoiders. Popular restaurant dining choices such as Mexican (Tex-Mex), Indian, Thai, Middle Eastern, and Japanese were all given a place too. With unlimited space I'd sing the praises of many more, so let this simply be the start of your culinary explorations.

I've described dishes in this section according to what they ought to or most usually contain, but there are always regional variations and no accounting for the additions cooks and companies may make to classic recipes. The severity of your allergy will determine how, when, and where you can experiment. Cross contamination with peanuts/nuts, gluten, and for severe allergics, dairy and egg are an issue in most restaurants. If in any doubt, the best place for you to try a new cuisine is in your own kitchen.

Italian

Great gluten-free choices include Polenta (p.81), risottos (see Risotto Milanese, p.144), and potato gnocchi (if flourless). There's no need to miss out on delicious sauces from piquant *arrabiata* to creamy *carbonara*, just ask for gluten-free pasta, which is available in some restaurants. Make the most of Parmesan, mozzarella, and other delicious cheeses but watch out for veined dolcelatte and gorgonzola. Finish with ice cream or zabaglione. **If you have to be dairy free,** enjoy antipasti from the classic melon and parma ham to grilled vegetables, salami, and most breads. For a main course, choose roasts, pan-fried fish and meat, and stews such as Fegato alla Veneziana (p.116) or Vitello tonnato (p.120). Proper pizza and calzone dough contain oil and water but no dairy; just make sure you pick cheeseless toppings or ask if you are allowed to bring your own dairy-free melting cheeses for the chef to sprinkle on just before your pizza goes into the oven. Sorbets and granitas are a good dessert choice in restaurants and you can make a dairy-free Panna cotta (p.161) at home.

Egg- and nut-safe first courses include the famous *insalate tricolore* with its colorful Italian flag of avocado, mozzarella, and tomatoes. Dried pastas are mostly egg free but fresh ones are egg-laden. Top pastas with rich gamey sauces of rabbit, venison, or luscious tomato but avoid *carbonara*, which contains egg and bacon. For the many nut-allergics who can tolerate pine nuts, there's the much-loved Pesto (p.211).

Restaurant desserts are tricky if you can't eat egg: ice creams (gelati) and custards are out of bounds and even sorbets may have had egg white added. If you don't want to risk it, order *frutti di stagione* (seasonal fruit) and make the sorbets (p.159) at home. Nut avoiders can indulge in most ice cream apart from nut flavors.

Mexican

Gluten avoiders have lots to choose from because Mexican is a corn- and rice-based cuisine. Tortillas (check they are just made with *masa harina*—corn flour—and that no wheat has crept in) are the basis for *burritos*, *tacos*, *enchiladas*, and *tostadas*, wrapped around delicious fillings of your choice. A good one to try at home is with Chili con carne (p.122), guacamole, salsas, sour cream, and cheese. Rice (*arroz*) and beans (*frijoles*) are green-light menu items for you.

For dairy-free choices avoid anything *con queso* (with cheese) or with sour cream. Opt for nachos with creamy guacamole, and salsas made from typical Mexican ingredients; tomatoes, peppers, cucumber, and spices with cumin and cilantro. Eggs (*huevos*) in various forms are an option, too, and authentic refried beans are made with lard rather than butter. A real treat is *horchata*—a refreshing drink made of rice and almonds that looks milky but is dairy free.

Egg-free and nut-free menu choices include; Gazpacho (p.85), taco salads, wraps, Chili con carne (p.122), and dips and salsas. Mango or guava are the characteristic flavors to round off a meal, typically eaten as pastelike sweets, or try Mango yogurt ice (p.158). Egg-allergics should avoid the vanilla flans and nut-allergics should avoid *mole* stews, which have nuts as a key ingredient.

Japanese

For dairy-avoiders this is definitely a cuisine to investigate and celebrate. Sushi is an excellent option that works well for most other allergies, too. With a wide range of fillings—vegetable, fish, or seafood—it is surprisingly satisfying to make at home in *temaki* form (see California temaki sushi, p.74). Try clear soups, *miso*- or *dashi*-based with tofu, meat, or vegetables and mains such as *teriyaki* beef, *yakitori* chicken, or *donburi*—bowls of rice topped with meat or vegetables.

Gluten-sensitives can also do well with sushi. Make dishes such as Miso marinated salmon (p.101) at home to ensure that soy sauce and miso are gluten-free. Wakame & cucumber salad (p.91) and many vegetable side dishes are safe as long as the soy sauce issue is resolved. When opting for noodle dishes, specify rice noodles or 100 percent

▲ Middle Eastern tagines served with couscous or quinoa.

buckwheat ones. If you like to eat out at Japanese restaurants, why not ask if you can bring your own soy sauce to season otherwise gluten-free safe dishes?

Egg is not much used in Japanese cooking, so many of the above options are safe for egg allergics. However, watch out for omelette-topped sushi, for *oyako donburi* (chicken and egg) and other egg-topped rice dishes. Make the most of *udon* and *soba* noodle dishes such as Noodles in hot ginger broth (p.142). For something sweet, opt for "mochi" (sweet sticky rice cakes) or a summer favorite, *kakigori*, made of shaved ice with a variety of sweet syrup flavorings.

Nuts and peanuts are not common ingredients in Japanese food. Nut-free choices include *tempura*, light as air batter-fried vegetables and seafood, and *gyoza*, a Japanese ravioli that is steamed or fried (sometimes called pot stickers). A popular choice to finish is Green tea ice cream (p.156).

▲ Southeast Asian dishes are great choices for dairy-avoiders because they are often naturally dairy free.

Southeast Asian & Chinese

These related cuisines, each with their own flavors and history, share the advantage that they are all virtually dairy-free and have rice at the heart of their cooking. The tradition is to share dishes between diners, so make sure you're not sharing spoons or transferring allergens as you do.

Good choices for dairy avoiders include soups, stir-fries, many *dim sum*, roast meats, and dipping sauces. Enjoy creamy coconut curries including Thai green chicken curry (p.111), as well as Singapore, Chiang Mai, and other noodle dishes. Southeast Asian sweet dishes tend to be based on coconut and bean paste rather than dairy.

For gluten-free eating, concentrate on rice. Fresh spring rolls (p.90) combine fresh herbs with pork and shrimp and Shrimp dumplings (p.103) are another option. Thai and Laotian curries and salads use mostly lime, fish sauce, chilies, and palm sugar for flavoring, but soy sauce is an issue, so cook at home or take your own gluten-free version to restaurants. There are numerous rice-based desserts including Thai sticky rice with coconut and mango.

Egg frequently declares itself as an ingredient in this cuisine in egg noodles (usually non-rice noodles), egg-drop and other egg-based soups and egg-fried rice. In Vietnamese food, avoid egg pancakes (*trung trang*), shrimp mousse on sugarcane, and shrimp toasts. Opt for salads, rice noodle dishes (such as Noodles in hot ginger broth, p.142), and stews. The fluffy white Chinese steamed buns called *mantou* use yeast as a rising agent rather than egg. The filled version *baozi* have fillings that are mostly egg free too.

If you are seriously allergic to nuts or peanuts, Southeast Asian and Chinese food is best made at home because chopped peanuts find their way into everything and use of peanut oil (mostly unrefined) is widespread. For the home cook try Thai green chicken curry (p.111), Vietnamese beef stew (p.124) and Asian slaw (p.212). In other recipes, replace chopped nuts with sesame seeds or toasted pine nuts, if you are able to eat them. Finish with Coconut sorbet (p.159) served with fresh tropical fruits.

Indian

If you are avoiding gluten, then problem-free Indian meals will be rice based. Most Indian cooks don't use flour as a thickener for curries, using almonds, yogurt or cream, or a vegetable-based sauce instead. Most Northern Indian flatbreads will be ruled out but check out split pea *moong dhal* pancakes—a popular snack food—and rice and lentil *dosas*, which are served hot with chutneys. *Dhals*, the bean and legume dishes that are an Indian staple, are the inspiration for Scallops and shrimps with lentils (p.105). The flavors of Indian food are so complex that even if you can't tolerate chili, you can omit it and still capture the essence of the cuisine.

Dig into Indian desserts such as *kheer*, an almond and cardamom-scented rice pudding, or *kulfi*—an ice cream made with condensed milk, pistachios, and almonds.

For dairy avoiders, grills and kebabs are the safest choices since many curries contain yogurt, ghee, or cream. One that doesn't, however, is vindaloo. Alternatively, make Indian dishes such as Spinach & yogurt lamb curry (p.131) in the dairy-free version at home. Opt for oven-baked flatbreads such as tandoori *roti* and *chapatti*, and check that fried breads like *poori* and *paratha* have been made using oil rather than ghee (clarified butter). Avoid *naan* and other breads with yogurt in them. For dessert, try Mango yogurt ice (p.158).

Eggs tend to be a named feature rather than a hidden ingredient in Indian dishes. So you can enjoy most breads (avoid *naan*, which may contain egg), rice, meat and vegetable curries, pickles and chutneys, as well as *lassi*, a cooling yogurt drink.

Nut- and peanut-allergics should beware of the ground almonds and pistachios in many curries, breads, and sweet dishes. In restaurants, check the oil used if ordering fried foods. Kebabs, grilled fish, and tandoori dishes are good choices with Raita (p.213), or make your own Tandoori fish (p.98). Enjoy sweet treats such as *gulab jamun*, fried milk balls in a rose-scented syrup.

French

Gluten-avoiders should steer clear of pastries and pâtisserie in the knowledge that you can make your own Croissants (p.54) and Chocolate croissants (p.66). Many *galettes de sarrasin*

(buckwheat pancakes) are made with no added wheat flour, but check first. Avoid stews, which may be thickened with flour, and opt for grills, *steak au poivre*, or fish dishes. Potato dishes are a good choice: gratins (see p.94), *pommes de terre à la lyonnaise*, or *boulangère*. If you can, bring your own bread to indulge in fine cheeses, but avoid veined ones such as Roquefort, which may contain mold cultured from bread. Gluten-free desserts include *îles flottantes* (poached meringues on a vanilla custard) and *crème brûlées*.

Dairy-allergics should avoid the buttery creamy dishes of northern France and opt for the southern cuisine, where olive oil is the rule. Choose classic salads like tuna-based *niçoise* and sauce-free grills and steaks (although *béarnaise* and *hollandaise* contain butter) or casseroles such as *boeuf bourguignon*. Opt for simple fruit-based desserts such as pears in wine or make dairy-free Petits pots au chocolat (p.154) at home.

> Even if you cannot tolerate chili, you can omit it in cooking and still capture the essence of Indian cuisine

Good egg-free choices for starters and mains include onion soup, *coq au vin*, *steak frites*, and *confit de canard*. Avoid sauces, most pastries, and desserts other than simple fruit ones or egg white-free sorbets. At home make egg-free versions of Crêpes (p.162) and Bacon & onion quiche (p.84).

Nuts more than peanuts find their way into many French dishes and hors d'oeuvres often involve nuts. You may be able to choose carefully from baguettes, *pains de campagne*, chocolate croissants, *palmiers*, and sweet fruit tarts because they don't usually contain nuts, but if nut traces are an issue avoid them all and make your own French-style bread (p.170), Chocolate croissants (p.66), and Apple tart (p.149).

Shopping

Strategies for food-sensitive people begin with smart shopping. There is lots of good food that you can eat if you know where to find it. Healthy, well balanced diets are a must for people with allergies and intolerances but you shouldn't have to miss out on treats and indulgences either. Different types of retailers have different strengths and they need to be approached in different ways.

Supermarket chains

Supermarkets have the widest ranges of fresh food and freezer sections and increasingly stock "allergy-friendly" ranges. The bigger retailers are becoming more health and environment aware and responsive to customers' concerns on these issues, but don't expect one-to-one service once you get there.

Health food stores & organic grocery stores

These are businesses, of course, but even the big chains still have vestiges of the whole-food hippie ethos with which they were founded. As a result, you can ask detailed questions about the food and have a good chance of getting some helpful answers. They are not always as competitively priced as supermarkets, but they stock a wider range of allergen-free and celiac-friendly goods. You will find smaller, less well-known brands, some of which were started for or by people with food sensitivities just like yours. The staff may have had some health-food training.

Local convenience stores

These concentrate on speed and ease of shopping. The good ones are friendly and become a real part of the community. They have to focus on core products, big brands, fresh produce, and frequent purchases, like bread and milk, but they may be happy to order your regular purchases for you, such as dairy-free soy milk or gluten-free bread. They tend to be very service oriented because customers are paying a premium for convenience.

▼ Sourcing fresh ingredients is easy, but stores and mail order companies are also waking up to the needs of allergy-free cooks.

Delicatessens

These can be an invaluable source of freshly prepared food and hard-to-find gourmet and specialty foods, but they are subject to similar catering hazards such as unlabeled or poorly labeled food and cross contamination described in Eating Out (p.29). However, if you take the time to talk with the owners and chefs, you may get inspiration and ideas for your own cooking.

Specialist food stores

I'm a big fan of authentic cultural food, as you can see from the recipes in this book. Southeast Asian and Japanese are useful specialist stores if you can't eat dairy, since there are little, if any, milk products used in their cooking and they are naturally dairy-free as a result. Other cuisines, such as Mexican, have rice and corn as staples but not much wheat, and are a useful shopping source for those on gluten-free diets. I recommend specialist stores because they supply ingredients you can't find in supermarkets. Many now offer online and mail order purchasing. The down side can be unfamiliar labeling, sometimes in a foreign language, which may not be subject to the same legal requirements that we're used to.

Mail order & online

Ideal for unusual foods and indispensable if you don't live in a city or town or near a health food store or supermarket. The range available online is impressive; from allergy-free prepared meals to gluten-free cakes, dairy-free chocolates and cookies, and nut, dairy, egg, and gluten-free pumpkin pie, plus all the staples that food-sensitive people need in their pantries, refrigerators, and freezers. The benefits of online shopping are that you can research products and compare prices and delivery options from the comfort of your own home—no lines, no baffled staff and no wasted trips. You do, however, have to make sure someone will be available to receive the food and there will probably be delivery charges. Some useful sites are given in the Resources section (pp.218–219), but new ones are emerging all the time. Your allergy or celiac organization should keep you up to date.

Manufacturers & food brands

Manufacturers and food brand companies depend on your business, so you shouldn't hesitate to ask for information about their products and ingredients. They put their addresses on their products and have "contact us" sections on websites because they want to hear from you. They use what they hear to change and develop products in order to suit shifting consumer needs. Individuals and lobbying organizations can tip the balance toward more and better products for people with food sensitivities. They can assist manufacturers to think through the consequences of decisions such as moving the production of popular allergen-safe foods to an area with

QUESTIONS TO ASK MANUFACTURERS

Food sensitivities are now so widespread that companies are addressing the issues and risks involved. Major brands and manufacturers will be able to provide you with literature and a website or helpline, and to answer most, if not all, of the following questions.

- **Who can I contact about** your products with respect to my allergy, food intolerance, or celiac disease?
- **Do you draw up lists** of foods that are "free from" the eight major allergens? (It may be more likely that their foods are clearly labeled with the federally mandated "contains" box.)
- **What is your company** policy on catering for customers with food sensitivities?
- **What is your policy** on allergen labeling? What are you doing to make it clearer and less ambiguous?
- **What is your policy** on "may contain traces" allergen warnings?
- **What advice do** you give to caterers and businesses handling your products on how to avoid cross contamination?
- **Do your manufacturing** decisions take allergy considerations into account?
- **What other foods** are made on the same production line as the product I wish to buy?
- **Do you test foods to** see if they are really what they claim to be—for example, that they are actually suitable for a dairy-free diet?

contamination risk. This can be upsetting for allergic or food-sensitive children because it reduces the already limited number of foods that are available to them.

What's on the label?

Most countries have a list of foods that are responsible for 90 percent of food allergies and must therefore be included on any package labeling. In the US, there are eight groups of these allergens: Milk, eggs, fish, crustacean shellfish (such as shrimp), peanuts, tree nuts, wheat, and soy. The US Food and Drug Administration enforces the Food Allergen Labeling and Consumer Protection Act (FALCPA, 2006) regulations that require manufacturers to declare allergenic ingredients, additives, and substances involved in food processing on their packaged food.

> You can tip the balance toward more and better products for people with food sensitivities

Health Canada and the Canadian Food Inspection Agency (CFIA) work together to provide information to consumers and the food industry in Canada, including pamphlets on each of the nine major allergens that have been identified for labeling (milk, eggs, fish and shellfish, peanuts, tree nuts, wheat, soy, sesame seeds, and sulfites). When the CFIA discovers a potential hazard, such as a potential allergen that hasn't been included on the label, the food is recalled and a warning posted on the CFIA web site.

Although good labeling of allergens is still very much in its infancy, it is good news for people with allergies, since shopping for food without sufficient information is a minefield. Labeling has reduced the risk but not eliminated it and, ultimately, what you eat remains your responsibility. Progress worth celebrating includes:

Labels must list major allergens. Requirements vary depending on where you live but in most areas, manufacturers must list at least the following allergens on labels: Cereals that contain gluten, eggs, peanuts, nuts, milk and dairy products, soy, fish, and shellfish (crustaceans and mollusks). The European Union countries require some 14 groups to be listed—in addition to those mandated for Canada, they also list celery, mustard, and lupin.

Any newly identified major potential allergens will be added to the list. A recent addition in the European Union is lupin. Lupin flour is used in pastries and the seeds eaten as a snack. Most reactions have been in children, and in adults allergic to peanuts and mollusks, specifically cuttlefish, squid, abalone, oysters, and snails.

Latex allergy, not yet on the official list, is a growing problem. This allergy to the sap of rubber trees causes symptoms that may progress rapidly and unpredictably from skin contact reactions to anaphylaxis on subsequent exposure.

All allergens should be listed irrespective of the quantity in the finished food. Manufacturers must now list all subingredients of a compound ingredient to reduce the problem of hidden or undeclared ingredients. For example, they can no longer list "rusks" as an ingredient without saying that these are made from cereals that contain gluten.

Manufacturers are asked to use plain language and common names for labeling, so for instance ingredients such as "casein," "whey," and "lactose" should be declared with a reference to milk in which they are found. Similarly, milk should be referred to as an ingredient in unfamiliar cheeses.

Although manufacturers are required to reduce or eliminate cross contamination with allergens that are not the intentional ingredients of a food, there are no legal controls governing cross contamination in the manufacturing. You may find "may contain nuts" or "manufactured in a factory that also produces nuts" on the label but this information is voluntary.

Packaged food can still be risky. It may be old stock from before the new regulations were in force or be mislabeled or become contaminated if it was unpacked to serve loose. It may also have been refined and come into contact with potential allergens during the process. Currently, non-allergenic ingredients derived from an allergen do not have to be declared. If you can refine peanut oil in a way that removes the allergenic proteins, or produce from wheat glucose a syrup that no longer contains gluten or other wheat proteins, these derivative products don't have to be labeled as allergens.

What I would like to see

Standardized labeling that is clear, prominent, and unambiguous would be a great start. At the moment inconsistencies and different terms across food brands and countries are confusing. Studies in the US have shown that in some cases fewer than 10 percent of children with milk allergies were able to correctly identify products containing milk. This is a risky state of affairs.

Plain language on labels: One manufacturer's view of plain language may not be another's and neither may correspond with yours. You may know that Cantal and Parmesan are cheese and that if listed as an ingredient the product must contain dairy—but is it obvious to everyone? It remains essential to teach children with food problems all the possible terms that might be used (see pp.38–42).

Improved procedures to avoid cross contamination in factories and a more considered use of "may contain traces of…" on labels. Nut trace contamination warnings are contentious because the suspicion is that manufacturers are simply covering themselves. Consumers need proper information: If the tiniest trace of a substance can cause a serious reaction, then people need to know that there is a trace risk. The more products without nuts as an ingredient that carry warnings, the less credible the warnings become. Credibility has been shown to be at its lowest among teenagers and children allergic to nuts—the group most at risk.

TIPS ON COST

Feeding people with food sensitivities need not be expensive as long as you use a little foresight and planning. Special foods such as gluten-free pastas, bread, and cake mixes, as well as egg replacers, are often stocked by supermarkets. Nondairy infant formulas can be found both at supermarkets and pharmacies. Ask your allergist for more information.

- **Various manufacturers**, particularly of gluten-free foods, will send free samples. Contact suppliers directly or via allergy organizations and trade shows.

- **Research supermarket** prices before you buy because some supermarkets increase the prices. The internet is invaluable for comparing prices.

- **Buy special pantry staples** in bulk from a wholesaler. Find them via the internet or ask your local health food store for help.

- **Egg replacers,** which are soy based, are often actually lower in price than eggs—an easy way to save!

- **Fresh fruit and vegetables** are likely to form the major part of your diet, but they don't have to be prepackaged in plastic in a supermarket. Check out your local fruit and vegetable stores and stands, which often sell bruised and slightly damaged produce for less.

- **Start growing your own** food to guarantee your food is allergen and additive free. Plant windowsill herbs or a tomato plant in a pot. Enthusiastic gardeners could turn part of their yard into a vegetable plot.

- **Shop via mail order** and the internet, especially for allergy-friendly foods and free-from ranges. They cut costs by not having store premises and should pass some savings on to you. (See Resources pp.218–219).

- **Make your own.** Homemade cookies and treats are invariably cheaper than store bought and make terrific presents—try making Chocolate truffles (p.207).

What not to eat

The simplest way to be sure of ingredients is to buy fresh foods and cook from scratch but I'm well aware that it isn't always practical. However, as soon as you stray into the aisles of prepared and processed foods, life becomes much more complicated. The ingredient list is located on the food label below the nutrition facts (serving size; calorie count; fat, cholesterol, sodium, carbohydrate, and protein content; and vitamins and minerals). Although this will alert you to potential pitfalls, these labels cannot be exhaustive because new foods come on to the market all the time. Unless you are severely allergic, you won't need to avoid everything on the list for each allergen.

Gluten
Gluten occurs naturally in an unprocessed state in wheat, barley, rye, oats, spelt, triticale, and kamut.

Ingredients and terms used: Bran, bulgur wheat, couscous, durum flour, flour, rusk, semolina, wheatgerm, whole wheat, modified starch, or starch. Malt, maltose, malt extract, malt syrup, and malt flour almost always refer to barley and wheat derivatives. Dextrin and maltodextrin can be derived from any starch; in the US it is usually corn; in Europe it is commonly barley or wheat.

Foods that may contain gluten
• **Alcohol**: All beers—lager, stout, and ales—are made from grain; cider may have barley added.
• **Baby food** often contains gluten.
• **Bread and baking**: Baking powder, brewers yeast, bread and breadcrumbs.
• **Cakes and cookies and pastries** of all types.
• **Candy and chocolate**: Some (including chewing gum) are dusted with flour.
• **Caramel color** is derived from barley malt.
• **Cereals** (unless specified as gluten free).
• **Cheese**: Grated cheese and processed cheeses and spreads may contain flour. Check veined cheeses such as Roquefort, stilton, and dolcelatte.
• **Desserts**: Ice creams and frozen yogurts may contain gluten if thickeners have been used. Avoid wafers and cones.
• **Drinks—nonalcoholic**: Flavored tea and coffees, barley-flavored soft drinks, malted drinks.
• **Meats and fish**: Burgers, sausages, and other processed meats may contain cereal or rusk.

Crabsticks or fish sticks may contain wheat. Avoid anything breadcrumbed or battered.
• **Nuts** may have flour as a coating.
• **Sauces**: Stock cubes, soups, and gravies may contain hydrolyzed vegetable protein, usually made of wheat or soy. Some salad dressings contain gluten. Many soy sauces contain wheat.
• **Seasonings and spices**, packet mixes, and mustard may contain flour as thickener, as may white pepper. Avoid malt (barley) vinegar. Distilled vinegars are safe.
• **Snacks**: Pretzels, corn chips; some corn tortillas contain wheat flour.
• **Soups** may contain barley and wheat-based thickeners or pasta as in minestrone.
• **Vegetables**: Frozen fries may have a flour coating.

Hidden traps: Vitamins and supplements may contain gluten.

Things that sound risky but aren't: Buckwheat is not wheat and does not contain gluten. Laverbread is just fried seaweed. Sweetbreads are organ meats.

Nuts
Many medical experts advise people with peanut allergies to avoid tree nuts and vice versa. Foods containing peanuts are listed separately but if you are allergic to either, read both lists. Nuts include almonds, Brazils, cashews, hazelnuts, macadamias, pecans, pistachios, and walnuts.

Ingredients and terms used: Chipped nuts, flaked nuts, nut butters, nut paste, nut extracts, nut oils, some blended vegetable oils. Marzipan, *frangipane*, and almond essence/extract are made from almonds; pralines are made from pecans. *Prunus* is a term used for nuts in cosmetics.

Foods that may contain tree nuts
• **Alcohol**: Liqueurs such as *amaretto*.
• **Baking ingredients**: Nut flours, all baking mixes.
• **Beans, peas, lentils, and seeds** may contain nuts as part of a mix or may be processed on the same factory line as nuts.
• **Breads**: Specialty breads, flatbreads, naan bread. Fresh or store-baked breads may be cross contaminated with nuts.
• **Cakes and cookies**: Plain cakes, fruitcakes, cheesecakes, tortes, gâteaux, baked breakfast goods such as croissants, cereal bars, cookies, and crackers (check labels).
• **Candy and chocolate**: Praline and nut chocolates. Many chocolates contain nut traces.
• **Cereals**: Crunchy nut cereals, mueslis, granolas, some rice cereals, mixed cereals that incorporate fruit and nuts, some instant oat cereals.
• **Cheese**: Some contain or are coated in nuts.
• **Desserts**: Many contain nuts or have nut toppings sprinkled on them.
• **Drinks**: Some milk/yogurt drinks and brands of hot chocolate.
• **Nut oils**, spreads, and butters.
• **Ice creams**: May have nuts added or as toppings. Some ice cream wafers and cones contain nuts.
• **Meat and fish**: Check labels on breaded/battered meats and fish, meat pies, some burgers and sausages, and salamis and other cold meats.
• **Milk**: Some spray dried milk powders and fortified milks.
• **Salads**: Mixed salads such as rice and pasta salads and coleslaws.

As soon as you stray into the aisles of prepared and processed foods, life becomes much more complicated

• **Sauces**: Satay sauce (mainly peanut but other nuts may be used); curry sauces such as *korma*.
• **Snacks**: Chocolate and yogurt covered peanuts and raisins; mixed and salted nuts.
• **Spreads**: Chocolate nut spreads; peanut butter-style nut butters; praline spreads.
• **Vegetarian food**: Nut roasts, cutlets, and burgers. Prepared and frozen meals may contain nuts.
• **Yogurts**: Cereal and nut yogurts.

Things that sound risky but aren't: Chestnuts and water chestnuts rarely cause allergic reactions. Other so-called "nuts" are not true nuts. Coconut is a fruit; nutmeg and pine nuts are seeds; soy nuts are dried beans; tiger or chufa nuts are roots—all are often safe for people with tree nut allergies.

Peanuts
Peanuts in their natural state are also known as ground nuts, earth nuts, and monkey nuts.

Ingredients and terms used: arachis oil is peanut oil found in food but also watch out for it in cosmetics and personal care products. Peanut oil is most frequently used in food.

Foods that may contain peanuts (see also nut entries)
• **Drinks**: Smoothies sometimes have peanut butter added to them.
• **Hydrolyzed vegetable protein (HVP)**: This may be of peanut origin and currently does not have to be disclosed as a source of nuts.
• **Meats and fish**: Thai, Indonesian, Vietnamese, and Malay dishes often contain peanuts.
• **Nuts**: If you can eat tree nuts but not peanuts, watch out for artificial nuts such as "mandelonas" that are actually reflavored peanuts.
• **Oils, margarines, and butters**: Refined peanut oil is unlikely to cause an allergic reaction. Unrefined oil, often used in Chinese food, should be avoided because there is a clear risk. Blended vegetable oils may contain peanut oils. Nut butters are often produced on factory lines that make peanut butter.
• **Seeds** may be packed on the same lines as peanuts.
• **Sauces** such as Satay sauce (Southeast Asian); *bang bang chicken* (Chinese) contains peanuts.
• **Seasonings**: Check any oriental seasoning mixes.

Eggs

All eggs in their natural or unprocessed state and all eggs and egg-derived products.

Ingredients and terms used: egg, egg white (sometimes called *egg albumen*), egg yolk, egg protein. Whole egg, dried egg, or powdered egg includes yolk and white. The terms *ova* and *albumin* mean the product contains egg and are often used in compounds such as *conalbumin* or *ovoglobulin*. *Lecithin* (E322), an emulsifier in many products including chocolate, is made from soybeans or egg yolk but does not cause reactions in people who are allergic to soy or eggs.

Foods that may contain eggs
• **Alcohol**: Advocaat, eggnog, and eierpunsch.
• **Baby food**.
• **Baking**: Mixes for breads, cookies, doughnuts, muffins, pancakes, pastries, pretzels. Baked goods such as quiches and soufflés and almost all cakes and many cookies. Bread may be glazed or enriched with egg.
• **Candy and chocolate**: Check cookie-based or glazed sweets, such as nougat, for egg.
• **Desserts**: Custards, ice creams, iced yogurts, parfaits, meringues, puddings, dessert mixes, cream-filled pies. Sorbets may contain egg white.
• **Jams and spreads**: Fruit spreads called butters, curds, and occasionally cheeses contain egg.
• **Meat, chicken, fish, and seafood** that has been breadcrumbed or battered usually has egg in it. Hamburgers, hot dogs, meatloaf, salami, and crab cakes may use egg for binding. Fish croquets or fishsticks may contain egg whites.
• **Pasta**: The dried variety is often egg-free. Most fresh pasta, especially ravioli types, contain egg.
• **Sauces and dressings** may be thickened with egg. especially mayonnaise-style dressings, hollandaise, béarnaise, tartare sauce, and Caesar salad dressing.
• **Soups**: Broths and bouillons may be clarified with egg white.

Hidden traps: Some commercial egg substitutes are designed for weight loss and actually contain egg, so check the label on your egg replacer. Some vaccines and anesthetics may contain egg.

Dairy

Dairy includes all cows' milk (whole, skim, low-fat, or UHT), all canned milk, cream, crème fraîche, ice cream, yogurt, fromage frais, Quark, butter and buttermilk, and all cheeses, whether soft or hard.

Ingredients and terms used: Milk powder, milk by-products, dry milk solids, and non-fat dry milk, *casein* or *caseinate*, whey, whey powder, curds, yogurt, yogurt powder, powder, lactose. Check any unfamiliar ingredients with *lact-* in them but note that lactic acid is produced from sugar by bacteria and is not derived from milk.

Foods that may contain dairy products
• **Alcohol**: Cream liqueurs.
• **Baby food**.
• **Baking**: Cake mixes, cakes, cookies, snacks, granola and fruit bars, and breakfast goods. Breads may contain milk, dried milk, or dairy products.
• **Drinks**: Milky, creamy, yogurt drinks and smoothies; coffees, hot chocolate, and malted drinks.
• **Butter, fats, ghee, and many margarines** contain milk products, as do egg and fat substitutes.
• **Candy and chocolate**: All milk and white chocolate contains dairy, as do many brands of dark chocolate, toffee, and fudge.
• **Cereals**: Some breakfast cereals contain lactose.
• **Desserts**: Assume ice creams and yogurts contain dairy unless proved otherwise.
• **Dips and spreads**.
• **Fried foods**: Check batter is dairy-free.
• **Jams and spreads**: Fruit curds contain butter but fruit cheeses are generally dairy-free jellies.
• **Meats and fish**: Some meats and canned tuna contain casein. Dishes with sauces may contain dairy.
• **Sauces and dressings**: Creamy sauces and salad dressings may contain lactose.
• **Soups and soup mixes**.
• **Vegetables, canned or processed**: Creamed corn may have butter; instant mashed potato may contain lactose.

Hidden traps: Some products such as "nondairy" coffee whiteners may have ingredients derived from milk. Some rice cheese contains casein.

So much food to enjoy

Whether you are a passionate or practical cook, there's an extensive range of foods available to you, even if substitutions have to be made to a recipe because of egg, dairy, or nut allergies, or gluten intolerance. Everything in the vegetable store and on the fresh fish and meat counters is on the menu in this book. Pamper an adult, have fun cooking with children, or just make sweet small indulgences for yourself—you'll find plenty of opportunities in the baking section, which has more than a sprinkling of chocolate recipes.

Vegetable side dishes and salads are such an obvious idea when cooking for people with allergies that I've allowed myself only a few full recipes for them in the book, since I preferred to concentrate on tricky dishes like breads, pies, pastries, and other desserts. But there are lots of vegetable ingredients in the recipes as well as in tips and serving suggestions. Pick the best from leafy greens, peppery salads, potatoes for every use and occasion, winter root vegetables and squashes, fragrant herbs and spices and fresh, dried, and seasonal fruits.

Likewise, if you are not allergic to fish or shellfish the entire fish counter is open to you. You'll find nostalgic treats like Fish pie (p.96), future classics like Miso marinated salmon (p.101), or barbecue specials such as Marinated swordfish (p.99). Adapt the recipes to suit whatever your fish store has available, whether it's mussels, sardines, anchovies, sole, sea bass, monkfish, mackerel, lobster, or skate.

Meat dishes are often the centerpiece of a meal, so I wanted recipes with staying power—both as common sense cooking and inspirational starting points. Choose from quick dishes such as Lemon thyme grilled chicken (p.109), slow simmered Ragu Bolognese (p.117) and Moussaka (p.128), and classic roasts for the whole family.

MY FOOD HEROES

Having an allergy or food intolerance doesn't mean doing without. Recipes for breads, pies, desserts, and pastries are made possible in this book by what I call my "food heroes":

- **Dairy-free milks** like soy are now familiar but rice, oat, and nut milks are also healthy and delicious in their own right. Soy cream makes an excellent dairy cream substitute.

- **Dairy-free cheeses** work well in many toppings and sauces.

- **Xanthan gum** acts as a gluten substitute, adding essential springiness to breads and helping to hold together gluten-free pastry that could otherwise be crumbly and difficult to work with. You only use a little at a time so a pack lasts a long time.

- **Flours made from corn** have a multitude of uses and have a delicious color and flavor. Use cornmeal for breads and tortillas (p.68) and finely ground cornflour to thicken sauces, stews, and gravies.

real problem-solving substitute ingredients that mean crusty, light-textured breads, creamy desserts, sponge cakes, and ice creams are no longer out of bounds. I've listed them here.

- **Prepared gluten-free flour mixes** are available in many supermarkets. Most are based on rice flour but having a mix gives a better balance of flavor, texture, and weight.

- **Potato flour** gets top marks for its binding properties. You can also use it with liquid as an egg substitute in baking.

- **Commercial egg-replacer powders:** Use them to adapt cake and quiche recipes.

- **Tofu:** Soft, silken, and firm varieties are good in dips and dressings, and replace cooked eggs in recipes.

- **Pine nuts** are my problem-solver for nuts in baking, toppings and sauces, as are sunflower, sesame, and other seeds.

Your pantry

Living an allergen-free lifestyle doesn't mean you have to cut out all the foods you love. Here are some tips to build up your pantry to include allergen-free staples. Use the substitutions table on pages 48–49 to help you with your cooking, and the resources on pages 218–219 for useful sources of these foods.

The gluten-free pantry

Here are the essentials you will need for a gluten-free pantry. If you are allergic to wheat but not gluten, then you can add back in products that contain gluten or gluten-like proteins, but are not related to wheat, such as oats, rye, and barley.

Breakfast: Gluten-free baked breakfast goods, including breads and croissants, are available in normal, long-life, frozen, and part-baked form. Stock up on gluten-free muffin, pancake, and bread mixes and gluten-free cereals such as granola and muesli—or you can buy the ingredients and make your own. If you can tolerate oats, opt for traditional oatmeal, otherwise hot millet cereal is an excellent alternative.

Breads and bread flours: Gluten-free breads and bread mixes are improving and becoming more widely available all the time. Pick from a wide range, from wraps to hamburger buns and fruit breads. To make your own, stock up on corn, rice, potato, tapioca, soy, and chickpea flours or buy ready-prepared gluten-free flour for bread making. Xanthan gum—a gluten substitute that adds springiness to bread—is essential, as are eggs and yeast.

Cookies, cakes, and pastry: To bake these you will need gluten-free baking soda, baking powder, and lighter flours such as cornflour, rice, and potato flour. Xanthan gum and eggs are vital supplies. Stock up on polenta, almonds, and other nuts—frequent ingredients in home-baked gluten-free cakes. There

are many delicious varieties of gluten-free cookies and cakes available by mail, and a smaller selection in health food stores.

Snacks and treats: Corn chips, rice cakes and crackers, seed mixes, and tortilla chips are good for eating on their own or with cheese or dips.

Pasta, pizza, and prepared meals: There is a great choice of dried pasta available made of corn, rice, 100 percent buckwheat, or chickpea flours. Gluten-free pasta-based meals, long-life or frozen pizza bases and pizzas are good choices for quick, pick-up meals.

Good grains, cereals and legumes: Stock up on staple gluten-free grains; white, brown, and wild rice, corn/polenta, quinoa, buckwheat, and millet. Experiment with less-known grains such as sorghum, and red camargue rice. Potatoes and fresh, dried, or canned legumes, beans, and lentils are good sources of carbohydrate and protein.

Sauces, seasonings, and soups: Cornflour, rice flour, and arrowroot are good thickeners for sauces. Build up a collection of gluten-free flavorings such as soy, ketchups, spices, and seasonings for all types of cooking, because these are not always readily available. For dressings, have safe non-malt vinegars available: Wine, rice, and balsamic. Buy gluten-free soups in cans and packages, and gluten-free stock cubes.

Alcohol and beverages: Liquor, wine, cider, and liqueurs based on wines and liquor are usually gluten-free, but check the label to ensure no malt or gluten-containing ingredients have been added. You will need to buy gluten-free beer.

◀ Your gluten-free pantry essentials:
Top shelf L–R: balsamic vinegar, gluten-free spaghetti, polenta, buckwheat flour, potato flour, white wine vinegar, xanthan gum.
Middle shelf L–R: corn tortillas, wild rice, lentils, seed mix, corn crispbreads, maize meal. **Bottom shelf L–R**: rice pasta, gluten-free muesli mix, puffed quinoa, gluten-free tamari soy sauce.

▲ Egg-free food heroes from left to right: commercial egg replacer, vanilla pods, and potato flour.

The egg-free pantry

Simplify cooking and eating by keeping egg-replacers and substitutes for egg-containing ingredients such as mayonnaise on hand. Buy special items online or at health food stores.

Baking: Stock a good supply of rising agents: egg-replacers, baking powder, baking soda, cream of tartar, and dried yeast. Vanilla pods and extract can add "eggy" flavor back in. Corn oil and condensed milk contribute richness to cakes. Soy and potato flour are useful binding agents.

Desserts: Cornflour-based egg-free custards are a great staple, although many fresh brands are egg free too. Keep cornflour or arrowroot to thicken homemade sauces. Packaged and canned desserts such as instant mousses and steamed fruit are useful. For homemade egg-free "set" desserts you'll need gelatine powder or leaf gelatine.

Savory: Have store-bought egg-free mayonnaise in your refrigerator for sandwiches, dips, and salads. Tofu, both firm and silken, adds "eggy" texture to homemade dips, mayonnaise, and cooked dishes.

Pasta: The most useful staple is the many varieties of egg-free pasta, from basic noodles and spaghetti to more elaborate shapes, multicolored pasta twists, and lasagne sheets.

Snacks: If the rest of the household regularly snacks on egg-containing pastries and cakes, make sure there are a range of snacks such as chocolate, fruit jellies, chips, and nuts for the egg-avoider to enjoy.

The dairy-free pantry

Dairy-free essentials include dairy-free milks, spreads, cream, yogurt, cheese, and ice cream. If you are allergic to cow's milk you may be able to tolerate products made from other animals such as goats and sheep, but they are often just as problematic.

Beverages: The staple is soy milk in myriad varieties: sweetened, flavored, fortified with vitamins and calcium, long-life or refrigerated. Naturally sweet dairy-free milks include rice milk (good for soy allergics) and tiger nut milk. Buy nut and oat milks for variety. Potato milk is best in dried form. Dairy-free baby formulas and infant food in jars or frozen form are also available.

Creams, yogurts, and toppings: Coconut milk and cream are essential for Southeast Asian dishes and also a good substitute for milk and cream in many custards and desserts. Use soy cream to serve with pies and tarts; for thicker toppings stock up on dairy-free custards, almond and other nut-based creams and desserts, as well as silken tofu. Soy yogurts come in fruit flavors—perfect for snacks or breakfast. Buy plain soy yogurt for making creamy salad dressings and dips.

Spreads, fats, and dips: Check the labels of margarine because some non-dairy margarines contain milk products. Buy hard vegetable fats for pastry making. Flavorless oils such as corn oil are good for baking and frying, but for savory dishes, use olive, seed, and nut oils to compensate for the lost "buttery" taste. Non-dairy dips such as hummus and guacamole, tofu, and nut-based spreads are invaluable for snacks and appetizers.

Cheese: Substitutes based on soy, rice, or nuts are surprisingly good and worth seeking out. Choose from non-dairy cream cheese, Parmesan, mozzarella, herbed cheeses, Monterey Jack, Cheddar-style, and those specifically designed to be good melting cheeses. Otherwise, nutritional yeast flakes add "cheesiness" and color to sauces and Dijon or mustard powder is a useful addition.

Ice creams, desserts and treats: Stock your freezer with non-dairy ice creams and desserts. Keep a supply of dairy-free chocolate. Dairy-free cookies, muffins, and long-life cakes are also available.

The nut-free pantry
A difficult allergy to live with but less problematic in the home where cross contamination is less of an issue once you have checked labels carefully. If you are allergic to peanuts or nuts, it is safer to keep your pantry nut free.

▼ Dairy-free staples include (clockwise from back left) grated Cheddar-style cheese, whipped soy cream, soy milk, yeast flakes, soy cream cheese, herb tofu, and vegan Parmesan.

Breakfast: Stock up on cereals: Nut-free cornflakes, puffed rice, wheat-based, and oatmeal. Source nut-free muesli and granola or make your own. Most basic bread is nut free or nut safe. If you make bread, invest in a breadmaker and fill shelves with flours, seeds, and yeast.

Snacks and spreads: Good snacks include dried fruits, fruit bars, oatmeal bars, and seeds. Keep safe treats such as dried fruits, jelly sweets, chocolates, and cookies for when others have nut-containing cakes and chocolates. Fruit preserves, yeast spreads, and nut-free chocolate spread can replace nut-based spreads. For pre-dinner nibbles use olives, caperberries, crispbreads, root vegetable and potato chips, and Japanese rice crackers and cocktail snacks.

Sauces and toppings: Include pesto among your other pasta sauces if pine nuts are not a problem. Toasted pine nuts are also a good substitute for chopped nuts in sweet, savory, and baked recipes. Keep a selection of seeds such as sunflower, pumpkin, and poppy seeds for decorative toppings on breads and desserts and sesame seeds for stir-fries and oriental dishes or in place of chopped peanuts. Invest in a small bottle of unblended sesame oil, since a dash adds flavor to salads and other recipes that call for off-limits nut oils.

Substituting ingredients

If you're cooking a dish that calls for ingredients you need to avoid, find the problem ingredient in the left-hand column, the substitutes and alternatives in the middle, and any tips on how to use them on the right.

DAIRY	substitutes & alternatives	notes & tips
Milk	Soy milk, rice milk, oat milk, coconut milk or thin coconut cream, nut milks such as almond, cashew, tiger nut milk (chufa), or potato milk.	Substitutes may be thinner or have a noticeable flavor. Some are available in dried form. Fruit juice, purées, and stocks can be used in some recipes.
Butter	For baking: Soy, sunflower, olive oil, and vegetable fat-based spreads. For other cooking: Oils, animal fats such as lard, and hard vegetable fats.	Choose according to the taste desired. Some dairy-free spreads contain too much water to be used for baking.
Cheese soft	Soy-based cream cheese.	Textures and spreadability will vary. Soy cream cheese in icing or toppings is softer and runnier than dairy and may need refrigerating.
Cheese hard	Substitutes (sometimes called "cheezes") made of soy, rice, tofu, or nuts. Types include mozzarella, cheddar, Monterey Jack, Parmesan, herb.	Textures, flavor, and saltiness vary. Melting varieties are useful for pizzas and other toppings.
Cream/ Yogurt	Soy cream, silken, firm, and soft tofu, and thick coconut cream. Tofu and other soy-based yogurts.	Soy and coconut cream alternative for savory dishes. Soy cream alternative with vanilla extract is an excellent pouring cream or make your own Chantilly Topping (p.216). If soy yogurt curdles during cooking, stir in a teaspoon of flour to stabilize.

Note: Cross reactivity in dairy is quite high but if cow's milk in particular, rather than dairy in general, is the problem, you may be able to tolerate goat or sheep's milk, cheeses, and yogurts.

NUT	substitutes & alternatives	notes & tips
Peanuts and tree nuts	Pine nuts or seeds such as sesame, pumpkin, or sunflower. For cakes, crumbles, or curries, use grated desiccated coconut (not a nut but a fruit).	Toast pine nuts and seeds to bring out flavor.
Nut-based oils	Vegetable, olive, or seed oils if tolerated.	A mix of flavorless oil and toasted sesame oil makes a tasty alternative to walnut oil in salads.
Toppings with nuts or peanuts	Crushed potato chips, corn chips, or rice crackers add crunch to a savory topping. If tolerated, seeds such as sesame, pumpkin, flaxseed, linseed, pine nuts; toasted jumbo oats; or shredded coconut.	Breadcrumbs fried with finely chopped garlic on cooked vegetables or salads. On cold desserts, make a sweet crumble topping (see Plum Crumble, p.146), cooked in the oven and then cooled.

Note: If only peanuts are the problem, you may possibly be able to use nuts or vice versa, but many people are allergic to both (see Cross reactions, p.16). Some people with nut allergies, but not all, can tolerate pine nuts and sesame seeds.

GLUTEN	substitutes & alternatives	notes & tips
Flour and baking powder	Ready-made gluten-free flour mixes and baking powder or make your own using rice, corn, potato, buckwheat, chickpea (gram), lentil, soy, or chestnut flours.	Gluten-free dough can be crumbly but don't add more water. Soy, potato, chickpea, and lentil flours have marked flavors. Lighter flours for breadmaking and baking include rice and corn flours and tapioca.
Bread, pizzas, tortillas	Various packaged gluten-free breads, pure corn tortillas, croissants, and pizza bases are available. Check the freezer section, too.	In recipes, use eggs and xanthan gum, if specified, or the bread will lack springiness. Use stale loaves to make gluten-free croûtons and breadcrumbs.
Pasta and noodles	Corn- or rice-based gluten-free pastas are available in many shapes and sizes. Rice noodles or 100 percent buckwheat noodles are gluten-free too.	In some recipes use other carbohydrate-rich foods such as rice, polenta, potatoes, yams, cassava, sweet potatoes, breadfruit, or legumes.
Flour thickeners	Cornflour, rice flour, arrowroot, sago, and tapioca.	Use 1 tbsp cornflour to thicken 1 cup liquid. To thicken soups, add cooked rice, cooked cubed potato, or bread and blend briefly in a food processor.
Cereals	Rice, corn, quinoa, millet, and buckwheat-based cereals as flakes or in "puffed" form. Millet flakes instead of oats for gluten-free porridge.	Make your own granola (p.52) and then add fruit and nuts to taste.

Note: If wheat rather than gluten is the problem, you can use products made of rye, barley, and oats.

EGG	substitutes & alternatives	notes & tips
For baking	Commercial egg replacers for either whole egg or egg white. Or make your own with potato flour and water. Use extra baking powder or yeast and liquid as rising agents in cakes and cookies that require it.	Egg replacers may have a drying effect; if so, add 1 tsp oil and also 1 tsp vanilla extract for flavor. To replace an egg, use 1 tsp baking powder, 1 tbsp vinegar, and 1 tbsp of extra liquid; or use 1 tsp yeast in 4 tbsp warm water.
In dressings and dips	Use soft, silken, or firm tofu for eggy texture.	Use bought or homemade egg-free Mayonnaise (see p.210). Use 2–3 tbsp tofu per egg to thicken dips, etc.
For binding or thickening	Potato flour for binding. Wheat flour, rice flour, or cornstarch for thickening.	Use flours to thicken cooked sauces or add double cream near to the end of cooking.
For glazing	Milk, cream, or gelatine (for extra shine).	See Chicken Pie recipe on page 106 for a gelatine glaze.
In desserts	Cornflour for custards and savory sauces. Thick whipped cream and/or gelatine in set desserts.	To thicken, use 1 level tbsp cornflour to 1 cup milk; add sugar and vanilla for sweet custard sauce. 1 tsp gelatine dissolved in 2 tbsp liquid approximates setting of one egg.
Whole cooked eggs	Use firm tofu cubed and cooked; scallops in fishy dishes with egg such as Kedgeree (p.67).	For breakfasts, try scrambled tofu and mushrooms. Add butter beans to salad niçoise instead of egg.

Note: Most people who are allergic to hens' eggs are allergic to other birds' eggs, too.

The recipes

Honey granola

A delicious and healthy breakfast cereal, easy and worth making yourself, especially if it's difficult to find packaged versions without gluten or nuts. Make the crunchy honey clusters in advance and then add, according to taste, nuts, other cereals, seeds, dried fruit, fresh fruit, or whatever takes your fancy just before serving. The main ingredients keep well, so it's worth stocking up on your favorite toppings.

nut & egg free

flavorless nut-free oil
¼ cup honey
1½ cups rolled oats
suggested nut-free additions
½ cup golden raisins
2 tbsp chopped, dried apricots
3 tbsp pumpkin seeds
2 tbsp pine nuts, toasted
  (optional)
½ cup puffed rice or wheat
1 cup corn flakes
1½ cups bran flakes
3 tbsp chopped, dried apple or
  pineapple pieces

to serve
fresh fruit in season, such as
  raspberries and bananas
milk or yogurt

PREPARATION TIME 5 minutes
COOKING TIME 10–15 minutes
SERVES 4–6

1 Preheat the oven to 350° F. Oil a large baking sheet.
2 Spoon the honey into a medium-sized bowl. Gently heat the honey first if it isn't quite runny enough to mix easily. Add the rolled oats and stir gently to make sure they are evenly coated.
3 Spread the oats thinly on the oiled baking sheet and toast in the oven for 10–15 minutes or until golden, checking once or twice to make sure that the oats are not burning.
4 Remove from the oven and let cool. Store in an airtight container if preparing ahead of time.
5 When ready to use, mix the clusters with the other dried ingredients. Add fresh fruit and serve with milk or yogurt.

WATCH OUT FOR pine nuts, which are tolerated by most people with nut allergies, but omit if in any doubt.

TIP Vary fresh fruit according to season. Try grated apple with a little ground cinnamon or tropical dried fruits such as pineapple, mango, and papaya.

gluten free
also egg free

Follow the recipe on the left, but replace the rolled oats with rice flakes. For the additional ingredients, substitute buckwheat or millet flakes for the bran flakes and use puffed rice or rice bran in place of puffed wheat. Add 3 tablespoons of pistachios, 2 tablespoons of flaked almonds, and 3 tablespoons of toasted hazelnuts.
Pictured opposite ▶

dairy free
also egg free

Follow the recipe on the left, but choose a dairy-free topping or milk. Try soy milk, rice milks, or tiger nut milk (which doesn't contain nuts). Oat milks are highly recommended if you can tolerate gluten. Similarly, hazelnut or almond milk are great if nuts aren't a problem. Use a combination of the dried ingredients and fruit that are suggested in the other versions.

Croissants

The ultimate breakfast food made from the flakiest of pastries, croissants are best made in a cool kitchen with a cool head. Equally delicious plain, with jam or honey, or filled with ham and just-melted cheese (or dairy-free melting varieties), they take a little time and effort but are worth it—especially if store-bought ones are off-limits, as they are for gluten avoiders.

🌾 gluten free

2 cups gluten-free all-purpose
  flour, plus extra for dusting
½ tsp salt
2 tsp superfine sugar
2 tsp xanthan gum
1 tbsp instant yeast
¼ cup cold butter, cut in
  ½-in dice
⅔ cup milk
1 egg
vegetable oil for baking sheet

for the glaze
1 egg, beaten
1 tsp confectioners' sugar

PREPARATION TIME 25 minutes
  plus proofing
COOKING TIME 15 minutes
MAKES 6

TIP These don't look as puffy as the wheat-based croissants (see nut-free recipe, right) but they are spongy and buttery and a tasty breakfast treat.

1 Sift the flour with the salt, sugar, and gum into the food processor with the dough attachment. Add the yeast and diced butter.
2 Warm the milk very briefly until just lukewarm then whisk in the egg. Add to the processor and run the machine for 1 minute to knead to a soft ball.
3 Tip the mixture out onto a lightly floured surface. Roll out to a rectangle. Fold the top third down and the bottom third up over. Give the dough a quarter turn and roll and fold again. Turn, roll, and fold once more.
4 Dust the rolling pin with flour and roll out the dough into an oblong about three times as long as it is high and about ¼ inch thick. Trim the edges and cut into 3 equal squares.
6 Cut each square in half to form triangles. Oil a baking sheet.
7 Beat the egg with the confectioners' sugar and brush the triangles. Starting from the long edge, roll up each triangle, curve each roll slightly into a crescent shape then place on the baking sheet. Cover loosely with oiled plastic wrap and leave in a warm place until well risen, about 45 minutes.
8 Meanwhile, preheat the oven to 400° F. Brush the croissants with the remaining glaze. Bake until spongy and golden, about 15 minutes.
9 Best served while still warm or transfer to a wire rack to cool before wrapping and storing.

nut free

2 cups bread flour,
  plus extra for dusting
¾ tsp salt
2 tsp superfine sugar
2 tsp instant yeast
⅓ cup cold butter
7 tbsp milk
1 egg, beaten
vegetable oil for baking sheet

for the glaze
1 egg
1 tsp confectioners' sugar

PREPARATION TIME 30 minutes
  plus chilling and proofing
COOKING TIME 15 minutes
MAKES 8

1 Sift the flour, salt, and sugar into a food processor with the dough attachment. Add the yeast.
2 Put 1 tbsp of the butter in a saucepan and melt. Remove from the heat and add the milk. The mixture should be just warm, not hot. Add to the flour mixture and run the machine to form an elastic dough. Run the machine for another minute to knead it thoroughly.
3 Transfer the dough to a work surface, dusted with flour. Knead gently until smooth. Roll out with a rolling pin, dusted with a little flour, to a rectangle about ½ inch thick.
4 Dot with a third of the remaining butter over the bottom two-thirds of the dough. Fold the top plain dough over the center portion then fold the bottom third up over. Press the edges together with the rolling pin. Give the dough a quarter turn and roll, dot, and fold again. Repeat with the final third of the butter.
5 Wrap the dough in plastic wrap and chill for at least 30 minutes.
6 Unwrap the dough, roll out on a floured surface again to a rectangle, but without adding butter. Fold as before, turn, roll, and fold again.
7 Dusting the rolling pin with flour, roll out to a large square about ¼ inch thick, trim the edges, and cut into 4 equal squares.
8 Cut each square in half to form triangles. Oil a large baking sheet with vegetable oil.
9 Beat the egg with the confectioners' sugar and brush on triangles. Starting from the long edge, roll each triangle, curve each into a crescent shape, and place on the baking sheet. Brush with remaining glaze. Cover loosely with oiled plastic wrap and leave in a warm place to proof until doubled in bulk, about 40 minutes.
10 Meanwhile, preheat the oven to 425° F. Bake the croissants until puffy and golden, about 15 minutes.
11 Best served warm. Otherwise, transfer to a wire rack and let cool before wrapping and storing.

 dairy free
also nut free

Follow the nut-free recipe, but substitute lard or vegetable shortening for the butter and dairy-free soy, rice, or oat milk, or water for the cow's milk.

 egg free
also nut free

Follow the nut-free recipe, but omit the egg. Add an extra 2–3 tablespoons of milk, if necessary. Use 3 tablespoons of light cream (or soy alternative to light cream) and 1 teaspoon of confectioners' sugar for the glaze instead of the egg yolk, water, and confectioners' sugar.

TIP All four versions can be reheated and they also freeze well.

Pancakes

My image of the great American breakfast is hot fresh coffee plus a stack of pancakes with soft brown crusts and the light inner sponge that soaks up honey or maple syrup so well. You can add more toppings—fresh fruits or soft dried fruits with a squeeze of lemon to cut through the sweetness, or even cream cheese or crumbled bacon.

 ## nut free

generous 1 cup all-purpose flour
pinch of salt
2 tsp baking powder
2 tbsp superfine sugar
1 large egg, beaten
1 scant cup milk
nut-free vegetable oil for frying

to serve
maple syrup or honey
handful of raspberries (optional)
lemon wedges (optional)

PREPARATION TIME 5 minutes
COOKING TIME 20 minutes
MAKES 8

1 Sift the flour with the salt, baking powder, and sugar.
2 Make a well in the center, add the egg and half the milk and whisk (but do not overmix) to form a smooth creamy batter. Stir in the remaining milk.
3 Heat a little oil in a frying pan over a medium heat. Pour off the excess. Add enough batter to the pan to make a pancake about 5 inches in diameter and cook until bubbles appear and pop on the surface and the pancake is almost set and brown underneath, about 1¼ minutes. Flip with a spatula and quickly cook the other side. Slide out onto a plate and keep warm while you cook the remainder. Heat the pan with a little more oil between each pancake. If you have a big pan, you could cook 2–3 pancakes at a time.
4 Serve the pancakes hot with maple syrup, honey, raspberries, or lemon wedges to squeeze over them.

TIP The pancakes are best made fresh, so keep them warm on a plate over a pan of gently simmering water while you cook the remainder.

dairy free
also nut free

Follow the recipe on the left, but use soy, rice, or oat milk in place of the cow's milk.

egg free
also nut free

Follow the recipe on the left, but in step 1, whisk 1 tablespoon of potato flour with ¼ teaspoon of xanthan gum and 2 tablespoons of water until thick and frothy and add to the flour. In step 2, omit the egg and add an extra 3–4 tablespoons of milk to form a creamy consistency. Continue with steps 3 and 4, left.
◀ Pictured opposite

gluten free
also nut free

Follow the recipe on the left, but use ½ cup buckwheat flour and ½ cup gluten-free all-purpose flour instead of all-purpose flour.

Corned beef hash

Golden brown crispy fried potatoes are a great easy-to-cook breakfast or brunch meal. Combine them with corned beef for the famous deli specialty corned beef hash or, more simply, just cook hash browns (see variation). Whichever you choose, it feeds a crowd and doesn't need split-second timing. There are endless additions and variations; my favorite is red flannel hash served with lots of chopped parsley.

dairy, egg, gluten, & nut free

4 tbsp flavorless nut-free oil
1 large onion, finely chopped
1 lb red-skinned or
  all-purpose potatoes, cooked,
  and cut into $\frac{1}{2}$-in cubes
12 oz corned beef, cut into
  $\frac{1}{2}$-in cubes
salt and freshly ground black
  pepper
1 tbsp Worcestershire sauce
  (optional)
chopped fresh parsley

PREPARATION TIME 25 minutes
COOKING TIME 10–15 minutes
SERVES 6

WATCH OUT FOR Worcestershire sauce; it can contain gluten. Make sure you use a gluten-free version.

VARIATIONS Add 2–3 chopped, cooked beets to the recipe at step 2 for a tasty red flannel hash.

For hash browns, prepare as for the recipe on the left, but use 1 $\frac{3}{4}$ lb of potatoes and omit the corned beef and Worcestershire sauce. At step 3, when the hash browns are golden brown underneath, use a spatula to flip them either as a single "cake," or cut into halves or quarters and then turn. If needed, sprinkle a few more drops of oil into the pan. When golden brown on both sides, the hash browns are ready to serve. Popular additions to hash browns include diced green bell peppers, bacon, cheese (not for the dairy-sensitives), and fresh chopped chilies, but note the caution (left).

1 Heat the oil in a heavy-bottomed frying pan and fry the onions over a fairly high heat, stirring occasionally, until lightly browned and turning crispy at the edges (about 4 minutes).
2 Add the cubed potatoes and corned beef and toss a few times to coat evenly in oil. Season with salt and pepper and sprinkle with Worcestershire sauce, if using.
3 Reduce the heat to medium. Spread the potatoes and corned beef out in the pan and press down with a large spatula. Cook for 10–15 minutes on a gentle heat until the bottom is brown and crispy—be careful not to cook it too quickly or it will burn.
4 Sprinkle with the chopped fresh parsley, cut into wedges, and serve hot.

SERVING SUGGESTION Serve with poached or fried eggs (if eggs are tolerated). It is also delicious with chili sauce or ketchup, but be aware that some people cannot tolerate chilies and some bottled ketchups are not suitable for people sensitive to gluten.

Smoothies

One of the most popular new breakfast foods, a good smoothie needs a balance of fruit, creaminess, and sweetness. Since more people are enjoying dairy-free milks for taste and health reasons, even if they can eat dairy, I've used soy and oat milks as well as cows' milk and yogurt. Use the recipes or create your own combinations with whatever ingredients you have on hand.

 egg free

banana oatie
1 large banana, chopped
1 cup oat milk
1 cup orange juice
½ cup ground almonds
1 tbsp honey
ground cinnamon to dust

apricot and mango
1 cup canned apricot
 halves, chopped
4 tbsp syrup from canned
 apricots
½ mango, chopped
1 cup orange juice
1 cup soy yogurt
½ tsp vanilla extract
a squeeze of lime juice
a handful of ice cubes

melon, grape, and pear
1 cup Galia melon (or other
 melon), chopped
2 pears, peeled and chopped
1 cup grape juice
2 ice cubes
mint sprig to garnish

mixed berry
1½ cups mixed red soft fruit
1 cup Greek yogurt
½ cup milk
2 ice cubes
3 tbsp honey

raspberry coulis (optional)
½ cup raspberries
2 tbsp confectioners' sugar

PREPARATION TIME 3–5 minutes
SERVES 1–2

 dairy free
also egg free

The smoothies are dairy free except for the mixed berry. Prepare as for the recipe on the left, but replace the yogurt and milk with soy or other dairy-free alternatives.

gluten free
also egg free

The smoothies are gluten free except for the banana oatie. Prepare as for the recipe on the left, but replace the oat milk with any gluten-free milk.

nut free
also egg free

The smoothies are nut free except for the banana oatie. Prepare as for the recipe on the left, but replace the almonds with ¼ cup of coconut milk and reduce the oat milk to ½ cup.

1 Put all the ingredients in a blender and blend until smooth. For a thick shake add ice cubes before blending.
2 Pour into glasses and garnish. Serve as soon as possible.
3 For the raspberry coulis, mix the raspberries with the confectioners' sugar, and press through a sieve. Swirl the coulis on top of each glass just before serving.
Pictured on next page ▶

BREAKFASTS

Delicious dairy-free smoothies (see p.59) and mouth-watering
egg- and nut-free Cinnamon, raisin, & apple muffins (see p.62).

Cinnamon, raisin, & apple muffins

There's a delicious cinnamon aroma from these as they bake and from time to time you'll catch a whiff of apple too. Popular with all ages, the muffins have a lovely texture and are particularly good eaten warm for breakfast, but are also ideal as part of a packed lunch. You can even treat them as a snack and serve them split and buttered.

 **egg & nut free**

2 cups all-purpose flour
pinch of salt
1 tbsp baking powder
1 tsp ground cinnamon
3 tbsp soft brown sugar
3 tbsp butter or margarine,
  melted
2 apples, unpeeled and grated
⅓ cup raisins
¾ cup milk
raw sugar to sprinkle
  (optional)

PREPARATION TIME 8 minutes
COOKING TIME 20 minutes
MAKES 12 muffins

1 Line 12 sections of a muffin pan with average-sized paper muffin cups or butter the pan well. Preheat the oven to 400° F.
2 Sift the flour, salt, baking powder, and cinnamon into a bowl.
3 Add the remaining ingredients and mix well. You will have a thick wet dough.
4 Spoon into the prepared sections (they should be full). Bake in the oven until risen, pale golden, and firm to the touch, about 20 minutes.
5 Transfer to a wire rack to cool.
◀ **Pictured on previous page**

TIP These muffins keep well for a few days in an airtight container and can also be frozen.

 dairy free
also egg & nut free

Follow the recipe on the left, but substitute dairy-free spread for the butter or ordinary margarine and soy, rice, or oat milk for the cow's milk.

 gluten free
also egg & nut free

Follow the recipe on the left, but substitute gluten-free all-purpose flour for the ordinary flour and make sure the baking powder is gluten free too. Add an extra 4 tablespoons of milk in step 3.

"A wonderful breakfast treat if you usually have to turn them down"

Blueberry muffins

For many, the blueberry muffin reigns supreme. Quick and easy to make, these light vanilla-flavored muffins are oozing with juicy fruit. They are an excellent weekend treat for breakfast or a midmorning snack and are ideally eaten fresh from the oven. We've been known to take an egg- and nut-free batch into our local coffee shop, so the whole family can enjoy coffee and muffins together.

nut free

¼ cup butter or margarine
2 cups all-purpose flour
1 tbsp baking powder
pinch of salt
¼ cup superfine sugar, plus extra
   for dusting (optional)
⅔ cup milk
2 tsp lemon juice
½ tsp vanilla extract
1 egg, beaten
1 cup blueberries
ground cinnamon for dusting
   (optional)

PREPARATION TIME 15 minutes
COOKING TIME 20 minutes
MAKES 6 large or 10 small muffins

1 Line 6 large or 10 small sections of a muffin pan with paper muffin cups or butter the pan well. Preheat the oven to 400° F.
2 Melt the butter or margarine in a saucepan. Remove from the heat and let cool.
3 Sift the flour, baking powder, and salt into a bowl. Stir in the sugar.
4 Make a well in the center, pour in the milk, lemon juice, vanilla extract, and egg. Fold the mixture quickly to combine, but don't worry if there are a few lumps. Fold the blueberries carefully into the mixture.
5 Spoon the mixture into the prepared pan (they will be almost full).
6 If desired, sprinkle lightly with cinnamon and sugar.
7 Bake in the oven until risen, lightly golden in color, and the centers spring back when lightly pressed, about 25 minutes. Transfer to a wire rack, dust with superfine sugar and let cool.

dairy free
also nut free

Follow the recipe on the left, but substitute dairy-free spread for the butter or ordinary margarine and soy, rice, or oat milk for the cow's milk.

egg free
also nut free

Follow the recipe on the left, but substitute 1 tablespoon of potato flour mixed with 3 tablespoons of water for the beaten egg. The egg-free muffins will be slightly paler and smoother on top, but equally delicious.

gluten free
also nut free

Follow the recipe on the left, but substitute gluten-free all-purpose flour for the ordinary all-purpose flour and check that the baking powder is gluten free as well. Add an extra 4 tablespoons of milk.

Chocolate croissants

Although these are a little complicated to make, they are so delicious for breakfast with a cup of fresh coffee and a glass of orange juice, you'll be glad you did. They are especially popular with children so you could make a batch or two in advance to freeze until you need them. Best eaten freshly baked, this croissant, also called *pain au chocolat*, can be warmed briefly in a microwave or oven before serving.

 nut free

2 cups bread flour,
   plus extra for dusting
1 tsp salt
2 tsp superfine sugar
2 tsp instant yeast
1/3 cup cold butter
7 tbsp milk
1 egg, beaten
vegetable oil for baking pan
to finish
1 egg

1 tsp confectioners' sugar, plus extra
   for dusting
24 squares of nut-free semisweet
   chocolate

PREPARATION TIME 30 minutes,
plus chilling and proofing
COOKING TIME 15 minutes
MAKES 8

1 Follow steps 1–6 of the nut-free croissant recipe on page 55.
2 Unwrap the dough, roll out on a floured surface again to a rectangle, but without adding butter. Fold as before, turn, roll, and fold again.
3 Dusting your rolling pin with flour, roll out the dough into a large rectangle, twice as long as it is high and about ¼ inch thick. Trim the edges, and cut into 8 equal squares.
4 Oil a large baking sheet.
5 Beat the egg with the confectioners' sugar and brush all over the surfaces of the squares. Put 3 squares of chocolate side by side on each square of dough. Fold the dough over the filling, so that you can just see the chocolate at each end, and place on the baking sheets, sealed sides down.
6 Cover loosely with oiled plastic wrap and leave in a warm place to proof until doubled in bulk, about 40 minutes.
7 Meanwhile, preheat the oven to 425° F. Bake until puffy and golden, about 15 minutes.
8 Transfer to a wire rack to cool. Dust with a little sifted confectioners' sugar. Best served warm.
◀ **Pictured opposite**

dairy free
also nut free

Follow the nut-free recipe, but substitute vegetable shortening for the butter and use dairy-free chocolate.

egg free
also nut free

Follow the nut-free recipe, but omit the egg. Add an extra 2–3 tablespoons of milk, if necessary. Use 3 tablespoons of light cream (or soy alternative to light cream) and 1 teaspoon of confectioners' sugar for the glaze instead of the egg and confectioners' sugar.

 gluten free
see overleaf

See overleaf for the gluten-free recipe.

Chocolate croissant continued

gluten free

2 cups gluten-free all-purpose
  flour, plus extra for dusting
½ tsp salt
2 tsp superfine sugar
2 tsp xanthan gum
1 tbsp instant yeast
¼ cup cold butter, cut in ½-in dice
⅔ cup milk
1 egg
vegetable oil for baking pan

to finish
1 egg, beaten
1 tsp confectioners' sugar, plus extra
  for dusting
18 squares semisweet chocolate

PREPARATION TIME 25 minutes
COOKING TIME 15 minutes
MAKES 6

1 Follow steps 1–4 of the gluten-free croissant recipe on page 54.

4 Cut into 6 equal squares.

5 Oil a baking sheet.

6 Beat the egg with the confectioners' sugar and brush over the surfaces of the squares. Lay 3 squares of chocolate in the center of the dough in a line. Fold the dough over and place, fold sides down, on the baking sheet. Cover loosely with oiled plastic wrap. Leave in a warm place to proof until well risen, about 45 minutes.

7 Meanwhile, preheat the oven to 400° F. Brush the chocolate croissant with the remaining glaze. Bake until spongy and golden, about 15 minutes.

8 Dust with a little confectioners' sugar. Best served warm or transfer to a wire rack to cool before wrapping and storing.

TIP These don't look as puffy as the wheat-based version, but they are spongy, buttery, chocolatey, and delicious. Eat them warm, either freshly baked or heated very briefly in the microwave or the oven.

Kedgeree

People get nostalgic about the country-house appeal of this traditional British breakfast dish of rice, fish, and eggs in a lightly curried sauce—but it also makes a great lunch or supper dish, especially with green vegetables or salad to accompany it. The lentils were in the original Indian dish adapted by the British, so I've reinstated them as a healthy and tasty option.

  ## gluten & nut free

3 tbsp green or brown lentils (optional)
9 oz undyed smoked haddock fillet or other smoked fish
1¼ cups milk
2 tbsp flavorless nut-free oil
1 onion, chopped
1 cup long-grain rice
¾ tsp curry powder
¼ tsp ground turmeric

2 eggs
4 tbsp heavy cream
2 tsp lemon juice
salt and freshly ground black pepper
3 tbsp chopped fresh parsley

PREPARATION TIME 10 minutes
COOKING TIME 17 minutes plus lentils, if using
SERVES 4

1 If using, cook the lentils according to the package instructions. When cooked, drain and set aside.
2 Poach the fish in the milk in a saucepan until it flakes easily with a fork, about 5 minutes. Lift the fish out and flake, discarding any skin and bones. Reserve the milk for the rice if you like your kedgeree with plenty of fishy flavor.
3 Heat the oil in a frying pan and fry the onion until softened but not browned, 2 minutes. Stir in the rice and spices until coated in the oil.
4 Measure 1¾ cups of liquid in a measuring cup. Use the poaching milk, topped with boiling water, or just use boiling water. Pour onto the rice, onion, and spice mixture. Bring to a boil, stirring. Reduce the heat to low, stir once, and cover the pan. Cook the rice for 10 minutes or until all the liquid is absorbed and the rice is cooked, but not mushy. Fluff the rice with a fork and keep warm.
6 Meanwhile, in a separate saucepan, boil some water, reduce to a simmer, add the eggs, and cook for 5–7 minutes. Plunge the eggs immediately into cold water until cooled. Peel and cut into quarters.
7 Mix the fish and lentils, if using, into the rice with a fork. Stir in the cream and lemon juice. Gently fold in the egg, season to taste, and heat through very gently.
8 Garnish with chopped parsley before serving.

 ## dairy free
also gluten & nut free

Follow the recipe on the left, but substitute soy, rice, or oat milk (as long as there are no sensitivities to gluten) for the cow's milk and soy cream for the heavy cream.

egg free
also gluten & nut free

Follow the recipe on the left, omitting the eggs and substituting ⅓ cup of firm tofu, cut into 1 inch pieces and steamed for 5 minutes. Alternatively, use 4 large scallops, sliced horizontally into two or three pieces and brushed with a thin film of oil. Sauté the scallop slices in a hot pan until just cooked but still soft, 30 seconds to 1 minute, and add in step 7 instead of the eggs.

TIP Garnish with cilantro leaves instead of parsley, if desired.

Tortillas

Tortillas are so versatile; use them to scoop up Chili con carne (p.122), wrap around fillings for lunchtime treats, or turn stale ones into tortilla chips to serve with dips (p.70). Mexican cooks make small tortillas by pressing out balls of *masa harina* (ground corn) and water—but this can be quite complicated to do. This batter-based version makes lovely, soft rollable tortillas.

 dairy & nut free

½ cup all-purpose flour
½ cup cornmeal
a pinch of salt
1 large egg, beaten
⅔ cup water

PREPARATION TIME 5 minutes
COOKING TIME 20 minutes
MAKES 8

1 Mix the dry ingredients together in a bowl.
2 Beat in the egg in the water to form a fairly thin batter. Pour into a measuring container.
3 Dust a sheet of paper towel with flour on the work surface.
4 Heat a small nonstick heavy frying pan. Turn down the heat to medium.
5 Pour in an eighth of the batter, lift the pan up to quickly swirl the batter around the pan to coat the base and a little way up the sides. Cook over medium heat until the edge of the tortilla begins to curl slightly. Flip over and quickly dry out the other side.
6 Slide onto the paper towel and dust with a little more flour. Cover with a second sheet of paper towel to keep the tortilla soft. Repeat, reheating the pan slightly between each tortilla, and stirring the batter every time until all of them are made. If you're not planning to use the tortillas immediately, cool and store in an airtight container. They are suitable for freezing.
7 See the serving suggestion on the right for delicious lunchtime wrap ideas.
Pictured opposite ▶

 egg free
also dairy & nut free

Follow the recipe on the left, but omit the egg and substitute ¼ cup of potato flour for half of the cornmeal and increase the water to 1 cup.

gluten free
also dairy & nut free

Follow the recipe on the left, but substitute gluten-free all-purpose flour for the ordinary all-purpose flour and increase the water to 1 scant cup.

SERVING SUGGESTION Try the following ideas for lunch-box wraps. For herb dip with roasted peppers, use the Herb dip recipe on page 71. Spread generously onto a tortilla, add a handful of roasted red peppers, and roll up into a wrap.
   For smoked salmon with crème fraîche, spread some crème fraîche (or, if you can't tolerate dairy, soya cream cheese thinned with soy cream and a squeeze of lemon) onto a tortilla. Add a slice of smoked salmon and roll up into a wrap.

Tortilla chips

It's worthwhile making your own tortilla chips, because although store-bought tortilla chips may be gluten and egg free, some may contain traces of nuts or milk powder, so aren't suitable for everyone. They are really easy to make using the tortilla recipe that suits you on page 68. In Mexico, tortillas are made every day and any leftover stale ones are fried to serve with dips—so they're never wasted.

dairy, egg, gluten, & nut free

1 quantity stale tortillas in appropriate version (p.68)
nut-free vegetable oil for frying
salt (optional)
for the salsa
1 ripe avocado, pitted and finely diced
juice of 1 lime
1 small onion, finely chopped
1 green bell pepper, finely diced
1 red chili, seeded and finely chopped

2 tbsp olive oil
pinch of superfine sugar
2 tbsp fresh chopped cilantro
freshly ground black pepper

PREPARATION TIME 2 minutes
COOKING TIME 8 minutes
SERVES 4

1 Cut each tortilla into 6 wedges.
2 Heat about ¼ inch of oil in a frying pan.
3 Add the tortilla wedges a few at a time and fry, turning once or twice until crisp and golden, 1–2 minutes. Remove with a slotted spoon and drain on paper towel.
4 Repeat until all the chips are cooked. Sprinkle with salt, if desired, and let cool.
5 Mix all the salsa ingredients together and transfer to a small bowl. Place on a large plate and surround with the tortilla chips.

WATCH OUT FOR chilies, since some people are sensitive to them.

SERVING SUGGESTION For nachos, top tortilla chips with grated cheese (or a dairy-free melting variety) and chopped mild green jalapeños (if tolerated) and broil until the cheese has melted.

"Serve these at a party—and you can be sure that absolutely all your guests can dip in"

Herb dip

This garlic herb dip has a fresh summery taste that is perfect for serving with crisp crudités and is equally delicious as a snack on toasted brown bread. An excellent idea for a buffet is to use the herb dip as a topping on halved cherry tomatoes or baked new potatoes, scattered with a little sea salt. Vary the fresh herbs according to what is available.

egg, gluten, & nut free

1 scant cup plain Greek-style
  yogurt or sour cream
1 cup cream cheese
2 tbsp olive oil
grated zest and juice of ½ lemon
1 small garlic clove, skinned
  and crushed
2 tbsp finely chopped fresh
  parsley
1 tbsp finely chopped fresh basil
1 tbsp finely chopped fresh
  chervil
4 scallions, finely chopped
salt and freshly ground black
  pepper to taste

PREPARATION TIME 5 minutes
SERVES 4

1 Place all the ingredients in a food processor or blender and pulse until well blended. Season the dip to taste.
2 Serve chilled with crudités, tortilla chips, or potato chips. This dip also makes a delicious filling for tortilla wraps (p.68).
3 This dip can be stored, covered, in a refrigerator for up to a day.

TIP This recipe makes enough to top 20 baked new potatoes or cherry tomato halves.

dairy free
also egg, gluten, & nut free

Follow the recipe on the left, but substitute soy-based yogurt for the yogurt or sour cream and replace the cream cheese with soy-based cream cheese alternative (tofutti) or silken tofu. Reduce the olive oil to 1 tablespoon, since the dairy-free version needs less liquid.

Crostini & toppings

Literally "little toasts," crostini are slices of bread, rubbed with garlic, brushed with olive oil, and then toasted. Served as appetizers or snacks, they work best with gutsy Mediterranean flavors as toppings, such as olives, eggplant, tomatoes, basil, and peppers. If you can't buy Italian or French bread to suit you, use the recipes for French-style bread (pp.170–171) or Focaccia (p.173).

dairy, egg, gluten, & nut free

eggplant & mushroom

4 tbsp olive oil plus extra for
   brushing
1 shallot, finely chopped
1 eggplant, finely diced
$\frac{1}{2}$ tsp ground cumin
$\frac{1}{2}$ tsp ground cinnamon
$\frac{1}{2}$ tsp dried oregano
$\frac{1}{2}$ cup button mushrooms,
   thinly sliced
salt and freshly ground black
   pepper
1 tbsp chopped fresh parsley

8 diagonal slices of allergen-free
   French-style bread (pp.170–171) or
   half slices of Focaccia (p.173)
2 garlic cloves, halved

PREPARATION TIME 10 minutes
COOKING TIME 6 minutes
MAKES 8

1 Heat the oil in a saucepan. Add the shallot and eggplant and fry over a fairly gentle heat until almost soft, about 4 minutes. Add the spices, oregano, and mushrooms and fry for another 2 minutes, stirring all the time. Season and stir in the parsley.
2 Meanwhile, rub the bread all over with garlic, brush both sides with olive oil and then toast.
3 Pile the eggplant and mushroom mixture on the toast and serve.

tomato & sweet basil

4 tomatoes, seeded and
   chopped
1 tbsp olive oil plus extra for
   brushing
few chopped fresh basil leaves
freshly ground black pepper
8 diagonal slices of allergen-free

French-style bread (pp.170–171)
   or half slices of Focaccia (p.173)
1 large garlic clove, halved

PREPARATION TIME 5
COOKING TIME 3–4 minutes
MAKES 8

1 Mix the tomatoes with the oil, basil leaves, and a good grinding of black pepper.
2 Meanwhile, toast the bread as above.
3 Place on a serving platter and spoon the tomato mixture on top.

SERVING SUGGESTION Try crumbling a little feta cheese or dairy-free alternative over the eggplant mixture before serving.

tapenade

1/2 cup olive oil plus
   extra for brushing
2/3 cup pitted black olives
2/3 cup pitted green olives
1 large garlic clove
3 tbsp chopped fresh parsley
2 tbsp capers in brine, rinsed
   and drained
1 x 2 oz can of anchovy
   fillets, drained
juice of 1/2 lime
1/4 tsp superfine sugar

freshly ground black pepper
8 diagonal slices of allergen-free
   French-style bread (pp.170–171) or
   half slices of Focaccia (p.173)

to finish
1 small onion, very finely chopped
juice of 1/2 lime

PREPARATION TIME 10 minutes
COOKING TIME 3–4 minutes
MAKES 8

1 Put all the tapenade ingredients in a blender or food processor, adding a good grinding of pepper. Run the machine to form a coarse paste, stopping and scraping down the sides as necessary.
2 Mix the onion and lime juice and let stand for at least 1 hour.
3 Brush the bread with oil and then toast.
4 Top each slice with a spoonful of tapenade and sprinkle with the onion and lime juice.

pepper, zucchini, & sun-dried tomato

1tbsp olive oil plus extra for
   brushing
2 shallots, finely chopped
1 small red or orange bell
   pepper, seeded and chopped
1 zucchini, chopped
1 tsp chopped fresh rosemary
2 tsp balsamic vinegar
salt and freshly ground black
   pepper

8 diagonal slices of allergen-free
   French-style bread (pp.170–171)
   or half slices of Focaccia (p.173)
1 garlic clove, halved
1 tbsp sun-dried tomato paste

PREPARATION TIME 15 minutes
COOKING TIME 7–8 minutes
MAKES 8

1 Heat the oil in a frying pan. Add the shallot, pepper, zucchini, and rosemary and fry over medium heat, stirring, until just soft, about 4 minutes. Stir in the balsamic vinegar and a little salt and pepper.
2 Rub the bread all over with garlic, brush both sides with olive oil, and then toast.
3 Spread each slice with a little sun-dried tomato paste and spoon the warm pepper mixture on top. Serve warm.

TIP You can bake the bread in the oven, if you prefer. Lay the prepared slices of bread on a baking sheet and bake at 350° F for 15 minutes or until crisp and golden, turning once.

SIDE DISHES, APPETIZERS, & LIGHT MEALS

California temaki sushi

Here's sushi that is fun to make at home since it doesn't need to look perfect. Hand-rolled cones of nori (Japanese seaweed) are folded around fillings—like wrapping a bunch of flowers—and eaten with bowls of wasabi, soy sauce, and pickled ginger. Serve as an appetizer or increase the quantities and arrange the ingredients on dishes, for guests to assemble their own party starter.

dairy, egg, gluten, & nut free

1 tbsp sushi vinegar
pinch of salt
1 tsp superfine sugar
2/3 cup short grain sushi
   rice, prewashed
1 1/4 cups water
4 nori sheets, cut in half
1/4 tsp wasabi paste
8 tsp appropriate version of
   Mayonnaise (p.210)
4 lettuce leaves, torn into
   1-in pieces

8 large shrimp, cooked and
   peeled
8 tsp flying fish or salmon roe
2-in piece of cucumber,
   seeded and cut into matchsticks
1/4 avocado, cut in 8 slices and tossed
   in lemon juice to prevent browning

PREPARATION TIME 40 minutes
COOKING TIME 20 minutes
SERVES 8

VARIATIONS Alternative fillings include sushi quality raw fish, lightly steamed asparagus, thinly sliced carrots, shiitake or other mushrooms cooked in a soy-flavored broth, crab sticks, scallions, snow peas, fresh or deep fried tofu, and sesame seeds.

WATCH OUT FOR seafood allergies. Use nonseafood variations such as vegetables or tofu (as listed above). If serving with soy sauce, make sure it is gluten-free if need be.

1 Mix the vinegar with the salt and sugar, stirring until dissolved.
2 Put the rice and water in a saucepan. Bring to a boil, stir, reduce the heat to as low as possible and cover and simmer very gently for 15–20 minutes or until the water has been absorbed and the rice is sticky. Remove from the heat and let stand, covered, for 10 minutes. Add the sushi vinegar mixture and fluff with a fork.
3 To assemble the maki, take a half sheet of nori and lay it rough side up across your left hand. Add 1 heaping tablespoon of rice to the left half of the nori sheet, covering half the sheet.
4 Mix the wasabi and mayonnaise. Take a teaspoon of wasabi mayonnaise and starting at the bottom left-hand corner, spread the mayonnaise in a diagonal line up to the top of the rice.
5 Place one piece of lettuce, one shrimp, 1 teaspoon of roe, and a slice each of the cucumber and avocado, on the top of half the rice, to the mayonnaise line.
6 Gently but firmly, lift the bottom left corner of rice-covered nori and fold it up over the filling to the top right corner of rice, using your left thumb to help roll it over. It is important to be firm and to get the corners to meet. Then wrap the top right-hand corner of uncovered nori over, down and around the back to form a cone. Dampen the last corner with water to stick it to the cone.
7 Repeat for the remaining nori sheets.

Blini with smoked salmon

These little buckwheat pancakes, an Eastern European favorite, are traditionally served with sour cream, caviar, and chopped onion. Like the smoked salmon version below, they can be served as an elegant appetizer, garnished with dill sprigs. Buckwheat, which is a seed, despite its name, does not contain gluten and gives a darkish flour with a slightly nutty taste; mix half and half with regular flour if preferred.

 nut, egg, & gluten free

for the pancakes
1 3/4 cups buckwheat flour
1/4 tsp superfine sugar
1/4 tsp salt
1 1/2 tsp instant yeast
2 tbsp butter
2 cups milk
2 tbsp warm water
nut-free vegetable oil for frying
to finish
12 thin slices of smoked salmon
2–3 onions, finely chopped
2/3 cup sour cream

to garnish
fresh chive stalks
lemon wedges

PREPARATION TIME 10 minutes
 plus standing time
COOKING TIME 30 minutes
SERVES 6 (makes about 30)

1 Sift the flour, sugar, and salt into a fairly large bowl and stir in the yeast.
2 Melt the butter in a saucepan. Remove from the heat and add the milk. Stir. It should be comfortably warm to the touch.
3 Gradually beat the milk and butter mixture into the flour mixture to form a thick, creamy batter. Cover the bowl with oiled plastic wrap and leave in a warm place until doubled in size, about 1 hour.
4 Beat again, then beat in the water to form a thick, creamy batter again.
5 Heat a little oil in a large heavy frying pan then pour off the excess. Put 3 separate tablespoonfuls of the batter well apart in the pan, swirling them gently with the tip of the spoon to make neat rounds, about 2 inches in diameter. Fry until the pancakes dry out and bubbles appear and burst all over the surface. Flip them over and quickly cook the other sides. Slide onto a plate and keep warm over a pan of gently simmering water while you cook the remainder (the batter makes about 30).
6 Put several blini on each plate with 2 rolls of smoked salmon, a small pile of chopped onion, and a spoonful of sour cream. Garnish with a wedge of lemon and a few chive stalks and serve while the blinis are still warm.

dairy free
also egg, gluten, & nut free

Follow the recipe on the left, but substitute dairy-free spread for the butter and soy, rice, or oat milk for the cow's milk. Serve with dairy-free sour cream alternative, tofu or plain soy yogurt instead of the sour cream.

TIP You may need to discard the first few blinis since, like pancakes, these season the pan for the remaining successful ones to come.
  Three blini may be enough for an appetizer. The rest will freeze beautifully and then can be reheated on a plate over a pan of simmering water or in the microwave.

Chicken fajitas

A riot of mouth-watering Mexican flavors; chicken sizzled in cumin, chili, and coriander, tossed with peppers, onions, and garlic and topped with cooling, creamy guacamole. Buy tortillas or make the right allergen-free tortilla for you (p.68), then roll the still sizzling filling into the warmed tortillas. You can also, more traditionally, make these with fried steak. Serve as an appetizer or a light meal.

dairy, egg, gluten, & nut free

for the fajitas
3 tbsp olive oil
1 red onion, halved and sliced
1 garlic clove, crushed
2 large red bell peppers, halved, seeded and cut into strips
2 large green peppers, halved, seeded, and cut into strips
4 tomatoes, cut into wedges
4 skinless chicken breasts, cut into strips
1/4 tsp chili powder
1/2 tsp ground cumin
1/2 tsp ground coriander
1/2 tsp dried oregano

for the guacamole
1 large ripe avocado, halved and pitted
juice of 1/2 lemon
2 tbsp chopped fresh chives
salt and freshly ground black pepper
few drops of Tabasco (optional)

to serve
8 tortillas (p.68)
large green salad

PREPARATION TIME 20 minutes
COOKING TIME 8 minutes
SERVES 4

1 To make the guacamole, scoop the flesh of the avocado into a small bowl and mash with the lemon, chives, and season to taste. Add a few drops of Tabasco, if desired, for added fire.

2 Heat the oil in a frying pan or wok. Add the onion, garlic, peppers, and tomatoes and stir-fry until nearly tender, about 4 minutes. Add the chicken and stir-fry for 2 minutes. Stir in the spices and herbs and season to taste.

3 Meanwhile, warm the tortillas on a covered plate over a pan of simmering water or wrapped in paper towel and warmed briefly in the microwave.

4 To serve, divide the chicken mixture among the tortillas, top each with a spoonful of guacamole and roll up. Place, rolled sides down, on warm plates and serve with a large green salad.

SERVING SUGGESTION Instead of guacamole, you may like to top the fajita filling with a spoonful of sour cream or plain yogurt. Use a dairy-free sour cream alternative or yogurt, if necessary. You can also add some shredded lettuce and grated cheddar cheese (or a dairy-free cheddar alternative).

WATCH OUT FOR chilies since some people can't tolerate them. Omit the chili powder if in any doubt.

Chicken drumsticks

A really useful recipe, popular with all ages, these chicken drumsticks can feed a crowd and you'll have none of the big allergens to worry about. They are great for lunch or dinner and ideal for barbecues, especially if serving with grilled corn. Add a baked potato for a filling and nutritious meal. The easy-to-make barbecue sauce scores over store-bought versions since it contains neither wheat nor dairy.

dairy, egg, gluten, & nut free

3 tbsp corn or other flavorless
  nut-free oil
2 tbsp molasses
4 tbsp tomato purée
1 tsp mustard powder
2 tbsp wine vinegar
2 tsp Worcestershire sauce
1/4 tsp smoked paprika (pimentón)
salt and freshly ground black
  pepper
8 chicken drumsticks

PREPARATION TIME 5 minutes
  plus chilling
COOKING TIME 14–16 minutes
SERVES 4

1 Mix all the ingredients, except the drumsticks, in a shallow sealable container, seasoning well with salt and pepper.
2 Make several slashes in the flesh on each chicken leg before adding them to the marinade—this lets the flavor in and also helps them to cook more evenly. Turn the drumsticks to coat them thoroughly.
3 Cover and chill for at least 4 hours or overnight.
4 Remove the chicken from the marinade and shake off the excess.
5 Cook under a preheated broiler or on the grill for 7–8 minutes on each side or until richly browned and the juices run clear when the skewer is inserted into the thickest part of the meat.

WATCH OUT FOR Check that the mustard powder, Worcestershire sauce, and paprika are gluten free.

SERVING SUGGESTION These are delicious served with grilled corn on the cob. Roll the cobs in a mixture of salt, pepper, and chilies, with lime squeezed over, and cook under a broiler or on a grill. Note that some people are sensitive to chilies, so omit if in any doubt.

"This is tasty, unpretentious finger food for the whole family to enjoy"

SIDE DISHES, APPETIZERS, & LIGHT MEALS

Soy-honey glazed sausages

I've used cocktail sausages as an appetizer or party snack for this recipe, but if you use full-sized sausages it makes an excellent main course for a meal served with mustardy mashed potatoes, wilted greens, and Vegetable gravy (p.215). Alternatively, serve the sausages with lentils or beans and fries for a fail-safe, popular supper for children.

dairy, egg, & nut free

1 lb 2 oz cocktail sausages
1 tbsp soy sauce
1 tbsp honey
1 tbsp sesame seeds

PREPARATION TIME 2 minutes
COOKING TIME 30 minutes
SERVES 4

1 Preheat the oven to 350° F. Arrange the sausages in a single layer in a roasting pan and cook until just beginning to brown, 10 minutes.

2 Mix together the soy sauce and honey. Remove the sausages from the oven, spoon over the soy mixture, and toss to coat. Return to the oven until glazed and browned, about 20 minutes. Turn once or twice during cooking.

3 Sprinkle with the sesame seeds and toss to coat before serving.

WATCH OUT FOR sesame seeds, since some people are allergic to them.

 gluten free
also dairy, egg, & nut free

Use pure pork or other gluten-free sausages and a gluten-free soy sauce. If serving with mustard, check that it is gluten-free too.

"Children love these sausages— the soy-glaze adds a barbecue flavor"

Grilled polenta

Use these polenta toasts for canapé bases or as a snack or appetizer with toppings such as Parmesan, arugula, and lightly steamed green vegetables; prosciutto; Pesto (p.211), or any of the toppings described in the Crostini recipe (pp.72–73). You can also stop halfway through this recipe for a soft, stirred version of polenta, which makes a great side dish for stews and casseroles.

 **egg, gluten, & nut free**

1³/₄ cups water
1 tbsp olive oil plus extra for brushing
½ tsp salt
scant ²/₃ cup instant polenta
salt and pepper to season
1 heaping tbsp grated Parmesan

PREPARATION TIME 20 minutes
COOKING TIME 4–5 minutes
SERVES 4

1 Place the water, olive oil, and salt in a medium-sized saucepan. Bring to the boil.
2 Add the polenta to the boiling water in a thin stream and stir constantly. Reduce the heat to a low simmer and cook, stirring constantly throughout, for 15 minutes or until the polenta has thickened. Add the grated Parmesan and stir to mix. Season to taste with salt and pepper. Remove from the heat.
3 Spoon the polenta onto a large flat plate or baking tray and spread it out evenly, smoothing it with the back of a large spoon, to form a circular cake about ¾ inch thick. Let cool. You can store it at this stage in the refrigerator for up to a day.
4 To grill, cut the polenta cake into strips or wedges. Brush with a thin layer of olive oil and then grill or broil until browned on both sides. Serve with a choice of toppings.

 dairy free

also egg, gluten, & nut free

Replace the Parmesan with an equal quantity of dairy-free cheese. I have tried it with both dairy-free Parmesan and dairy-free cheddar and they both work well—though the Parmesan can be a little salty.

VARIATION For a soft, stirred version of polenta, just stop at the end of step 2. As well as working well with stews and dishes that have lots of sauce or juice, this is a classic accompaniment to Osso bucco (p.118).

Seven-layer dip

This is an unabashed and lavish layered party dip that is a riot of colors and flavors. It looks stunning served in a deep glass dish. For a speedier version, follow the recipe, but use store-bought guacamole in place of the avocados and store-bought salsa for the tomatoes, or take a little longer to make the mouth-watering fresh version below. Serve with tortilla chips (p.68) or toasted flatbreads.

egg, gluten, & nut free

3 avocados
juice of 1 lime or lemon
1 lb canned refried beans
2 ¼ cups sour cream
¼ tsp chili powder
2 green bell peppers, seeded and finely chopped
2 cups drained pitted black olives, halved
8 tomatoes, chopped
½ red onion, chopped

6 ½ cups cheddar or Monterey Jack cheese, coarsely grated
chopped cilantro and scallions to garnish

PREPARATION TIME 20 minutes
SERVES 16–20

dairy free

also egg, gluten, & nut free

Follow the recipe on the left, but replace the sour cream with the same quantity of dairy-free sour cream or soy yogurt, and the cheddar or Monterey Jack cheese with the same quantity of the non-dairy equivalent.

1 Peel and mash the avocados with the lime juice, using a fork.
2 To assemble, layer the refried beans over the base of a large glass dish. Add the mashed avocados and then the sour cream and sprinkle the chili powder on top.
3 For the green pepper layer, sprinkle the chopped pepper around the perimeter of the dish first, to ensure that the layer is visible, and sprinkle the rest evenly over the center. Layer the halved olives carefully on top and spoon over the chopped tomatoes and red onion. Finally, add the cheese and the cilantro and scallion garnish. Chill until ready to serve.
◀ **Pictured opposite**

WATCH OUT FOR chili powder, since some people cannot tolerate chili. Substitute with an equal quantity of ground cumin if this is a problem.

VARIATION If you like things spicier, add 3 tablespoons of chopped jalapeño peppers to the green pepper layer and replace the chili powder with 1 oz of taco seasoning.

SIDE DISHES, APPETIZERS, & LIGHT MEALS

Bacon & onion quiche

A baked dish of eggs and cream in a pastry crust is not an obvious recipe for this book! But here are four versions, each with crisp pastry shells and a creamy, slightly wobbly custard encasing the filling of bacon, onion, herbs, and cheese. Mix the filling well into the custard, and do add the mustard into the egg version—it makes all the difference.

 nut free

1 quantity of nut- and egg-free Piecrust pastry (p.180)
1 tbsp flavorless nut-free oil
2 onions, chopped
6 slices bacon, rind removed and diced
3 eggs
1⅓ cups light cream
1 cup grated hard cheese, eg cheddar
2 tbsp chopped fresh parsley

1 tbsp chopped fresh sage
salt and freshly ground black pepper

PREPARATION TIME   30 minutes
   plus pastry chilling time
COOKING TIME   35 minutes
SERVES   6

1 Preheat the oven to 400° F.
2 Roll out the pastry and use to line a 10 inch flan dish. Place on a baking sheet. Prick the base with a fork and fill with crumpled foil or waxed paper and baking beans. Bake in the oven for 10 minutes. Remove the foil or paper and beans and bake for about 5 minutes, until lightly golden and dried out. Remove from the oven. Reduce the temperature to 375° F.
3 Meanwhile, heat the oil in a frying pan and fry the onion for 2 minutes, stirring, until translucent. Add the bacon and continue to fry for another 2 minutes. Remove from the pan with a slotted spoon and reserve.
4 Beat the eggs and cream together with half the cheese and herbs. Season with salt and pepper.
5 Transfer the bacon and onion mixture to the flan case and spread out. Spoon over the egg and cream mixture. Sprinkle the remaining cheese on top. Bake in the oven for 35 minutes until bubbling, set, and turning pale golden. Serve warm or cold.

 dairy free
also nut free

Follow the recipe on the left, but use the dairy-free Piecrust pastry recipe on page 180. Use soy cream in place of the light cream and a cheddar-type soy cheese instead of the cheddar cheese.

 egg free
also nut free

Follow the recipe on the left, but omit the eggs. At step 4 put 6 tablespoons of potato flour in a bowl with 1½ teaspoons of xanthan gum and 1 scant cup water. Whisk with an electric beater until thick and white and the mixture stands in soft peaks. Whisk in the 1¼ cups of cream and a tablespoon of English or Dijon mustard. Beat together with half the cheese, the herbs, and salt and pepper to taste. Continue from step 5.

gluten free
also nut free

Follow the recipe on the left, but use the gluten-free Piecrust pastry recipe on page 182.

SIDE DISHES, APPETIZERS, & LIGHT MEALS

Gazpacho

An easy-to-make chilled tomato soup, perfect for a hot summer day. Recipes vary depending on which region of Spain you find yourself in—this is based on the Andalucian version. Serve it in bowls with a garnish of finely chopped vegetables or in glasses, as they do in Spanish restaurants and bars. Gazpacho has been described as "liquid salad" and is every bit as healthy.

 dairy, egg, & nut free

2¼ lb fresh ripe tomatoes, skinned and quartered
½ small onion, quartered
½ green or red bell pepper, seeded and quartered
1 cucumber, peeled, seeded and quartered
2 garlic cloves, peeled and halved
⅔ cup olive oil
1 small day-old bread roll or thick slice of bread (about 2 oz), soaked in water
3 tbsp wine vinegar
good pinch of sugar

½ red or green chili, seeded and chopped (optional)
salt and freshly ground black pepper
ice water to thin (optional)
to garnish
a selection of any of the following: small croûtons; finely diced tomatoes; red and green peppers; cucumber; onion; or chopped fresh parsley

PREPARATION TIME 15 minutes, plus chilling time
SERVES 4–6

1 In a food processor blend together the tomatoes, onion, pepper, cucumber, garlic, olive oil, bread (squeeze out the water just before using), vinegar, sugar, and chili, if using. Blend for 1 minute or until smooth. Season to taste with salt and pepper. Chill for at least 2 hours before serving and thin with ice water, if necessary.

2 Serve with your choice of garnish or arrange the garnish in small bowls at the table and allow guests to choose their own.

SERVING SUGGESTION If eggs are tolerated, a little very finely chopped hard-boiled egg is an attractive garnish.

gluten free
also dairy, egg, & nut free

Follow the recipe on the left, but use a gluten-free bread roll and substitute gluten-free croûtons to garnish, if using.

WATCH OUT FOR chili, since some people can't tolerate it. Omit if in any doubt.

Leek & butternut squash soup

Homemade soups, both delicious and nourishing, call for homemade stock, but if you don't have time, find a bouillon powder you can trust. I've gone to town with the toppings: herbs, seeds, bacon, and cream, but just one or two will turn a plain soup into something substantial or fancy. A tip for gluten-avoiders is to keep a supply of gluten-free croûtons handy for soup and salad garnishes.

 **egg, gluten, & nut free**

1 tbsp nut-free flavorless vegetable oil
1 good-sized butternut squash
2 tbsp butter
2 leeks, white parts only, finely chopped
1½ tsp curry powder
½ tsp ground cumin
4¼ cups chicken or vegetable stock
1 tsp molasses or dark brown sugar (optional)
salt and freshly ground black pepper to season
2 tbsp chopped fresh cilantro or parsley
3 tbsp light cream

PREPARATION TIME 1¼ hours
COOKING TIME 20 minutes plus reheating
SERVES 8

1 Preheat the oven to 375° F. Halve the butternut squash lengthwise and scoop out the seeds. Brush the cut surfaces with the oil and bake face down on a baking sheet for 1 hour or until the flesh is soft. When cool enough to handle, scoop out the pulp and discard the skin.
2 Melt the butter in a heavy-bottomed pan. Add the leeks and cook gently for about 3 minutes until softened, but not browned. Add the curry powder and cumin and cook for 1 minute.
3 Add the roasted squash, stock, and the molasses or sugar. Season lightly. Bring to a boil, reduce the heat, cover, and simmer for 20 minutes.
4 Purée in a blender or food processor until there are no lumps. You may need to do this in two batches if it won't fit in your blender or food processor. Return to the saucepan. Stir in the chopped cilantro or parsley and the cream. Taste and re-season, if necessary. Reheat but do not reboil. Ladle into warm soup bowls, season to taste with salt and pepper and garnish lavishly (see suggestion, right).
Pictured opposite ▶

dairy free
also egg, gluten, & nut free

Follow the recipe on the left, but replace the butter with dairy-free spread and use soy cream alternative instead of the cream.

SERVING SUGGESTION Serve garnished with a swirl of heavy cream, chopped parsley or cilantro, toasted pumpkin seeds, or crumbled fried bacon (shown right).

WATCH OUT FOR stock cubes and bouillon. Check that they are dairy free or gluten free as necessary. Some people are sensitive to chili, so omit the curry powder if need be.

Crispy squid

If you thought you couldn't have light crispy fried food without egg or wheat, try this. It's inspired by the Chinese restaurant staple "salt and pepper squid," where seafood is rolled in seasoned cornstarch and deep fried. Serve the squid (also known as *calamari*) with sweet chili sauce and lime wedges or some Mayonnaise (p.210) with a dash of chili sauce and lime juice stirred into it.

dairy, egg, gluten, & nut free

½ cup cornstarch
½ tsp chili powder
½ tsp five-spice powder
½ tsp ground turmeric
½ tsp celery salt
salt and freshly ground black
   pepper to season
4 large squid, about 2¼ lb,
   (cleaned and slit open, and
   tentacles cut in short lengths)
corn oil or other nut-free
   flavorless oil for frying

for garnish
roughly chopped cilantro leaves
finely chopped red bell pepper or red
   chilies, seeded (if tolerated)
grated or pared zest of ½ a lime
1 lime, cut into quarters

PREPARATION TIME 15 minutes
COOKING TIME 5 minutes
SERVES 4–6

WATCH OUT FOR chilies since some people cannot tolerate them. Omit the chili powder and chili garnish, if necessary. This is not suitable for people with a shellfish allergy.

TIP If you can't find large squid, buy baby squid—remove the tentacles and trim off the hard core at the base of them. Split and score each squid as in the recipe, but leave whole—they will curl beautifully when fried. Alternatively, if you can only buy squid rings, dust these in the cornstarch mixture and fry in exactly the same way.

1 Mix the cornstarch with the chili and five-spice powders, ground turmeric, and celery salt. Season with salt and pepper.
2 Wash the squid and pat them dry. Open out, score the inside surfaces lightly with a sharp knife in a cross-hatch pattern, and cut the squid into 1 inch pieces.
3 Heat the oil for deep-frying in a deep-fat fryer or wok to 375° F or until a cube of day-old bread browns in 20 seconds.
4 Coat the squid pieces and the tentacles in the cornstarch mixture and deep fry in batches for 45–60 seconds or until the squid pieces turn a light golden color. A good rule of thumb is that the pieces are ready when the bubbling sound dies away— but be careful not to overcook or the squid will turn rubbery.
5 Drain on paper towel. Keep warm in a low oven until all the batches are fried. Pile in small warm dishes and garnish each with chopped cilantro leaves, finely chopped red pepper, or chilies, lime zest, and a wedge of lime.

Fresh spring rolls

Basically a shrimp, herb, and pork salad rolled in a soft rice paper wrapper, this is one of the most refreshing and elegant appetizers. Unlike most spring rolls it isn't deep-fried. A Vietnamese specialty, serve it with Vietnamese dipping sauce (p.210), hoisin sauce, or even a peanut sauce—you'll have to get a recipe elsewhere as I just couldn't include peanut sauce in an allergy friendly cookbook!

dairy, egg, gluten, & nut free

rice paper wrappers (*banh trang*)
8-in in diameter
4 large leaves of soft lettuce,
  each torn in half
1 oz rice vermicelli, cooked
  according to package
  instructions and drained
1 carrot, peeled and cut into
  julienne strips
4 oz cooked pork (ideally
  pork belly), cut into thin strips
½ cup bean sprouts

8 leaves of Thai basil (optional)
16–24 medium-sized cooked shrimp
8 sprigs of cilantro
8 leaves of mint

PREPARATION TIME 40 minutes
COOKING TIME 5 minutes for
  vermicelli
SERVES 4 as an appetizer (makes
  8 rolls)

TIP The trick to wrapping rice papers is to do it when they have just reached the soft and pliable stage. Place the filling at the bottom of the wrapper and fold the sides in neatly. If you haven't done it before, have a few extras to practice with first.

WATCH OUT FOR seafood. This dish is not suitable for seafood (crustacean) allergy sufferers. Omit the shrimp and increase the pork or bean sprouts if necessary.

1 Have a large shallow bowl of warm water ready to soften the rice paper wrappers. Drop a wrapper into the water for 20 seconds and then place on paper towel.

2 Place half a lettuce leaf on the edge of the rice paper nearest to you. Place a tablespoon each of rice vermicelli and carrot strips on the lettuce and add a few strips of pork, several bean sprouts and a Thai basil leaf, if using.

3 Bring up the nearest edge of the rice paper wrapper and roll it over the contents. Fold in the sides. You should now have the beginnings of a fairly tight cylinder.

4 Place 2–3 shrimp in the crease between the rolled and unrolled portions of the rice paper and a sprig of cilantro and a mint leaf next to the row of shrimp. When fully rolled, the shrimp and herbs will show through the translucent wrapper.

5 Now roll the rice paper into a cylinder. Place the roll, seam side down, on a large, flat plate to help seal it, and cover with a damp towel while you make the remaining spring rolls.

6 Serve immediately or store at room temperature, covered with plastic wrap, for up to 2 hours.

Tabbouleh

This refreshing salad of parsley and tomatoes includes bulgur wheat—but the gluten-free version, using quinoa, is every bit as delicious with a slightly nutty flavor. It is excellent as an appetizer or a side dish.

 **dairy, egg, & nut free**

½ cup bulgur wheat
½ cup water
2 cups chopped fresh parsley
4 tbsp chopped fresh mint
1 small onion, chopped
4 scallions, chopped
4 medium tomatoes, chopped

4 tbsp olive oil
4 tbsp lemon juice
salt and freshly ground black pepper

PREPARATION TIME 10 minutes
COOKING TIME 5–10 minutes
SERVES 4

1 Rinse the bulgur wheat in a strainer and drain. Bring the water to a boil, add the bulgur, bring back to a boil, reduce the heat and simmer gently until tender and the grain has absorbed the liquid, about 5–10 minutes.
2 Tip into a bowl and let cool.
3 Add the remaining ingredients, seasoning to taste with salt and pepper. Chill and serve on the day of making.

 gluten free
also dairy, egg, & nut free

Folow the recipe on the left, but substitute quinoa for the bulgur wheat and cook in ¾ cup of water. Cook for 5–10 minutes until all the liquid has been absorbed.

TIP In Lebanese restaurants, tabbouleh is sometimes served with lettuce leaves. Wrap a spoonful in a leaf and eat with your fingers.

Cucumber & wakame salad

This light, fresh tasting salad (pictured on page 100) is a perfect accompaniment to grilled fish and meats and is a version of a popular Japanese salad called *sunomono* (literally, "things of vinegar").

dairy, egg, gluten, & nut free

½ oz dried wakame seaweed
1 cucumber, peeled, seeded, and diced
3 scallions, sliced (optional)
for the dressing
2 tbsp rice vinegar
2 tsp mirin

2 tsp soy sauce
½ tsp honey

PREPARATION TIME 15 minutes
SERVES 4

1 Put the wakame in a bowl, cover with lukewarm water and let soak for 10–15 minutes. Drain and trim away any rough stems, then cut the seaweed into strips. Place in a bowl with the cucumber and scallions, if using.
2 Mix the dressing ingredients together until thoroughly blended and pour over the salad. Mix gently and serve immediately.

TIP Wakame, sometimes called sea vegetable, is seaweed sold in dried form in many Asian supermarkets and health food stores (see Resources, pp.218–219). When placed in water it softens to a glossy green vegetable that tastes and looks a little like spinach but needs no cooking.

SERVING SUGGESTION This is a delicious accompaniment to Miso marinated salmon (p.101).
  Garnish with sesame seeds. If allergic to sesame seeds, a few pink pickled ginger slivers make an attractive alternative.

Middle Eastern salad

This simple salad is made special by the addition of two uniquely Middle Eastern ingredients. The bright pink pickled turnips get their color from being pickled in beet juice and add tanginess to the salad. Deep red sumac powder is a popular seasoning made from the berries of the same name and has a pleasant lemony taste. If you have trouble finding it, just use paprika instead.

dairy, egg, gluten, & nut free

1 pink pickled turnip, drained
  and finely diced
1-1½ cucumbers, peeled,
  seeded and thinly sliced
2 medium tomatoes, finely
  diced or 8–10 cherry tomatoes,
  halved
1 scallion, finely chopped
4 tbsp lemon juice
2 tbsp olive oil
powdered sumac or paprika to
  garnish (optional)

PREPARATION TIME 5 minutes
SERVES 4

1 Mix the chopped vegetables together.
2 Just before serving, dress with the oil and lemon juice and season with salt and pepper to taste. Sprinkle with powdered sumac or paprika and serve.

SERVING SUGGESTION Serve with dips such as Red pepper dip (p.211) or hummus and flatbreads as an appetizer, or as part of a main course with grilled lamb chops.

"Looks pretty in a glass bowl for a summer party or a girls' lunch"

Gratin gallois

This is a version of the classic French *gratin dauphinois* made near us in Wales. Unsurprisingly, it incorporates the national vegetable, leeks, and it is utterly delicious served bubbling hot. The vermouth brings out the flavors of the leeks, and the potatoes are deliciously crispy on top and creamy underneath. Serve with Honeyed Welsh lamb (p.132) or any roast or stew.

 egg, gluten, & nut free

1½ tbsp flavorless nut-free oil, plus extra for baking dish
1 lb leeks, white parts only, finely chopped – yields around 12 oz
2½ cups light cream
1 bay leaf
2 tbsp dry vermouth
2 lb floury potatoes, peeled and thinly sliced
2 garlic cloves, finely chopped
salt and freshly ground black pepper to season
freshly grated nutmeg to season

PREPARATION TIME 30 minutes
COOKING TIME 1¼ hours
SERVES 4–6

dairy free
egg, gluten, & nut free

Prepare as for the recipe on the left, but substitute an equal quantity of soy cream alternative for the heavy cream.

TIP Nutmeg is a fruit, not a nut, and therefore safe for people with nut allergies.

1 Preheat the oven to 350° F. Oil a 1 quart gratin dish.
2 In a heavy-bottomed saucepan, fry the leeks in the oil until softened, but not colored.
3 Add the cream, bay leaf, and vermouth and simmer for 5 minutes.
4 Bring the cream mixture to a boil and add the potatoes. Mix carefully with a large spoon to ensure the potatoes are evenly coated with the cream mixture.
5 Spoon half of the potato mixture into the gratin dish. Sprinkle with the garlic and season with salt and pepper. Add the remaining half of the potato mixture and season again with salt and pepper. Grate fresh nutmeg over the top.
6 Bake for about 1¼ hours or until brown and bubbling. The potatoes should be tender when a knife is inserted in the center.

SIDE DISHES, APPETIZERS, & LIGHT MEALS

Roast potatoes with garlic & sea salt

These are everything a roast potato should be—crisp, crunchy, and brown on the outside and fluffy on the inside. Don't just serve them with roasts; they work well with grilled and braised dishes and stews, too. Mix it up by sprinkling with herbs, such as rosemary or sage leaves, 20 minutes before the end of cooking or shake in a few drops of balsamic vinegar or pinches of paprika just before serving.

dairy, egg, gluten, & nut free

8 medium-sized potatoes, peeled and quartered
4 tbsp olive oil
1 head of garlic, separated into cloves
sea salt

PREPARATION TIME 8 minutes
COOKING TIME 30–40 minutes
SERVES 4–6

1 Preheat the oven to 425° F.
2 Measure the oil into a large roasting pan and place in the oven to heat through.
3 Place the potatoes in a pan of boiling water for 2 minutes. Drain and cool under cold water. Dry them well, using a dish towel.
4 Carefully place the potatoes and unpeeled garlic cloves in the hot oil in the roasting pan. Turn them around to coat them evenly with the oil. Sprinkle with the sea salt and return to the oven.
5 Roast for 30–40 minutes until the potatoes are nicely browned with crispy edges. Turn the potatoes twice during cooking.

"Everyone loves them—it would be hard to imagine Sunday lunch without roast potatoes"

SIDE DISHES, APPETIZERS, & LIGHT MEALS

Fish pie

A winning combination of firm white fish and shrimp in a creamy, parsley-flecked béchamel sauce under a mound of crispy-topped mashed potato makes this a fabulous lunch or supper dish. You can vary the fish according to taste or season. Serve with buttered samphire, mixed peppery greens, or a tomato salad to add contrasting flavor and color.

 ### egg & nut free

1 lb 10 oz cod, halibut, or
  other white fish, filleted
8 1/2 oz smoked haddock
  or other smoked fish
2 1/2 cups milk
1 small onion, roughly chopped
bay leaf (optional)
scant 1/2 cup butter
1/4 cup all-purpose flour
3 1/4 lb potatoes
  peeled and quartered
2 tbsp light cream or milk

salt and freshly ground black
  pepper to season
8 oz cooked peeled shrimp
1 tbsp capers in brine, drained, rinsed
  and chopped (optional)
2 tbsp chopped fresh parsley leaves
2 tbsp grated Parmesan cheese

PREPARATION TIME 1 1/4 hours
COOKING TIME 45 minutes
SERVES 4–6

1 Preheat the oven to 375° F.
2 Put the fish in a large saucepan, add the milk, and poach the fish gently for 5 minutes; it should be slightly undercooked at this stage.
3 Transfer the fish to a plate with a slotted spoon. When cool, remove the skin, cut the fish into large chunks, and place in a 1.5 quart ovenproof dish.
4 Add the chopped onion and bay leaf (if using) to the fish milk. Bring to a boil. Remove from the heat and let stand for 10 minutes. Strain.
5 Make a white sauce by melting 3 tbsp butter in a saucepan and stirring in the flour. Cook, stirring for 1 minute. Whisk in the infused milk a little at a time, ensuring there are no lumps. When all the milk is incorporated, bring to a boil and cook for 2 minutes, whisking all the time. Remove from the heat.
6 Meanwhile, boil the potatoes for about 15 minutes or until cooked through. Mash with the remaining butter and the cream or milk and season with salt and pepper.
7 Add the shrimp, capers, and parsley to the fish, season with salt and pepper, and pour over the white sauce. Top with the mashed potatoes and use a fork to rough up the surface for crispy bits when cooked. Dust with Parmesan, if desired. Bake for 45 minutes until the top is crispy and golden.
Pictured opposite ▶

 ### dairy free
also egg & nut free

Follow the recipe on the left, but substitute dairy-free spread for butter; dairy-free soy, rice, or oat milk for cow's milk; and soy cream alternative for light cream. Use dairy-free Parmesan.

 ### gluten free
also egg & nut free

Follow the recipe on the left, but for the white sauce, substitute gluten-free all-purpose flour or a half and half mix of rice flour and cornstarch for the all-purpose flour. You may need to increase the milk slightly to get a thick pouring sauce if using all gluten-free all-purpose flour.

WATCH OUT FOR fish and crustaceans. If allergic to crustaceans but not white fish, omit the shrimp and increase the fish to a total of 2 3/4 lb.
  If you follow a gluten-free diet, make sure you buy capers in brine rather than malt vinegar.

Tandoori fish

This quick-to-cook recipe makes an excellent light supper dish. In restaurants, red and yellow food coloring is used to achieve the brilliant orange color of this famous Indian marinade, but I've made it optional, since the spices on their own give a mustardy golden color, which is just as attractive. Marinate for at least two hours to allow the subtle mixture of yogurt and spices infuse the fish.

 egg, gluten, & nut free

for the tandoori marinade
1 cup plain yogurt
2 tbsp nut-free vegetable oil
2 garlic cloves, crushed
2 tsp grated fresh ginger
1 tsp garam masala
½ tsp ground turmeric
½ tsp chili powder or paprika
  salt to season
to finish
4 white fish fillets, about 8 oz
  each, skinned if desired

lemon or lime wedges (to garnish)
1 quantity of egg-, gluten-, and
  nut-free raita (see page 213)

PREPARATION TIME 5 minutes,
  plus marinating
COOKING TIME 15 minutes
SERVES 4

1 Mix all of the marinade ingredients together in a glass or other nonmetallic bowl. Add the fish and coat thoroughly with the marinade.
2 Cover and chill for at least 2 hours or overnight.
3 Make the raita recipe.
4 Preheat the oven to 425° F. Remove the fish fillets from the marinade and drain off any excess. Place in an ovenproof dish and bake toward the top of the oven until the fish flakes easily with a fork, about 15 minutes. Transfer to warm plates. Garnish with lemon or lime wedges. Serve with the raita, a small side salad, and other accompaniments (see right).

WATCH OUT FOR chili because some people cannot tolerate it—use paprika instead of chili powder.

TIP If you decide to use red and yellow food dyes then add 1 teaspoon of yellow and 1½ teaspoons of red to the marinade. Make sure neither contain tartrazine, a known allergen.

dairy free
also egg, gluten, & nut free

Prepare as for the recipe on the left, but substitute soy yogurt for cow's milk yogurt in the marinade. Make the dairy-free Raita recipe on page 213.

SERVING SUGGESTION Serve with plain boiled or coconut rice and steamed green vegetables.

Marinated swordfish

This meaty fish suits Asian accents hence this fusion-style salsa verde. This makes a great dish for a barbecue since you can prepare the salsa in advance and the fish cooks in minutes. Keep an eye on it since it dries out quickly; it's best broiled or grilled to medium. Serve the steaks with the salsa verde, lime wedges, and salads or noodles.

dairy, egg, gluten, & nut free

2 swordfish steaks,
 1–1¼-in thick (1lb) each,
 halved

for the marinade

2 tbsp gluten-free tamari or
 soy sauce
2 tbsp Thai fish sauce
1 tbsp sesame oil
1 small red onion, finely chopped
2 garlic cloves, finely chopped
2 tsp rice vinegar
2 tsp mirin (or dry sherry)
2 tbsp chopped fresh coriander
1 dried red chili, crushed
flavorless nut-free oil for
 basting

for the Asian salsa verde

1 bunch fresh cilantro leaves,
 roughly chopped
1½ tbsp grated fresh ginger
2 tbsp rice vinegar
2 tsp superfine sugar
4 tbsp flavorless nut-free oil
6 scallions, finely chopped
1 tbsp lime juice
salt and freshly ground black pepper

PREPARATION TIME 10 minutes
 plus marinating time
COOKING TIME 8–10 minutes
SERVES 4

WATCH OUT FOR sesame oil; some people are allergic to sesame, in which case replace the sesame oil with a flavorless nut-free oil. Make sure that the soy or tamari sauce is gluten free if necessary.

TIP The steaks are also great barbecued. Place in a hinged wire rack and cook, 2–3 in from the coals. Cook for 4–5 minutes each side, brushing frequently with oil.

1 Mix the marinade ingredients together in a shallow bowl. Marinate the steaks for at least an hour, turning once or twice. Shake the marinade from the steaks before cooking.
2 Preheat the grill. Grill the fish, 4 inches from the heat, for 4–5 minutes each side, until cooked through, brushing with oil occasionally.
3 For the Asian salsa verde, put the cilantro, ginger, rice vinegar, sugar, and oil in a food processor and blend to a still-chunky, rough-textured paste, stopping and scraping down the sides as necessary. Stir in the chopped scallions and the lime juice. Season to taste.

Miso marinated salmon

Marinating fish in miso and sake overnight is a traditional Japanese technique that works brilliantly with salmon. Miso, made from fermented soy beans, is a thick, salty paste with an underlying sharpness from the fermenting process and a rich caramel aftertaste that contributes well to the crisp browning of the fish. This easy dish is impressive enough for casual entertaining or a dinner party.

dairy, egg, gluten, & nut free

3 tbsp mirin (rice wine)
2 tbsp sake
3 tbsp superfine sugar
generous ½ cup sweet rice
  miso paste
4 salmon fillets (with skin on),
  about 6 oz each
Cucumber and wakame Salad
  (see p.91)

PREPARATION TIME 5 minutes plus
  cooling and marinating
COOKING TIME 6 minutes
SERVES 4

1 For the sweet miso marinade, put the mirin and sake in a small saucepan. Add the sugar and heat gently, stirring until dissolved.
2 Bring to a boil, remove from the heat, and stir in the miso until thoroughly blended. Cool completely.
3 Place the salmon in a single layer in a nonmetallic dish. Spoon the marinade over and turn the fish over to coat completely. Leave in the fridge to marinate for at least 4 hours or overnight.
4 When ready to serve, preheat the broiler. Lay the fish, skin sides up, on foil on the grill rack. Broil for 3 minutes.
5 Turn the fish over and broil until lightly browned and the fish flakes easily with a fork, another 3 minutes.
6 Serve with Cucumber and wakame salad (pictured right—see page 91 for recipe).

WATCH OUT FOR some varieties of miso that include other grains such as barley and wheat. Traditionally miso is made from fermented soy beans and koji, a fermented rice product, but some varieties include other grains. Check the ingredients before buying.

TIP If white miso paste (pale gold in color) is difficult to get hold of, there are darker blends that work well in this recipe. However, avoid the red miso (actually brown in color), which is by far the saltiest form.

SERVING SUGGESTION Good side dishes include rice, noodles (avoid egg- or wheat-based noodles, if you can't tolerate them), spicy salad greens such as mizuna or watercress, and shredded daikon, turnip, or radishes. Sprinkle with black and white sesame seeds for stylish dinner party entertaining (if you can tolerate them).

Potato-crusted halibut

An unbelievably simple and effective recipe for halibut fillets with a crisp golden-brown potato topping and braised beets on the side. It's a recipe with mercifully little peeling involved and the one version works for all—dairy, egg, gluten, and nut free. Start the fish off in a frying pan and then transfer to the oven, where the beets are already cooking away.

dairy, egg, gluten, & nut free

for the braised beets
4 even-sized beets about
  1¼ lb in total, washed,
  but not trimmed or peeled
2 tbsp balsamic vinegar
for the halibut
4 thick halibut fillets, about
  7 oz each, skinned if
  desired

salt and freshly ground black
  pepper
2 large potatoes, scrubbed, but
  not peeled
3 tbsp flavorless nut-free oil

PREPARATION TIME 20 minutes
COOKING TIME 1¼ hours
SERVES 4

SERVING SUGGESTION This is also delicious served with lemony green beans. Steam green beans until just tender, about 6 minutes, and toss with olive oil, lemon zest, and juice.

1 Preheat the oven to 400° F.
2 Wrap the beets individually in foil, sprinkling 1 tablespoon of water on each before sealing the foil.
3 Place on a baking sheet and cook for about 1 hour, or until the beets are tender all the way through. The peel slips off easily once they are cooked.
4 Top and tail the beets, cut in quarters, and keep warm. Sprinkle with the balsamic vinegar just before serving and season with salt and pepper.
5 Meanwhile, when the beets are nearly cooked (after about 40 minutes), season the halibut fillets with salt and pepper.
6 Coarsely grate the potatoes and squeeze out as much excess water as possible. Pat the grated potatoes dry with paper towels.
7 Top each fillet with a thick, even layer of grated potato and press the topping down onto the fish.
8 Heat the oil in the frying pan until hot, almost smoking.
9 Using two spatulas or a fish spatula, one on the top of the fillet, one underneath, add the halibut fillets to the pan, potato-side down. Push any stray potato back under the fish.
10 Fry until the potato crust is golden brown, about 5 minutes, then turn the fillets over carefully, again using both spatulas.
11 Place the frying pan in the oven if it is ovenproof. Otherwise, transfer fillets to a roasting pan. Cook until the fillets are just cooked through, 8–10 minutes.
12 Transfer the fish and beets to warm serving plates. Serve with lemony green beans, also, if desired (see right).

Shrimp dumplings

These little Asian morsels are filled with chopped shrimp, scallions, fresh ginger, and Thai fish sauce. They are cooked quickly in boiling water then served with a sweet chili dipping sauce. They make an attractive appetizer for a dinner party or can be served for lunch or supper with a vegetable stir-fry. Tapioca flour is often used in Asian cuisine and is gluten free.

 dairy, egg, & nut free

for the dumplings
½ cup all-purpose flour, plus extra for dusting
½ cup tapioca flour
a pinch of salt
½ cup warm water

for the filling
2 scallions (plus extra for garnish, if desired)
7 oz raw shelled tiger shrimp, chopped
½ tsp grated fresh ginger
1 tsp Thai fish sauce

for the chili dipping sauce
½ cup granulated sugar
½ cup hot water
1 tsp red pepper flakes
1 tbsp paprika
1 tsp grated fresh ginger
1 large garlic clove, crushed
1 tbsp Thai fish sauce
1–2 tbsp lime juice

PREPARATION TIME 30 minute plus dough resting time
COOKING TIME 5 minutes
SERVES 4–6

1 Sift the flours and salt into a bowl. Mix with the warm water to form a soft dough. Knead gently on a floured surface until smooth and elastic. Wrap in plastic wrap and let rest for 30 minutes.

2 For the filling, finely chop the 2 scallions. Mix with the chopped shrimp, ginger, and fish sauce.

3 Make the chili sauce. Put the sugar in a saucepan with the water and heat, stirring, until melted. Stir in the remaining ingredients except the lime juice, bring to a boil and boil for 1 minute. Stir in the lime juice to taste. Tip into 4 small bowls and let cool.

4 On a floured surface, divide the dough into 24 balls and roll out to thin pancakes, about 2½ inches in diameter. Loosen from the work surface, using a palette knife or spatula.

5 Put a spoonful of the filling on each pancake. Brush the edges with water. Fold over and pinch the edges together well.

6 Bring a large pan of water with a pinch of salt to a boil. Drop in the dumplings. Bring back to a boil, then simmer for 5 minutes, stirring gently to keep the dumplings separate. They will float to the surface as they cook.

7 Use a slotted spoon to transfer to warm serving plates. Serve with a small pot of chili dipping sauce on one side. Garnish with scallion curls, if liked (see right).

gluten free
also dairy, egg, and nut free

Follow the recipe on the left, but substitute ½ cup gluten-free all-purpose flour, plus extra for dusting, for the ordinary all-purpose flour. Add 2 teaspoons of xanthan gum to the flours and use an extra 3–4 teaspoons of warm water to mix. There is no need to rest the dough before use.

WATCH OUT FOR chilies, because some people can't tolerate them.

SERVING SUGGESTION Garnish with scallion curls. Trim 4 scallions to about 3 inches long from the white end. Make several cuts down the length of the white part, so they resemble tassels, then place in a bowl of ice water to curl up.

TIPS If you prefer, use all-purpose flour instead of half tapioca flour.

Check the consistency of the chili dipping sauce and thin with a dash of cold water, if necessary.

Use store-bought sweet chili dipping sauce instead of the homemade, if you prefer. It is usually egg free, dairy free, and gluten free, but check the label carefully since it may contain traces of nuts or sesame.

Scallops & shrimp with lentils

An inspired pairing of aromatic simmered lentils with quick-cooked seafood that makes an excellent prepare-ahead dish for those not allergic to crustaceans and shellfish. Influenced by the heady spice mix of red lentils in the Indian *masoor dhal*, the coral-colored lentils turn a nice mustardy yellow when cooked. The dish works well with green, brown, or Puy lentils although cooking times may vary.

egg, gluten, & nut free

12 large scallops without coral
12 jumbo shrimp
3 tbsp sweet chili sauce (optional)
3 tbsp lime juice (optional)
1 tbsp butter
1 onion, finely chopped
2 garlic cloves
1 tbsp finely chopped fresh ginger
1 tsp ground cumin
1 tsp ground coriander
½ tsp chili, cayenne, or paprika powder

generous 1 cup red lentils
4¼ cups water or stock
1 tbsp lime or lemon juice
2 tbsp heavy cream
salt and pepper to season
nut-free flavorless vegetable oil for grilling scallops
1 tsp finely chopped red chili
2 tbsp fresh cilantro leaves

PREPARATION TIME 10 minutes
COOKING TIME 30 minutes
SERVES 4

1 Pat the scallops dry on paper towels. Marinade the shrimp in the chili sauce and lime juice, if using.
2 Melt the butter in a saucepan and fry the onion, garlic, and ginger, stirring, for 2 minutes until softened. Add the cumin, coriander, and chili, cayenne, or paprika to the mixture and fry for 1 minute, stirring.
3 Add the lentils and water or stock. Bring to a boil, then reduce to a simmer. Simmer for 25 minutes or until the lentils are soft but not mushy, stirring occasionally. Remove from the heat and stir in the lemon juice and cream and season well with salt and pepper. Place on a serving dish and keep warm.
4 Preheat the broiler or grill pan to medium.
5 Slice the scallops horizontally into two or three horizontally, depending on their size, and brush all over with oil.
6 Grill or broil the shrimp for about 2 minutes on each side, until pink. Grill or broil the scallops for just 30 seconds each side or they will be overcooked.
7 Scatter the chopped chili and cilantro leaves over the lentils. Serve immediately.
◀ **Pictured opposite**

dairy free

also egg, gluten, & nut free

Follow the recipe on the left, but substitute an equal quantity of soy or other dairy-free cream for the 1 tablespoon used in the recipe.

TIP If grilling, place the shrimp directly on the grill 4 inches from the coals and cook for about 2 minutes each side. Skewer the scallops through the middle, brush with oil, and grill 3 inches from the coals, turning once, for 30–60 seconds each side.

WATCH OUT FOR lentils—some legumes (lentils) are processed in factories that also process products that contain gluten. Check for seafood allergies—shrimp are crustaceans and scallops are mollusks. Some people cannot tolerate chilies—omit if in any doubt.

Chicken pie

A classic supper dish—ideal for family and guests. The vegetables are sautéed first for extra flavor and the chicken is lightly poached in stock and wine. Cornstarch is used to make the sauce and the whole thing is combined under a crisp glazed pastry crust. Even the egg-free version (pictured) has its own glaze, for a pie that looks as good as it tastes.

 ## nut free

2 tbsp flavorless nut-free
  vegetable oil
5 oz button mushrooms
2 leeks, thinly sliced
2½ cups chicken stock
⅔ cup dry white wine
1 bay leaf
2 carrots, sliced
2¼ lb chicken fillets, cut
  into bite-sized pieces

3½ tbsp cornstarch
salt and freshly ground black pepper
½ tsp chopped fresh thyme
1 quantity egg and nut-free Piecrust
  (p.180)
1 egg, beaten

PREPARATION TIME 40 minutes
COOKING TIME 40 minutes
SERVES 6

1 Preheat the oven to 400° F.
2 Heat the oil in a saucepan, add the mushrooms, and fry for 5 minutes. Remove the mushrooms to a plate. Add the leeks to the pan and fry for 2 minutes, stirring, and remove to a plate.
3 Add the stock, wine, bay leaf, and carrots to the pan, bring to a boil, reduce the heat, and simmer for another 5 minutes. Add the chicken and cook gently for another 5 minutes. Remove the chicken and carrots to a plate.
4 In a small bowl, blend the cornstarch with 4 tablespoons of stock and stir until smooth. Pour into the pan and cook, stirring for 3 minutes until thickened. Season and remove from the heat.
5 Spoon the chicken, all the vegetables, and the sauce into a deep 7 cup pie dish. Stir in the thyme.
6 Roll out the pastry on a floured surface to ¼ inch thick. Cut a 9 inch round for the pastry lid. Roll out the trimmings and cut a ½ inch strip, long enough to go around the rim of the dish.
7 Dampen the edge of the pie dish with water and press the strip of pastry around the rim. Dampen the strip.
8 Carefully lift the pastry lid and place over the top of the pie dish and firmly press it to the strip all around to seal. Crimp the edges together if you desire. Make a small slit in the center of the pastry to allow steam to escape. Glaze the pastry with beaten egg.
9 Bake until golden and the pie is hot through, about 40 minutes.

WATCH OUT FOR bouillon cubes, which may contain dairy or gluten.

 ## dairy free
also nut free

Follow the recipe on the left, using one quantity of dairy-free Piecrust (p.180).

egg free
also nut free

Follow the recipe on the left.
To glaze, replace the egg with 2 tablespoons of milk or, if a shinier glaze is preferred, use the following gelatin glaze. Put 2 tablespoons of water in a small bowl and sprinkle 1 tablespoon of gelatin over. Let soften for 5 minutes then stand the bowl in a pan of gently simmering water and stir until dissolved completely. Brush over the pastry using a pastry brush, being careful not to let puddles of the glaze collect in the pastry hollows or crimped edges.
Pictured opposite ▷

 ## gluten free
also nut free

Follow the recipe on the left, using one quantity of gluten-free Piecrust (p.182). The gluten-free pie crust will have a slight yellowish hue because of the cornmeal in the pastry.

Chicken, olive, & chickpea stew

A dish with characteristically North African flavors—sweet spices, chickpeas, lemon, and green olives meld together to make a meltingly delicious stew. It is easy to make and ideal for summer or winter eating. Serve with plenty of rice to soak up the juices. Alternatively, use couscous, either the real thing, or the quinoa version (see gluten-free recipe, p.135), or Basmati and wild rice pilaf (p.144).

dairy, egg, gluten, & nut free

4 tbsp light olive oil
4 chicken breasts on the bone
  with skins on
1 onion, chopped
2 garlic cloves, crushed
1 tsp ground cumin
2 tsp ground turmeric
½ tsp coriander seeds, crushed
4 cardamom pods, lightly
  crushed
1 cup chicken stock
juice of 1 lemon

1 x 15 oz can of chickpeas,
  drained and rinsed
12 pitted green olives, soaked in
  water for 2 hours if salty
salt and freshly ground black pepper

PREPARATION TIME 12 minutes
COOKING TIME 40–50 minutes
SERVES 4

1 Heat 2 tablespoons of the oil in a large flameproof casserole dish and brown the chicken pieces on both sides. Remove with a slotted spoon and set aside.
2 Heat the remaining oil and sauté the onions and garlic for 2 minutes until softened but not browned. Stir in the cumin, turmeric, coriander, and cardamom and cook gently for 1 minute. Stir in the stock, lemon juice, and chickpeas.
3 Bring to a boil, reduce the heat, cover, and simmer for 40–50 minutes or until the chicken is tender. Add the olives 10 minutes before the end of cooking.
4 Season with salt and pepper just before serving.

WATCH OUT FOR bouillon cubes, which may contain traces of dairy or gluten, if you're cooking for people with severe dairy or gluten sensitivities.

VARIATION If you like a lemony taste, add the squeezed halves of lemons into the stew and remove just before serving.

"This one-pot supper dish releases its wonderful fragrances as soon as you lift the lid"

Lemon thyme grilled chicken

Delicious, versatile, and quick, this herbed lemon-scented grilled chicken is perfect for any meal. If you can, buy chicken pieces with the bone still in since it contributes to the flavor, and keep the skin on because it crisps beautifully as it cooks. Noodles or boiled rice are a perfect match and all you need is a well-flavored salad to accompany it.

dairy, egg, gluten, & nut free

8 chicken thighs or drumsticks or
4 chicken breasts on the bone
  with skins
juice of 1 lemon
1 garlic clove, crushed
2 tsp fresh thyme leaves
½ tsp finely chopped fresh
  rosemary
4 tbsp olive oil
salt and pepper to season
finely grated zest of 1 lemon

PREPARATION TIME 5 minutes
  plus marinating
COOKING TIME 18–20 minutes
  (grilled or broiled), 30 minutes
  (roasted)
SERVES 4

SERVING SUGGESTION Serve with a salad of chopped tomatoes, chickpeas, and finely sliced red onions dressed with olive oil and wine vinegar, or mixed salad greens with a honey and mustard dressing.

1 Marinate the chicken pieces in the lemon juice (reserve the squeezed lemon halves for later), garlic, herbs, 2 tablespoons of the oil, and a little salt and pepper for at least an hour.
2 Preheat the broiler or grill to medium. Grill or broil the chicken pieces, skin side down, 4 inches from the heat for 10 minutes, then turn over. Brush with any remaining marinade and grill or broil until cooked through, another 8–10 minutes. Alternatively, roast in the oven at 375° F for about 30 minutes. Put the squeezed lemon halves into the roasting pan for added flavor.
3 Transfer to warm serving plates and spoon any pan juices over. Garnish with the lemon zest before serving.

VARIATION Replace the thyme and rosemary with a handful of torn fresh basil leaves, which should be scattered over the chicken 10 minutes before the end of the cooking time.

Thai green chicken curry

A virtually authentic Thai curry with the characteristic aroma and flavor of coconut, fish sauce, ginger, curry, and herbs. I've substituted colorful red and yellow peppers for the more traditional Asian eggplant used in Thailand. This version has plenty of kick from the green curry paste and the shredded red chili, but for those who like more firepower, there are optional extra green chilies.

🌀 ⊘ ⊛ ⊛ **dairy, egg, gluten, & nut free**

2 x 14 fl oz cans (3½ cups) of coconut milk

1 lb skinless chicken breasts, cut into 1-in pieces

4 kaffir lime leaves, 2 left whole and 2 finely shredded

a little nut-free vegetable oil

2–3 red, orange, or yellow bell peppers, sliced (optional)

2 tbsp Thai green curry paste

3 tbsp Thai fish sauce

2 tsp palm sugar or brown sugar

3–4 green chilies, seeded and crushed (optional)

3 stalks lesser galangal, peeled and shredded

5½ oz snowpeas (optional)

1 red chili, seeded and finely shredded

10–12 Thai sweet basil leaves, torn

PREPARATION TIME 10 minutes
COOKING TIME 20 minutes
SERVES 4

TIPS If you can't get lesser galangal, use a ½ inch piece of fresh ginger. Grated zest of ½ lime is a good substitute for the lime leaves.

If you don't like your curries too hot, replace the shredded red chili with a quarter of a red bell pepper, seeded and thinly sliced.

WATCH OUT FOR chili, since some people can't tolerate it. Omit if need be.

1 Open both cans of coconut milk and spoon the thick coconut cream that has risen to the top of the cans into a saucepan. Pour the thinner milk at the bottom of the cans into a measuring cup for use later.

2 Add the chicken and the 2 whole kaffir lime leaves to the thick coconut cream. Cook on a moderately high heat for 10 minutes or until the chicken is just cooked through. Remove the chicken to a plate using a slotted spoon.

3 Boil the coconut cream until it thickens and the oil separates out. It will look curdled at this stage but don't worry. It will be used to thicken and flavor the sauce (in step 5).

4 In a large frying pan, fry the bell peppers (if using) in oil for about 3 minutes. Set aside. Fry the curry paste in a tablespoon of the remaining coconut milk for 1–2 minutes until the fragrance is released. Add the fish sauce and sugar and stir.

5 Add the remaining coconut milk, green chilies (if using), lesser galangal, and snowpeas (if using). Stir and cook on medium heat for 5 minutes. Return the peppers (if using), chicken, and coconut cream to the pan and cook for about 5 minutes to make sure that the meat is heated through. Scatter the shredded kaffir lime leaves, red chili, and sweet basil leaves over the curry just before you've finished heating the meat through.

6 Serve immediately with steamed or boiled rice.

A heartwarming roast dinner for the family or friends with Chicken roasted in olive oil (p.114), gluten-free Chestnut stuffing (p.214), Roast potatoes with garlic & sea salt (p.95), steamed green beans, and Vegetable gravy (p.215).

Chicken roasted in olive oil

Everyone has their own recipe for chicken or other celebratory birds. This one is delicious and has the benefit of being naturally dairy free. If you are making a family meal or festive roast chicken or turkey, accompany it with Vegetable gravy (p.215), Roast potatoes with garlic & sea salt (p.95), lightly steamed green beans, and Chestnut stuffing (p.214).

dairy, egg, gluten, & nut free

2½–3 lb free range chicken
1 lemon
1 onion, halved
fresh parsley, chervil, or marjoram
4 tbsp olive oil
salt and freshly ground black
   pepper

PREPARATION TIME 5 minutes
COOKING TIME 1 hour
SERVES 4

1 Preheat the oven to 425° F.
2 Cut the lemon in half and squeeze the juice over the chicken. Place the squeezed lemon halves in the cavity along with the onion halves. Alternatively, for an attractive garnish, place the lemon halves in the roasting pan alongside the chicken.
3 Finely chop the herbs and mix them with a little olive oil. Gently pry the skin away from the chicken breast and use the herbs to stuff the gap between the skin and the chicken breast.
4 Using your hands, rub olive oil into the skin of the chicken and then season generously with salt and pepper.
5 Cook for 1 hour or until the chicken is browned and the juices run clear when a skewer is inserted into the thigh.
◀ **Pictured on previous page**

"This has crispy golden skin, soft white meat, and a hint of lemon in the juices"

Duck with apples & celeriac

Not just fabulous to eat, this special occasion duck is served on a bed of sautéed apple and celeriac with a delicious deep red wine and fig gravy. Its beautiful fall colors make it a feast for the eyes, too. Cooking the duck is an easy stove-top recipe, and if you make the more complex gravy ahead of time, the whole dish can be assembled in about 20 minutes.

egg, gluten, & nut free

for the gravy
1 cup red wine
½ cup well-flavored duck
  or chicken stock
1 sprig thyme or 1 bouquet garni
1 onion, quartered
2-in piece of orange peel
4 dried figs, halved
for the duck
2 large eating apples

1 lb 6 oz celeriac
1 tbsp wine or cider vinegar
2 tbsp butter
4 medium-sized duck breasts, skin on

PREPARATION TIME 25 minutes
COOKING TIME 50 minutes
SERVES 4

1 Place the gravy ingredients in a saucepan and bring them to a boil. Reduce to a simmer and simmer very low for 30 minutes or until the figs are soft. Discard the onion, thyme sprig (or bouquet garni), and orange peel. Put the figs and a minimal amount of the liquid (6–8 tablespoons) in a food processor and blend until smooth. Mix the blended figs back into the gravy and set aside.

2 Peel and chop the apples into ½-inch pieces. Peel and chop the celeriac into ½ inch pieces and cover with water acidulated with wine or cider vinegar to prevent discoloration.

3 Steam the celeriac pieces for 3–5 minutes until just tender.

4 Brown the apple pieces in the butter until golden but still firm.

5 On medium heat in a large frying pan, place duck breasts skin-side down. When the fat begins to run, turn the heat up to medium-high for about 5 minutes. When the skins are brown, turn the breasts over and cook for 10–12 minutes, depending on how rare you like your duck. Cover the pan if it spatters. Use a slotted spoon to remove the duck, and keep it warm.

6 Pour away the excess fat and add the gravy to the pan, scraping to incorporate any residues. Allow the gravy to bubble and reduce for 1–2 minutes. Season, remove from heat, and keep warm.

7 Add the celeriac to the frying pan with the apples. Sauté them together briefly to warm through.

8 Slice each duck breast into thin slices. Tip the celeriac and apple mixture onto a warmed serving dish and top with the duck slices. Surround with gravy and serve immediately.

dairy free

also egg, gluten, & nut free

Follow the recipe on the left. In step 3, replace the butter with 2 tablespoons of light olive oil.

TIP If you want to make this dish look really professional, arrange vegetables on individual warmed plates, then slice the duck breast in ¼ inch slices, and fan out over the vegetables. Pour red wine and fig gravy around the perimeter of the vegetables in a crescent.

VARIATION For a truly plutocratic touch, finely chop 1¾ oz of duck foie gras and stir into the apple and celeriac at the end of step 7 just before removing from the heat.

WATCH OUT FOR foie gras, if using, since some has added butter. Check your bouillion cubes because some may contain traces of gluten or dairy.

Fegato alla Veneziana

One of the best versions of liver and onions there is, this is also an easy, nearly instant supper dish. The advance preparation of frying the onions is simple and the finished dish only takes a couple of minutes. The vinegar is essential so don't leave it out. Serve with Grilled polenta (p.81), as they do in Venice, or with puréed potatoes and wilted spinach leaves or braised *cavolo nero* (Italian cabbage).

 egg, gluten, & nut free

2 tbsp mild olive oil
2 mild onions, thinly sliced
8–12 very thin slices of calves'
    liver, trimmed and cleaned
    1 lb in total
sea salt and freshly ground black
    pepper to season
3 tbsp butter
2 tbsp red wine vinegar

to garnish
chopped fresh parsley or sage

PREPARATION TIME 5 minutes
COOKING TIME 12 minutes
SERVES 4

dairy free
also egg, gluten, & nut free

Follow the recipe on the left, but use 2½ tablespoons of olive oil instead of butter in step 3.

1 Heat the olive oil in a large frying pan over moderate heat. Fry the onions, stirring frequently, until the onions are soft and golden brown, but not scorched, 8–10 minutes. Remove the onions from the pan with a slotted spoon and set aside on a warmed plate.
2 Season the liver slices with sea salt and freshly ground pepper.
3 Increase the heat to medium high and add the butter. When it is foaming, add the seasoned liver slices and brown them, preferably in batches to avoid overcrowding. The hot pan sears the liver quickly, so you should need no more than 15 seconds for each side.
4 Return the onions to the side of the pan and toss briefly to heat through. Sprinkle the wine vinegar, which will hiss and reduce quickly to a mere trace of liquid.
5 Transfer to warm plates, spooning over any pan juices and sprinkle with parsley or sage.

WATCH OUT FOR vinegars—please don't substitute grain-based or malt vinegars for red wine vinegar. It won't taste right and people who are gluten-sensitive can't tolerate grain or malt vinegars.

Ragu Bolognese

Delicious with spaghetti, this ragu works well with any pasta, which has plenty of surface area for the pasta to cling to. It's a winner with corn pasta too. Simmer it slowly and add the cream near the end, to make it as authentically Bolognese as possible. The best cheese to serve it with is Parmesan, and there are some pretty good dairy-free versions around now, too.

egg, gluten, & nut free

2 tsp olive oil
1 onion, finely chopped
2 garlic cloves, finely chopped
1 carrot, finely chopped
2 oz bacon, pancetta, or
  prosciutto, chopped into
  ¾ in pieces
10½ oz lean ground beef
3½ oz chicken livers,
  trimmed and chopped
½ cup dry white wine
14 oz can chopped
  tomatoes with their juice
2 tbsp tomato paste

sea salt and freshly ground black
  pepper to season
¼ tsp freshly grated nutmeg
1 bay leaf
4 tbsp heavy cream
chopped fresh parsley for garnishing
  (optional)

to serve
pasta of your choice
freshly grated Parmesan

PREPARATION TIME 20 minutes
COOKING TIME 2 hours
SERVES 4

dairy free
also egg, gluten, & nut free

Follow the recipe on the left, but use soy cream alternative instead of heavy cream and nondairy Parmesan alternative (sometimes called vegan Parmesan) —beware since it can be quite salty.

WATCH OUT FOR the pasta because many types of store-bought pasta contain gluten or egg, or both. However, if you check the labels carefully, you will be able to find pasta that you and your guests will be able to eat.

1 Heat 1 tablespoon of oil in a flameproof casserole dish or heavy-bottomed saucepan. Fry the onions for 2 minutes or until lightly golden. Add the garlic and carrot and fry for another 2 minutes. Add the bacon and cook for another 2 minutes. Remove from the pan with a slotted spoon and set aside.

2 Heat the remaining oil and fry the meat until browned, stirring all the time to break up the lumps. Add the chicken livers and mix in well. Return the vegetable and bacon mixture to the pan and combine with the beef and liver.

3 Add the wine, tomatoes, and tomato paste. Season with salt and pepper and add the grated nutmeg and bay leaf.

4 Bring to a boil, stirring; reduce to as low as possible and simmer very gently until rich and tender, 1¼ hours, stirring occasionally. Stir in the cream and continue to simmer very gently for another 45 minutes.

5 Serve the ragu stirred into pasta, with parsley, if desired, and a bowl of grated Parmesan.

Osso buco

This meltingly tender, rich, slow-simmered dish is a real treat. I didn't think the famous veal stew could be improved upon until I found an Italian recipe that suggested incorporating finely chopped carrots and celery into the rich tomato and wine sauce. Add the gremolata seasoning of parsley, lemon zest, and garlic right at the end for a wonderful, fresh, and tangy contrast.

dairy, egg, gluten, & nut free

2 tbsp nut-free vegetable oil
4 large pieces of shin of veal (*ossi bucchi*), each at least 2-in thick
2 carrots, very finely chopped
1 celery heart, very finely chopped
generous 1 cup very dry white wine
14 oz tomatoes, skinned and chopped (or a 14-oz can of chopped tomatoes)
1 tbsp tomato paste
salt and freshly ground black pepper

for the gremolata
grated zest of 1 lemon
2 tbsp finely chopped fresh parsley
1 garlic clove, finely chopped

PREPARATION TIME 15 minutes
COOKING TIME 1½–2 hours
SERVES 4

SERVING SUGGESTION Serve with saffron-scented risotto Milanese (pictured right—see page 145 for the recipe).

Dig out the marrow from the bones and stir into the risotto.

TIP You can add a pinch of superfine sugar with the tomatoes to bring out their flavor.

1 Heat the oil in a frying pan and lightly brown the veal pieces on both sides. Remove from the frying pan with a slotted spoon and set aside.

2 Gently fry the chopped carrots and celery in the pan for about 2 minutes, stirring, until softened, but do not allow them to brown.

3 Transfer the vegetables to a flameproof casserole dish that is just large enough to fit the veal in a single layer (this keeps the liquid ingredients to a minimum and avoids a thinner sauce). Arrange the veal on top.

4 In a bowl, combine the wine, tomatoes, and tomato paste and season with salt and pepper. Pour the mixture over the meat and vegetables—it should just cover the meat. If necessary, top off with wine.

5 Bring to a boil and then reduce the heat to the barest simmer. Cover and cook gently for 1½– 2 hours, removing the cover after the first hour. The stew is cooked when the meat is tender and loosening from the bones, and the sauce is slightly reduced. Taste and re-season if necessary.

6 Just before serving, mix the lemon zest, parsley, and garlic clove together to make the gremolata and sprinkle it over the meat.

Vitello tonnato

An elegant, classic dish for hot summer days. The slices of cold roast veal in a creamy tuna mayonnaise sauce need no more than rice or new potatoes and a green salad to accompany them. A favorite for buffet lunches, Vitello tonnato looks at its most decorative arranged as overlapping slices with the sauce poured over and then decorated with capers and thinly sliced lemon.

 dairy, gluten, & nut free

3 tbsp olive oil
1½ lb piece of boned veal
  loin
1 onion, quartered
1 carrot, chopped
1 celery stick, chopped
⅓ cup dry white wine
⅓ cup stock
1 bay leaf
salt and freshly ground black
  pepper
for the sauce
7 oz drained, best quality
  canned tuna in oil
2 tbsp lemon juice
3 anchovy fillets, chopped

1 tbsp capers in brine,
  plus extra to garnish
salt and freshly ground black pepper
½ cup store-bought mayonnaise or a
  1 quantity of Mayonnaise (p.210)
  or a ¼ quantity of Aïoli (p.209)
juices from the roast (to thin the sauce)
to garnish
½ lemon, thinly sliced (optional)
fresh parsley, roughly chopped
  (optional)

PREPARATION TIME 15 minutes
  plus chilling time
COOKING TIME 1 hour
SERVES 4

egg free
also dairy, gluten, & nut free

Follow the recipe on the left, but use store-bought egg-free mayonnaise or 1 quantity of egg-free Mayonnaise (p.210) or a ¼ quantity of Aïoli (p.209).

TIPS Buy topside or shoulder of veal loin, as preferred.
  If making in advance, slice and marinate the veal in a third of the sauce overnight for extra flavor.

1 Preheat the oven to 350° F. Heat the oil in a frying pan and brown the veal quickly on all sides.
2 Spread the onion, carrot, and celery out in a large casserole dish and place the browned meat on top.
3 Add the wine, stock, bay leaf, and a little salt and pepper. Cover with the lid and roast in the oven for 1 hour, until tender, basting once or twice. Remove from the oven and let cool in the liquid. When cold, wrap the veal in foil and chill until ready to serve. Strain the liquid; discard the vegetables, but reserve the liquid for thinning the sauce.
4 Make the sauce. In a food processor, blend together the tuna, lemon juice, anchovies, and capers to a smooth purée. Season to taste. Fold in the mayonnaise or aïoli, using 5–6 tablespoons of the reserved juices from the roast to thin the sauce to the consistency of thick cream.
5 Remove the veal from the refrigerator and allow it to come to room temperature. Arrange slices attractively on a serving dish. Pour the sauce over and decorate with thin slices of lemon and some scattered capers and fresh parsley, if desired.

Meatloaf

This is a great family meatloaf, crusty on top and juicily meaty underneath. It is comforting, nostalgic eating, especially when combined with mashed potatoes and Vegetable gravy (p.215). It's delicious, too, with a fresh tomato sauce or a big dollop of ketchup. I've suggested some additions but I'm sure you'll have your own. Enjoy the leftovers in sandwiches or cold with a green salad or coleslaw.

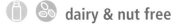 **dairy & nut free**

1 tbsp vegetable nut-free oil
  plus extra for the loaf pan
1 onion, chopped
1 lb ground beef
8 oz ground pork or sausage
1 tbsp Worcestershire sauce
  (optional)
2 garlic cloves, crushed
1½ cups breadcrumbs
1 tsp chopped fresh thyme
  leaves or ½ tsp dried
6 tbsp chopped fresh parsley
3 tbsp tomato purée

3 tbsp ketchup
salt and freshly ground black
  pepper to season
1 egg, beaten

PREPARATION TIME 10 minutes
COOKING TIME 1–1¼ hours
SERVES 4–6

1 Preheat the oven to 350° F. For a soft-sided loaf that is crusty on top, line a 9 x 15 in/2 lb loaf pan with wax paper. If you prefer to handmold the meatloaf, so that it will be crusty all the way around, line a baking sheet instead.
2 Fry the onion in the oil for 4 minutes, until softened and golden.
3 In a bowl, mix the meat, Worcestershire sauce, if using, garlic, breadcrumbs, herbs, tomato purée, and ketchup. Season well. Stir in the beaten egg to bind.
4 Transfer the mixture to the prepared pan or shape into a loaf roughly 9 x 5 inches on the baking sheet.
5 Bake in the oven for 1–1¼ hours until browned on top and the sides are beginning to shrink away from the pan.
6 Turn out onto a warm plate. Pour any juices in the pan over the loaf. Slice and serve with mashed potatoes and gravy.

WATCH OUT FOR ketchup, since it may contain traces of wheat or dairy, so check the labels carefully. Make sure the Worcestershire sauce is gluten-free if need be.

 egg free
also dairy & nut free

Follow the recipe on the left, but substitute 1 tablespoon of potato flour mixed with 2 tablespoons of water in place of the beaten egg and stir into the mixture in step 3.

gluten free
also dairy & nut free

Follow the recipe on the left, but use gluten-free breadcrumbs. If using sausage rather than ground pork, make sure that no fillers that contain gluten have been added to the meat.

VARIATIONS Other ingredients you can add include chopped green bell peppers, finely chopped chili peppers (if tolerated), cheeses (including dairy-free variants), or sautéed chopped mushrooms. A good tip is to fry a teaspoon of the mixture to check the taste and seasoning before you cook the loaf.

Chili con carne

This is what I would call a family Chili con carne, rather than a purist's version that bans tomatoes and beans. It's a joyous dish that is gloriously "everything free," as indeed are nearly all of the accompaniments suggested below. Great debates break out about the merits of ground beef versus chopped beef and red peppers versus green, so not wanting to cause a ruckus, I've put in both as options.

dairy, egg, gluten, & nut free

1 tbsp corn or vegetable oil
2 onions, finely chopped
2 garlic cloves, finely chopped
1 red or green bell pepper,
  seeded and diced
2 tsp hot chili powder or 2 tbsp
  mild chili seasoning
½ tsp red pepper flakes
½ tsp ground cumin
1 lb lean beef, ground or
  cut into small cubes

1 x 14 oz can of chopped tomatoes
1 scant cup tomato paste
1 scant cup water
1 x 14 oz can red kidney
  beans, drained and rinsed
salt to season

PREPARATION TIME 12 minutes
COOKING TIME 2 hours
SERVES 4

1 Heat the oil in a flameproof casserole dish. Fry the onion, garlic, pepper, and spices gently for about 4 minutes, until the vegetables are softened and lightly golden.
2 Add the beef and fry until browned. If using ground, use a wooden spoon and turn constantly to break up any lumps.
3 Add the remaining ingredients and season to taste. Bring to a boil, reduce the heat, cover, and simmer gently for 1 hour, stirring occasionally. Remove the lid and continue to simmer until rich and tender, another 1 hour, stirring occasionally to prevent sticking. Taste and re-season if necessary.

WATCH OUT FOR chili since some people can't tolerate it. Leaving out chili and red pepper flakes turns it into something closer to a ragu—still good, but definitely not a chili con carne.

TIPS This is a great "do ahead" dish, because it improves with reheating.
  You can make this serve 5–6 people by adding another drained can of red kidney beans.
  The amount of chili powder is very much a matter of taste. This one is fairly hot. You can use pure chili powder or the milder chili seasoning, which is a mix of chili with other spices and oregano. Add as little or as much as you like.

SERVING SUGGESTIONS Serve with cornbread (pp.174–76) or boiled long-grained rice. Top with wedges of fresh lime, parsley, chopped avocados, tomatoes, scallions, guacamole, and salsa.
  Sour cream and grated cheddar or Monterey Jack cheese are traditional accompaniments. If you are allergic to dairy, use nondairy sour cream and buy some of the excellent nondairy cheddar and Monterey Jack cheeses available.

Vietnamese beef stew

This delicious aromatic beef stew is warming enough for a winter dinner, yet unusual enough for entertaining. The Vietnamese excel at subtle mixtures that are fragrant rather than spicy. Here, the fresh ginger, lemongrass, curry, and chili powders blend during cooking into a rich brown sauce. You won't believe the delicious, cinnamon-scented aroma that fills the room when you make this.

dairy, egg, gluten, & nut free

for the marinade
2 tbsp grated fresh ginger
2 lemongrass stalks, trimmed and very finely chopped
2 tsp mild curry paste or powder
2 tsp ground cinnamon
2 tsp light brown sugar
4 tbsp tomato paste
2 red chilies, seeded and finely chopped
2 tbsp fish sauce

for the stew
2 lb lean stewing steak, cubed
3 tbsp corn or other flavorless nut-free oil

1 large onion, chopped
3 garlic cloves, crushed
2 cups water
1 tsp salt
2–4 star anise
freshly ground black pepper
2 carrots, cut into chunky pieces
2 potatoes, cut into chunky pieces
1 daikon or 2 small turnips, cut into chunky pieces

PREPARATION TIME 15 minutes plus marinating time
COOKING TIME 1½ hours
SERVES 4–6

1 Mix all the marinade ingredients together in a large bowl. Add the meat and toss with your hands to coat completely. Let marinate for at least 1 hour or overnight.

2 Heat 1 tablespoon of the oil in a flameproof casserole dish. Add the onions and garlic and fry, stirring, until softened and translucent, about 2 minutes. Remove from the dish with a slotted spoon.

3 Heat the remaining oil in the dish. Add half the meat and brown quickly on all sides. Remove from the dish. Add the remaining meat and brown quickly. Return the rest of the meat, any remaining marinade, and the onions and garlic to the pan.

4 Stir in the water and add the salt and star anise. Add a good grinding of pepper. Bring to a boil, reduce the heat, cover, and simmer very gently for 1 hour.

5 Add the prepared vegetables and simmer gently until everything is tender, another 30 minutes.

6 If necessary, remove the lid and boil the stew rapidly for 1–2 minutes to reduce the liquid slightly. Taste and re-season if necessary. Serve straight from the pot.

TIP As with most stews, this tastes even better when made in advance and then reheated, making it perfect for dinner parties.

SERVING SUGGESTIONS Serve the stew with rice and Asian slaw (p.212). To create a stylish meal with an Asian flavor that works for dairy, egg, gluten, and nut allergies, serve with Fresh spring rolls (p.90) as an appetizer, and end with coconut sorbet (p.159). This stew is also delicious over noodles or scooped up with French bread (pp.170–171).

WATCH OUT FOR chili since some people can't tolerate it. Omit if need be. Some noodles, especially fresh ones, contain egg or gluten; read the food labels carefully.

Chinese-style spare ribs

Serve these sticky, delicious glazed ribs on a big plate for everyone to help themselves. Roast in the oven, or partially cook and then barbecue. If you like, serve them on a bed of shredded Chinese cabbage (or other lettuce) and top with scallions and toasted sesame seeds. Kids love these, but they're definitely finger food, so paper napkins and finger bowls are strongly recommended.

 dairy, egg, & nut free

for the marinade
4 tbsp soy sauce
2 tbsp rice vinegar
4 pieces of stem ginger
   preserved in syrup, drained
   and very finely chopped or
   crushed in a garlic crusher
4 garlic cloves, crushed
2/3 cup hoisin sauce
1 tsp five-spice powder
4 lb pork spare ribs
   (1 lb per person), cut
   into separate ribs

to garnish
sliced scallions
sesame seeds (optional)

PREPARATION TIME 8 minutes plus
   marinating time
COOKING TIME 1½ hours
SERVES 4

1 Mix the marinade ingredients in a large nonmetallic or glass shallow dish. Add the ribs and turn to coat. Leave in the fridge to marinate for at least 3 hours, turning the ribs occasionally.
2 Preheat the oven to 375° F.
3 Place a sheet of foil in a roasting pan and transfer the ribs and their marinade to the foil. Wrap loosely.
4 Roast in the oven for 1 hour. After an hour, open up the foil and turn the ribs over.
5 Increase the oven temperature to 425° F and roast with the foil open for another 30 minutes or until the ribs are sticky and glazed. Turn the ribs once.
6 Serve immediately.

TIP To grill, follow the recipe up to step 5. Roast the ribs for 1 hour and transfer to the grill to finish. Brush with the remaining marinade just before grilling. You can cook them from raw, but they won't be as tender. Cook slowly on the grill (not too near the coals) since too high a heat will caramelize the sugars in the marinade and burn.

gluten free
also dairy, egg, & nut free

Follow the recipe on the left, but make sure that you use a gluten-free soy sauce. Also, some brands of Hoisin sauce may contain malt vinegar or wheat products, making them unsuitable for gluten-sensitives. If that is the case, you can make your own as follows, but note the cautions below.

Hoisin sauce
4 tbsp gluten-free soy sauce
4 tbsp black bean or yellow bean
   paste
2 tbsp molasses
2 tsp rice vinegar
¼ tsp garlic powder
2 tsp sesame oil
¼ tsp chili sauce (optional)
A good grinding of black pepper
Mix all of the ingredients together until smooth.

WATCH OUT FOR sesame seeds. If you are allergic to them, omit from the garnish and use corn oil instead of sesame oil if you are making the Hoisin sauce yourself. Some people cannot tolerate chili, so omit the chili sauce if necessary. Check that the black bean or yellow bean paste does not contain gluten.

Roast pork with fennel

Fennel and pork are a winning combination. In this dish, they're paired in two ways, with fennel seeds coating the roast and bulb fennel cooking around it. The pan juices are used to make a delicious gravy. Serve the pork with carrots and Roast potatoes with garlic & sea salt (p.95) for a perfect Sunday lunch or dinner. This is an easy meal to shop for since the recipe uses a cut of meat that is readily available in supermarkets.

dairy, egg, gluten, & nut free

3 fennel bulbs
6 tbsp light olive oil
1 tbsp light brown sugar
2½ lb boned pork loin
   (skin taken off, but fat left on)
1 tsp rock salt
1 tbsp crushed black peppercorns
3 tbsp fennel seeds
1 tbsp finely chopped fresh
   rosemary

1 cup vegetable or
   chicken stock
1 cup dry white wine
lemon juice (optional)

PREPARATION TIME 10 minutes
COOKING TIME 1 hour 40 minutes
   (including gravy)
SERVES 6–8

1 Preheat the oven to 375° F.
2 Cut the feathery fronds off the fennel. Cut the bulbs lengthwise into quarters or sixths, depending on their size.
3 In a bowl, toss the fennel pieces in 4 tablespoons of the olive oil and brown sugar to coat them evenly.
4 Tie the pork with string at regular intervals in four or five places along its length, so that it is cylindrical. This will give you a more evenly cooked and better looking roast.
5 Heat the remaining oil in a roasting pan. Brown the meat quickly all over. Mix together the rock salt, peppercorns, fennel seeds, and rosemary on a large flat plate, spreading it out evenly. Roll the meat in this mixture, pressing it into the meat with your hands.
6 Place the roast on a rack in the roasting pan. Arrange the fennel pieces around the meat.
7 Roast in the oven until cooked through and the fennel is golden and caramelized at the edges, but still slightly firm in the center, about 1½ hours. Turn the fennel once during cooking.
8 Transfer the pork and fennel to a carving dish and keep warm. Spoon off the excess fat from the roasting pan, leaving the juices. Add the stock and wine and stir, scraping any bits stuck to the pan into the liquid using a wooden spoon. Strain the gravy into a saucepan to remove any stray seeds or peppercorns. Boil rapidly for 5 minutes until reduced by a half. Season and sharpen with lemon juice, if desired.
9 Carve the pork, transfer to warm plates, and spoon the gravy over.

TIPS Pork loin is a lean cut and can overcook and dry out easily so buy meat with a layer of fat on top and leave it on during cooking.

If you like crackling, roast the skin alongside the meat. Score the skin, sprinkle with salt, and place on a flat baking tray. Roast on a high shelf for 20–30 minutes or until it is crisp.

WATCH OUT FOR bouillon cubes, which may contain traces of dairy or gluten, if you're cooking for people with severe dairy or gluten sensitivities.

Moussaka

This famous Greek specialty is an excellent make-ahead dish, particularly if you have a large number to feed. The layers of eggplant, lightly spiced ground beef, and creamy béchamel sauce should be served bubbling hot and it needs no more than a crisp salad to accompany it. I've suggested feta or Parmesan in the béchamel, but other cheeses, including dairy-free ones, work very well, too.

egg & nut free

3 eggplants
salt
olive oil
2 large onions, chopped
3 garlic cloves, finely chopped
½ tsp ground cinnamon
¼ tsp paprika or mild chili
   powder
1 lb 2 oz ground lamb
1 tbsp tomato paste
1 scant cup red wine

freshly ground black pepper
½ tsp dried oregano
6 tbsp all-purpose flour
1 quantity Béchamel sauce (p.208)
⅓ cup crumbled feta or grated
   Parmesan

PREPARATION TIME 1¼ hours
COOKING TIME 40 minutes
SERVES 6

1 Cut the eggplants lengthwise into ¼ inch slices. Place in a colander, sprinkle with salt, and leave for 30 minutes for the salt to draw out the bitter juices; then rinse and pat dry with paper towels.

2 Heat 2 tablespoons of olive oil in a heavy-bottomed casserole dish or frying pan and fry the onions and garlic for 2 minutes until softened. Stir in the spices.

3 Add the ground lamb and fry until browned. Using a wooden spoon, turn the lamb constantly to break up any lumps. Add the tomato paste and wine, season with salt and pepper, and stir well. Bring to a boil, reduce the heat as low as possible, and simmer uncovered, stirring occasionally, for 40 minutes. Remove from the heat and stir in the oregano.

4 Meanwhile, heat enough olive oil to coat the base of a frying pan, season the flour with salt and pepper and dip the eggplant slices in the flour. Fry in batches until golden on each side. Drain well on paper towels.

5 Make the béchamel sauce and stir in the feta or Parmesan.

6 Preheat the oven to 375° F. Line the base of a 8 x 10 inch ovenproof dish with a layer of eggplant slices, then half the meat, then eggplant, then the remaining meat, finishing with eggplant. Top with the béchamel sauce. Bake for 40 minutes until the top is lightly browned and bubbling.

Pictured opposite ▶

dairy free
also egg & nut free

Follow the recipe on the left, but use the dairy-free Béchamel sauce recipe (p.208). Use dairy-free crumbled feta or dairy-free grated Parmesan, Gouda, or cheddar-style cheese.

gluten free
also egg & nut free

Follow the recipe on the left, but substitute rice flour for all-purpose flour when coating the eggplant slices and use the gluten-free version of Béchamel sauce (p.208).

WATCH OUT FOR chili, since some people can't tolerate it. Omit the chili powder if need be.

TIP Do not stint on the paper towels when draining the oil from the cooked eggplant, since this prevents the moussaka from swimming in oil.

SERVING SUGGESTION Serve with a mixed salad topped with olives and cubes of feta cheese or a dairy-free alternative.

Classic shepherd's pie

A universally popular combination of ground lamb with finely chopped onion, celery, and carrots, simmered under a topping of floury mashed potatoes, with a dusting of nutmeg. Making shepherd's pie has never been an exact science, so add in chopped leftover roast meat and vary the vegetables and seasonings to taste; some people swear by the addition of peas and ketchup to the lamb.

 ## egg & nut free

3 tbsp nut-free vegetable oil
1 onion, chopped
1 celery stick, finely chopped
2 carrots, coarsely grated or
  finely diced
1 tbsp chopped fresh thyme
1 lb 10 oz ground lamb
⅔ cup beef or vegetable
  stock
1 tbsp all-purpose flour
1 tsp Worcestershire sauce
1 tbsp tomato paste
1 bay leaf

salt and freshly ground black
  pepper
for the potato topping
2½ lb floury potatoes,
  peeled, quartered, and rinsed
¼ cup butter
1 tbsp milk
1 large pinch of freshly grated nutmeg

PREPARATION TIME 50 minutes
COOKING TIME 45 minutes
SERVES 4–6

1 Heat 2 tablespoons of the oil in a heavy-bottomed pan and fry the onion, celery, and carrot for about 5 minutes, stirring, until softened. Remove from the pan and reserve.

2 Heat the remaining oil and fry the lamb until evenly browned, stirring constantly with a wooden spoon to break up the meat.

3 Add the stock and flour to the meat. Add the reserved vegetable mixture, Worcestershire sauce, tomato paste, bay leaf, and seasoning to taste.

4 Bring to a boil, stirring, until thickened. Reduce the heat, cover, and simmer very gently, stirring occasionally, for 30 minutes, until tender. Transfer to a shallow ovenproof serving dish, discarding the bay leaf.

5 Meanwhile, cook the potatoes in boiling, lightly salted water for about 15 minutes, until tender. Drain and mash with 3 tablespoons of the butter and the milk using a potato masher or a fork. Season with nutmeg and salt and pepper to taste.

6 Preheat the oven to 350° F. Spread the potatoes over the top of the meat mixture, roughing up the surface with a fork for a crispier topping, and dot with the remaining butter.

7 Bake for about 45 minutes until piping hot and the potatoes are lightly browned.

 ## dairy free
also egg and nut free

Replace the butter with dairy-free spread and the milk with soy or rice milk or oat milk. Check that the stock is dairy free.

gluten free
also egg and nut free

Follow the recipe on the left, but at step 3 substitute 1½ teaspoons (half the quantity) of cornstarch for ordinary flour and blend until smooth with 1 tablespoon of water. Mix into the meat and stock.

TIP Use leftover cooked meat if preferred and adjust the seasoning.

WATCH OUT FOR bouillon cubes, which may contain traces of dairy or gluten. Make sure the Worcestershire sauce is gluten free if need be.

Spinach & yogurt lamb curry

This Indian curry is redolent of the heady aromas of the subcontinent. With a base of onions, garlic, cumin, coriander, and cloves, the lamb is simmered slowly in fresh ginger, spinach, and yogurt until it is tender and almost falling apart. Just add rice and Raita (p.213) and you have a real feast for the senses. Best done a day ahead and reheated.

 egg, gluten, & nut free

½ cup flavorless
   nut-free oil
2 onions, finely chopped
1 ½ tsp ground cumin
1 tsp ground coriander
pinch of cayenne
pinch of ground cloves
1 bay leaf
4 garlic cloves, crushed
1-in piece of fresh ginger,
   grated
1½ lb boned lamb shoulder or
neck fillets, cut into
   1-in cubes

⅔ cup plain yogurt
3 cups (1½ lb) fresh or thawed
   frozen spinach
salt and freshly ground black pepper
¼ tsp garam masala
2 tbsp chopped fresh cilantro

PREPARATION TIME 10 minutes
COOKING TIME 45–60 minutes
SERVES 4

dairy free
   also egg, gluten, & nut free

Substitute soy yogurt for the dairy yogurt. If serving with raita, use the dairy-free version.

WATCH OUT FOR cayenne pepper, which is chili based. Some people cannot tolerate chili, so omit if any doubt.

1 Heat the oil in a large, heavy-bottomed casserole dish and fry the onions for 2 minutes, stirring until softened but not browned.
2 Add the cumin, coriander, cayenne, cloves, and bay leaf and fry gently for 1 minute, stirring.
3 Add the garlic and ginger and fry for another minute. Add the meat and fry for 2 minutes, stirring, until browned all over.
4 Add the yogurt and mix well. The yogurt will curdle, but don't worry, it forms a rich sauce at the end.
5 If using fresh spinach, trim, wash, and roughly chop. If using frozen, squeeze out any excess water. Add the spinach to the pan. Stir and cook until the spinach has softened and wilted. Season with salt and pepper.
6 Cover and simmer very gently until the meat is tender, 45–60 minutes. Skim any excess oil from the top. If cooking ahead, allow to cool to room temperature, then chill overnight.
7 To serve, reheat gently, if necessary, stirring until piping hot. Stir in the garam masala and cilantro and serve with rice or flat breads (gluten-free if necessary), chutney, and raita.

Honeyed Welsh lamb

We spend a lot of time on our farm in Wales, which supplies organic lamb and beef to supermarkets. This recipe shows off delicious late summer Welsh lamb and honey—and is really a tribute to locally produced food. The cider gives a subtle apple taste to the gravy and the glaze roasts to a rich brown. Serve with leek-flavored Gratin gallois (p.94) and seasonal vegetables.

dairy, egg, gluten, & nut free

1 tbsp flavorless nut-free oil
4 tbsp clear honey
4 tsp finely chopped fresh
   rosemary
1 tsp grated fresh ginger
4–4½ lb leg of lamb,
   preferably Welsh!
4 tbsp dry cider
for the gravy
juices from the meat
⅔ cup meat or
   vegetable stock

½ tsp cornstarch (optional)
salt and pepper to season

PREPARATION TIME 10 minutes
COOKING TIME 2–2½ hours
SERVES 6–8

TIP You need plenty of foil to prevent the honey glaze from dripping into the roasting pan, where it's likely to burn and impart a bitter taste to the gravy.

WATCH OUT FOR bouillon cubes, since they may contain traces of dairy or gluten.

1 Preheat the oven to 375° F.
2 In a small bowl, mix together the oil, honey, rosemary, and ginger to form a thick paste.
3 Using a skewer, stab holes in several places on the surface of the lamb. Rub the honey mixture over the meat.
4 Cut a piece of extra-wide aluminum foil—big enough to wrap the leg of lamb loosely. Place the foil in a large roasting pan and place the leg of lamb on top. Pour the cider around the base of the lamb. Loosely fold the foil around the lamb and secure the edges.
5 Roast for 2–2½ hours, basting twice with the juices during the cooking. This timing will give you medium-rare lamb.
6 Remove the roasting pan from the oven, put the lamb onto a plate and let relax in a warm place for 20 minutes. Keep the meat juices in the pan and discard the foil.
7 To make the gravy, place the roasting pan on a moderately hot stove, add the stock to the meat juices, and simmer until thickened. If a thicker gravy is preferred, spoon a little of the hot stock into a cup and then stir in ½ teaspoon of cornstarch until smooth. Return the mixture to the roasting pan and stir until thickened. Season with salt and pepper to taste. Keep warm until ready to serve.

Lamb tagine

A savory-sweet combination of fruit, nuts, and meat gives this fragrant stew the characteristic taste of Morocco. It's best to use stewing cuts such as neck or shoulder and to simmer it as long and low as possible. Couscous is the traditional accompaniment but the saffron quinoa couscous is a terrific alternative—whether you need to be gluten free or not.

 ## dairy & egg free

4 tbsp light olive oil
2 lb stewing lamb, ideally from the shoulder or neck, cut into 1-in cubes
1 onion, finely chopped
2 garlic cloves, finely chopped
1 tsp ground cumin
1 tsp ground cinnamon
½ tsp ground ginger
2¼ cups vegetable or meat stock
1 tbsp honey
2 tbsp tomato paste
2-in piece of orange peel
1 cinnamon stick

salt and pepper to season
½ cup pitted prunes, halved
½ cup dried apricots, halved
½ cup blanched almonds, lightly toasted
1 tsp orange flower water (optional)

to garnish
sesame seeds

for the couscous
1⅓ cups couscous
1¼ cups boiling water

PREPARATION TIME   20 minutes
COOKING TIME   1¼–1½ hours
SERVES   4–6

1 In a large heavy-bottomed flameproof casserole dish, sear the lamb pieces, a few at a time, in 2 tablespoons of the oil. Remove the browned pieces with a slotted spoon and set aside.
2 In the same pan, on a medium-low heat, fry the onions and garlic in the remaining oil until softened but not browned (about 2 minutes). Stir in the powdered spices and cook for a minute longer.
3 Return the lamb to the casserole dish, add the stock, honey, tomato paste, orange peel, and cinnamon stick. Mix well and season with salt and pepper. Bring to a boil and then reduce the heat. Simmer, partly covered, for 1–1¼ hours. Stir in the prunes, apricots, almonds, and orange flower water, if using, and cook, covered, for another 15 minutes or until the dried fruit has absorbed some liquid and has softened.
4 Meanwhile, put the couscous in a bowl, add a pinch of salt, and pour the boiling water over. Stir well. Place the bowl over a pan of gently simmering water. Cover and leave until the water has been absorbed, at least 5 minutes, or until the tagine is ready.
5 Fluff up the couscous with a fork, spoon onto warm plates, and serve with the tagine. Garnish with sesame seeds.

nut free
also dairy, egg, & gluten free

Follow the recipe on the left, but replace the almonds with an equal quantity of toasted pine nuts, if these can be tolerated. If in any doubt, do not use.

 ## gluten free
also dairy and egg free

Follow the recipe on the left, but make the saffron quinoa couscous recipe as follows:
• Heat a scant 3½ cups of lightly salted water. Add ¼ teaspoon of powdered saffron or ½ teaspoon of saffron threads and stir.
• Bring to a boil, add a generous 2½ cups quinoa and reduce to a simmer. Cook, covered, for about 10 minutes (the quinoa is cooked when the germ separates and you can see a tiny threadlike white tail on each grain). Remove from the heat and let stand for 10 minutes.
• Fluff up with a fork before serving.
◀ Pictured opposite

WATCH OUT FOR bouillon cubes. Check that they are dairy-free or gluten-free as necessary. Some people are allergic to sesame seeds, in which case omit.

Lasagne al forno

A classic dish of pasta sheets layered with a rich meaty ragu and béchamel sauce and dusted with Parmesan. The ragu and béchamel can be made in advance and the dish assembled on the day. If you can't find gluten-free pasta sheets use the recipe on page 138. Or do as the Italians do and layer thin slices of precooked polenta in place of the pasta to create a *polenta pasticciata*.

 egg & nut free

for the filling
1 quantity Ragu Bolognese (p.117), omitting the chicken livers and cream and increasing the ground beef to 14 oz

for the topping
1 quantity Béchamel sauce (p.208)
½ cup grated Parmesan cheese

to finish
10 oz no-boil egg-free lasagne sheets

PREPARATION TIME 2½ hours (including cooking the sauce)
COOKING TIME 35–40 minutes
SERVES 4–6

1 Make the ragu Bolognese according to the instructions on page 117 and above.
2 Make the béchamel sauce according to the recipe on page 208.
3 Preheat the oven to 375° F. Put a spoonful of the meat mixture in the base of a 6-cup ovenproof dish and spread it out. Top with 2 lasagne sheets. Layer half the meat, then two more sheets of lasagne, then the rest of the meat and top with the last two sheets. Spoon the béchamel sauce over and sprinkle with the Parmesan.
4 Bake in the oven until bubbling and turning golden on top, 35–40 minutes. Serve hot.

SERVING SUGGESTION A fresh green or mixed salad is the perfect accompaniment to lasagne.

dairy free
also egg & nut free

Follow the recipe on the left, but use 1 quantity of the dairy-free version of Béchamel sauce (p.208). Top with ½ cup of grated dairy-free Parmesan equivalent.
Pictured opposite ▶

gluten free
see recipe overleaf

If you can't find gluten-free pasta sheets in the store or by mail order, use the simple recipe overleaf. Alternatively, layer thin slices of pre-cooked Polenta (p.81) in place of pasta.

Lasagne al forno continued

 gluten free
also nut free

For the lasagne sheets
¾ cup gluten-free all-purpose
  flour, plus extra for dusting
¾ tsp xanthan gum
¼ tsp salt
1 large egg, beaten
1 tbsp olive oil

PREPARATION TIME 2¾ hours
(including making the pasta and
cooking the Bolognese)
COOKING TIME 35–40 minutes
SERVES 4–6

1 Prepare as for the nut and egg-free recipe on page 136, but
  make the pasta first. Sift the flour with the gum and salt in a
  bowl. Work in the egg and oil to form a firm dough.
2 Knead gently on a work surface until smooth. Wrap in plastic
  wrap and let rest for 30 minutes.
3 Roll out the dough as thinly as possible and cut into six
  16 x 3 inch sheets, re-kneading and rolling the trimmings as
  necessary. Lay the sheets on a board to dry while you make the
  filling. Continue as for the nut and egg-free recipe on page 136.

TIP Try using buckwheat
flour instead of gluten-free
all-purpose flour.
  You can also cut the rolled-out
dough into thin ribbons for
homemade tagliatelle. Let it dry
for 30 minutes then simply boil it in
lightly salted water for a few minutes
until just tender.

"If you've never
made pasta before,
you'll be surprised
how easy this is"

Haddock & spinach pasta bake

This is a real old-fashioned supper dish; creamy pasta layered with smoky haddock and spinach, enhanced with scallions and mushrooms, and the whole thing topped with tomatoes and cheese. It can be made in advance and then just put in the oven to brown when you're nearly ready to eat. If you're making the gluten-free version, I recommend it with corn pasta.

 ## egg & nut free

8½ oz undyed smoked haddock
1¼ cups milk
8 oz dried durum wheat egg-free pasta shapes
2 tbsp butter
1 bunch of scallions, finely chopped
½ cup button mushrooms, sliced
¼ cup all-purpose flour
4 tbsp light cream

1 tbsp lemon juice
2 tbsp chopped fresh parsley
salt and freshly ground black pepper
1 cup (8oz) spinach, chopped, fresh or frozen and thawed
⅓ cup grated cheddar cheese
2–3 tomatoes, sliced

PREPARATION TIME 20 minutes
COOKING TIME 35 minutes
SERVES 4

1 In a saucepan, poach the fish in the milk for about 5 minutes or until the fish flakes easily with a fork. Lift the fish out and flake, discarding any skin and bones. Reserve the milk for the sauce.
2 Meanwhile, cook the pasta according to package directions. Drain.
3 Melt the butter in a saucepan. Add the scallions and gently fry for 2 minutes, stirring, until softened, but not browned.
4 Add the mushrooms and fry until softened, about 1 minute.
5 Remove from the heat and stir in the flour. Blend in the fish milk. Return to the heat and bring to a boil, stirring all the time. Simmer for 2 minutes, stirring.
6 Add the cream, lemon juice, and parsley. Fold in the haddock and the cooked pasta. Stir well and season to taste – carefully with the salt, since both the fish and the cheddar are quite salty.
7 Preheat the oven to 375° F. Transfer half the pasta mixture to a 5 cup shallow ovenproof dish. If using frozen spinach, squeeze the thawed spinach to remove excess moisture. Layer it over the pasta and top with the remaining pasta.
8 Sprinkle with the cheese and arrange the tomatoes around the edge. Bake in the oven for 35 minutes until it turns lightly golden. Serve hot.

WATCH OUT FOR egg in pasta. Dried pasta commonly contains just durum wheat and water, but check the label to make sure.

 ## dairy free
also egg & nut free

Follow the recipe on the left, but substitute dairy-free margarine for the butter; soy, rice, or oat milk for the cow's milk; and soy cream for the cream. You can add an extra pat of dairy-free margarine to enrich the sauce. Use dairy-free cheddar-style cheese for the topping, or mix 4 tablespoons of breadcrumbs with 1 tablespoon of melted dairy-free margarine and sprinkle over the surface instead of (or in addition to) the cheese substitute.

 ## gluten free
also egg & nut free

Follow the recipe on the left, but substitute rice or corn pasta for the wheat pasta, and cornstarch or another gluten-free flour for the all-purpose flour.

Pasta with arugula

If you like robust modern Mediterranean flavors, this simple-to-prepare but special pasta dish will appeal to you. The piquant garlic, chili and lemon mix contrasts well with the peppery arugula leaves and makes for a quick and stylish lunch or supper dish. It can be whipped up in less than 15 minutes: ideal if you have little time to spare for cooking.

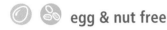 ## egg & nut free

12 oz dried egg-free
   spaghetti
4 tbsp olive oil
4 garlic cloves, finely chopped
1 red chili, seeded and
   chopped
zest of 1½ lemons
2 tbsp lemon juice
2 oz arugula torn into
   1-in pieces or shredded
   finely (chiffonade)
¼ cup grated Parmesan (plus
   extra to serve)
sea salt and freshly ground black
   pepper to season

PREPARATION TIME 3 minutes
COOKING TIME 10 minutes
SERVES 4

1 Cook the pasta in a large pot of boiling water according to the package instructions or until al dente.
2 While the pasta is cooking, heat the oil in a small pan over low heat. Add the garlic, chili, and lemon zest. Cook until the garlic has softened (about 2 minutes). Add the lemon juice.
3 Drain the pasta and pour the flavored oil over. Add the arugula and Parmesan and toss well.
4 Season to taste with salt and pepper and serve immediately, with extra Parmesan on the side.

WATCH OUT FOR chilies, since some people can't tolerate them. Omit if this is the case.

 ## dairy free
also egg & nut free

Follow the recipe on the left, but replace the Parmesan with an equal quantity of nondairy Parmesan (see Resources, pp.218–219). This can be quite salty so you may need to adjust the seasoning accordingly.
◀ Pictured opposite

TIP If nondairy Parmesan is not available, try other nondairy cheeses. An equal quantity of feta-style cheese chopped into ½ inch cubes or nondairy mozzarella both work well—especially if topped with black olives.

 ## gluten free
also egg & nut free

Follow the recipe on the left, but replace the egg-free spaghetti with an equal quantity of an egg-free pasta that is also gluten free. Corn pasta is ideal in this recipe since it holds the flavors well; 100 percent buckwheat pasta is fine, too.

Noodles in hot ginger broth

One of the most versatile dishes around, this is a version of the freshly-made, comforting, hot noodle bowls served in street stalls and restaurants around the world. Any noodles will work, from Chinese-style egg noodles, to rice noodles or 100 percent buckwheat noodles for gluten-avoiders. The dish itself cooks in only a few minutes—the ultimate healthy fast food.

 ## dairy & nut free

4¼ cups well-flavored chicken stock
scant ½ oz peeled fresh ginger, cut into fine (julienne) strips
3 tbsp light soy sauce
1 star anise
7 oz noodles
3 tbsp nut-free vegetable oil for stir-frying
8 baby corn, halved lengthwise
10 shiitake mushrooms, sliced
2 bok choy, roughly chopped

for garnish
4 scallions, sliced diagonally
½ cup bean sprouts

PREPARATION TIME 10 minutes
COOKING TIME 12 minutes
SERVES 4

1 Simmer the stock, ginger strips, soy sauce, and star anise for 3 minutes.
2 Cook the noodles according to the package instructions, until just tender. Divide the noodles between four bowls.
3 Heat the wok until nearly smoking and add vegetable oil. Stir fry the baby corn to give it a bit of color and then add the mushrooms and fry for 1–2 minutes.
4 Carefully pour the stock into the wok. Add the bok choy, bring to a boil and simmer for about 1 minute or until the bok choy is just tender.
5 Ladle the stock and vegetables over the noodles. Garnish with the scallion slices and a sprinkling of bean sprouts and serve immediately.

egg free
also dairy & nut free

Follow the recipe on the left, but avoid Chinese or other egg noodles and use rice noodles, wheat-based udon noodles, or soba buckwheat noodles instead.

 ## gluten free
also dairy & nut free

Follow the recipe on the left, making sure you use rice, corn, or 100 percent buckwheat noodles instead. Make sure the soy sauce is gluten free.
Pictured opposite ▶
with wide flat rice noodles

SERVING SUGGESTION Top the noodles and vegetables with 5½ oz of meat, fish, chicken, or duck that has been cut into fine strips and quickly grilled or wok-fried. If you have time, marinate first with sweet miso marinade (see steps 1 and 2 of the recipe on page 101).

WATCH OUT FOR bouillon cubes, since they may contain traces of dairy or gluten.

Basmati & wild rice pilaf

This pilaf, studded with dried cranberries, currants, and pine nuts is often described as "jeweled" rice, with the basmati and wild rice giving additional contrast to the texture and taste. If you have time, cook the basmati and wild rice separately; if you don't, buy a mix of wild rice and basmati and start at step two, using all the stock.

dairy, egg, gluten, & nut free

4¼ cups chicken or
   vegetable stock
½ cup wild rice
2 tbsp flavorless nut-free oil
1 onion, finely chopped
1 celery stalk, finely chopped
1 cup white basmati rice,
   washed and drained
leaves from 2 sprigs of fresh
   thyme
1 bay leaf
3 tbsp currants

2 tbsp dried cranberries
2 tbsp chopped fresh parsley
3 tbsp pine nuts, toasted
salt and freshly ground black pepper

PREPARATION TIME 10 minutes
COOKING TIME 50 minutes
SERVES 6

TIP If you prefer, use a good pat of butter or dairy-free spread to cook the onions.

1 Put 1¼ cups of the stock in a saucepan, bring to a boil and add the wild rice.
2 Cover and reduce the heat to low and simmer for 45–50 minutes until the rice is just tender and has absorbed the liquid (it will still have a nutty texture). If necessary, remove the lid and boil rapidly for a few minutes to evaporate the last of the stock.
3 Meanwhile, heat the oil in a separate saucepan and fry the onion and celery until softened but not browned, 3 minutes.
4 Add the basmati rice and stir until the grains are evenly coated and glistening. Stir in the thyme leaves. Add the remaining stock and bring to a boil. Reduce the heat to low, add the bay leaf, currants, and cranberries and cover and simmer very gently until the rice is tender and the water has been absorbed (about 10–12 minutes).
5 Remove from the heat. When the wild rice is cooked, add to the basmati with the parsley and pine nuts. Season to taste and fluff with a fork.
6 Tip into a warmed serving dish and serve immediately.

WATCH OUT FOR pine nuts, also known as pine kernels, which may not be tolerated by some people who are allergic to nuts. Omit if necessary. If using a bouillon cube, make sure that it is dairy free and/or gluten free as necessary.

Risotto alla Milanese

An authentic risotto alla Milanese is a yellow-hued and saffron-scented creamy delight. Serve as a starter or with Osso bucco (p.118). You will need to use short grain risotto rice and it does take a great deal of stirring, so don't leave it unattended. Use the recipe, minus the saffron, as the basis for your own vegetable, herb, meat, fish, or seafood risottos.

egg, gluten, & nut free

4¼ cups chicken stock
⅔ cup dry white wine
2 tbsp butter
2 tbsp olive oil
1 onion, finely chopped
1 oz prosciutto,
    finely chopped
1½ cups risotto rice such as
    arborio or carnaroli
½ heaping tsp chopped saffron
    strands or ½ level tsp
    powdered saffron dissolved in
    2 tbsp hot water
freshly ground pepper
2 tbsp freshly grated Parmesan
    cheese
salt to taste

PREPARATION TIME 10 minutes
COOKING TIME 20 minutes
SERVES 4

dairy free

also egg, gluten, & nut free

Follow the recipe on the left, but replace the butter with an equal quantity of dairy-free spread and the Parmesan with an equal quantity of dairy-free Parmesan or other grated dairy-free cheese. For extra creaminess, stir in 2 tablespoons of soy cream alternative in step 3, when adding the saffron.

WATCH OUT FOR bouillon cubes, since they may contain traces of dairy or gluten.

1 Place the stock and wine in a saucepan and bring to a simmer.
2 In a heavy-bottomed saucepan melt the butter and olive oil and fry the onion and prosciutto until the onion has softened.
3 Add the rice and cook for 2 minutes, stirring well to ensure that each grain is coated with the oil and butter.
4 Add a ladleful of stock to the rice and stir. When the rice has absorbed the stock, add another ladleful. Stir constantly to prevent the rice from sticking. When you have used up half the stock, add the saffron and continue to add the stock, stirring, until all the stock has been used and absorbed, and the rice is tender and creamy, but still firm and with some "bite" to it.
5 Season with freshly ground pepper. Add the Parmesan and check the seasoning before serving, only adding salt if needed.
Pictured with Osso bucco on page 118

Plum crumble

This is worth making just for the heavenly wafts of fall fruit, cinnamon, and allspice that fill the kitchen as it cooks. Serve the crumble when the fruit has just begun to bubble through and the topping is barely tinged with brown. Cream, Chantilly topping (p.216), custard, or vanilla ice cream are the ideal accompaniments. If nuts are not a problem, try chilled Cashew cream (p.216).

 ## egg & nut free

for the crumble topping
2 cups all-purpose flour
½ cup cold butter cut into
  1-in pieces
generous ¼ cup soft light or dark
  brown sugar
for the filling
2 lb pitted plums, halved
1⅔ cups granulated sugar
1 tsp ground cinnamon
large pinch of ground allspice

PREPARATION TIME 10 minutes
COOKING TIME 45 minutes
SERVES 4–6

1 Preheat the oven to 375° F.
2 Place the flour in a large bowl. Using the tips of your fingers, rub in the butter until the mixture resembles breadcrumbs. Stir in the sugar.
4 Place the fruit, sugar, and spices in the ovenproof dish and mix to combine. Spoon the crumble mixture on top. Bake for about 45 minutes or until the crumble is golden brown and the fruit is just beginning to bubble through the topping.
Pictured opposite ▶

TIP For apple or rhubarb crumble, use 2 lb of sliced tart apples sweetened with ½ cup of sugar plus 2 tablespoons of water, or 2 lb of rhubarb plus 1 tablespoon of chopped stem ginger.

SERVING SUGGESTION Serve with vanilla ice cream, or custard or with dairy-free Chantilly cream or Cashew cream (see page 216 for both).

 ## dairy free
also egg & nut free

Follow the recipe on the left, replacing the butter with an equal quantity of dairy-free spread.

 ## gluten free
also egg free

Follow the recipe on the left using the following ingredients for the crumble topping:
1½ cups gluten-free all-purpose
  flour mix
¾ cup ground almonds
⅓ cup cold butter, cut into 1-in pieces
⅓ cup soft light or dark brown sugar

Apple tart

This delicious classic and versatile Normandy *tarte aux pommes* works equally well as an elegant dessert or as a stylish snack-time treat. Served warm or at room temperature, the hint of vanilla in the apple is wonderful. Use tart apples such as Gala or Cortland for the purée and add pretty pink apples for a decorative top layer and serve with cream or ice cream.

 ## egg & nut free

1 quantity egg and nut-free
  sweet Piecrust (p.180),
  chilled for 30 minutes
1½ lb dessert or tart
  apples, peeled, quartered,
  cored and chopped
1 scant cup vanilla sugar
1 vanilla pod, split lengthwise
1 lb tart apples
  peeled, quartered, cored, and
  thinly sliced—about ⅛ in
  thick—or rosy dessert apples,
  thinly sliced with the skin left on

PREPARATION TIME 50 minutes
  plus chilling and cooling time
COOKING TIME 1 hour 5 minutes
SERVES 6–8

1 Preheat the oven to 400° F.
2 Roll out the piecrust pastry and line a 10-inch loose-bottomed tart pan. Place the chopped apples and ¼ cup of the vanilla sugar in a heavy-bottomed saucepan. Scrape the seeds out of the vanilla pod and add both the pod and the seeds to the apple and sugar mixture. Cook gently, stirring occasionally, until the apples are soft and can be pulped when pressed with a wooden spoon, about 15 minutes. If using dessert apples, add 1–2 tablespoons of water to ensure the apples break down easily. Remove the vanilla pod.
3 Beat the cooked apple well with a wooden spoon, adding another ¼ cup of the sugar. Let cool. Once cool, transfer to the piecrust.
4 Arrange the apple slices in circles overlapping each other on top of the apple sauce, starting from the outside in.
5 Bake in the center of the oven for 15 minutes. Remove the tart from the oven and sprinkle with the remaining ¼ cup of vanilla sugar. Return to a high shelf in the oven and bake until lightly browned and the sliced apples are tender, about 50 minutes.

 ## dairy free
also egg free

Follow the recipe on the left, but use the dairy-free sweet Piecrust recipe (p.180) and serve with soy cream alternative or dairy-free ice cream.

gluten free
also egg & nut free

Follow the recipe on the left, but use gluten-free sweet Piecrust (p.182).
◀ Pictured opposite

TIP You can make the piecrust and freeze it in its tart pan.

SERVING SUGGESTION Serve hot, warm, or cold, either on its own or with cream, crème fraîche, or vanilla ice cream (or a dairy-free alternative).

Classic rice pudding

This children's favorite has enjoyed a surge of renewed popularity recently in restaurants and home cooking. The dairy-free version is a particular delight, since rice milk enhances the flavor further. Using the risotto method, cooking the rice in the butter before adding the milk, gives an even richer and creamier pudding. Flecked with tiny vanilla seeds, this pudding is classy enough to serve for any occasion.

 egg, gluten, & nut free

1 tbsp butter
generous ¼ cup granulated sugar
scant ½ cup pudding or short grain rice
4¼ cups milk
1 vanilla pod
a pinch of salt
6 tbsp heavy cream

PREPARATION TIME 10 minutes
COOKING TIME 1½–2 hours
SERVES 4–6

1 Preheat the oven to 325° F.
2 Melt the butter in a 1.5 quart flameproof dish on a low heat. Add the sugar and mix well. Add the rice and stir, coating the rice grains with the butter and sugar mixture.
3 Split and scrape the seeds from the vanilla pod. Add the seeds and pod to the milk and stir. Pour the vanilla milk onto the rice and sugar mixture and stir well, using a wooden spoon to break up any lumps.
4 Stir in the salt and cream and bring slowly almost to a boil. Remove the vanilla pod. Transfer to the oven and bake for 1½–2 hours until thick and creamy and browned on top, stirring after 30 minutes and 1 hour.
5 Serve plain or with any of the serving suggestions (right).

TIP For a less rich rice pudding reduce the amount of heavy cream to 5 tbsp.

dairy free
also egg, gluten, & nut free

Follow the recipe on the left, but replace the butter with an equal quantity of dairy-free spread and replace the milk with 17 fl oz of soy milk and 17 fl oz of rice milk. Replace the cream with an equal quantity of soy cream. If desired, you can use vanilla-flavored milk substitutes and reduce the vanilla to ½ a pod.

SERVING SUGGESTION
Serve with cream or soy cream alternative, raspberry or strawberry jam, fruit compôte (see the cherry compôte recipe on page 161), or fruit sauce.

VARIATION Add 2–3 tablespoons of golden raisins in Step 4 with the cream and salt. Replace the vanilla pod with either the grated zest of ½ a lemon or a good dusting of freshly grated nutmeg.

Fragrant poached peaches

This is an excellent and versatile way to prepare fruit. I've used peaches but you can also use an equal weight of any stone fruits: apricots, nectarines, or plums. Pears can also be cooked in this way but take longer. These are all lovely, served in pretty glasses and drizzled with some of the syrup and with some Chantilly topping (p.216) or ice cream.

dairy, egg, gluten, & nut free

4 peaches (about 1lb)
  unpeeled
1 cup water
½ cup superfine sugar
thinly pared zest of ½ a lemon
1 vanilla pod

PREPARATION TIME 15–20 minutes
COOKING TIME 5–10 minutes
SERVES 4

1 Cut around the peaches to halve and give a sharp twist to loosen both sides. Lift out the pit or scoop out with a small knife.
2 Put the water, sugar, and lemon zest in a large, heavy-bottomed saucepan. Slit the vanilla pod and scrape out its seeds and add the pod and seeds to the pan. Stir over a low heat until the sugar has dissolved. Bring to a boil and boil for 1 minute. Reduce the heat until the syrup is simmering gently.
3 Add the fruit carefully to the pan. Cover and poach gently for 5–10 minutes, until the fruit is tender when pierced with a toothpick or the point of a sharp knife. Gently turn the fruit over in the juice halfway through cooking if it is not fully submerged. The poaching time will depend on the ripeness of the fruit. Remove carefully from the pan with a slotted spoon, set aside, and keep warm.
4 Boil the juice rapidly for 2–3 minutes, until reduced and syrupy. Spoon over the fruit. Serve warm.

TIPS For a lighter syrup, reduce the quantity of sugar to ¼ cup.
  If peeled peaches are preferred, immerse them in boiling water for 10 seconds, then cool immediately in a bowl of cold water. Use a small sharp knife to ease away the skin and brush with lemon juice to prevent discoloration.

VARIATIONS Apricots work well with the vanilla-lemon zest combination (left) and also with brown sugar and a large pinch of white pepper.
  Try poaching plums with a piece of cinnamon stick and the finely grated zest of an orange for a fragrant ruby-red syrup. Star anise and honey also work well with stronger-flavored fruit.
  Use a little fresh ginger, saffron threads, wine, or liquor to create your own syrup flavors.

SERVING SUGGESTION If there are any leftovers, these desserts are good for breakfast, chopped into granola, blended into smoothies, or broiled briefly under high heat and served on cinnamon toast.

DESSERTS

Decadent dairy-free Petits pots aux chocolat (p.154)
with dairy-free Chantilly topping (p.216).

Petits pots au chocolat

These rich, smooth, velvety—very decadent—creations turn eating chocolate into an art form. They're dense and truffley and very simple to make. I serve them in glass dishes but you could also use little espresso coffee cups or small ramekin dishes instead. They are the perfect dessert to linger over and taste as luscious and stylish as they look.

egg, gluten, & nut free

1½ cups (6 oz) nut-free
  semisweet chocolate with at
  least 70 percent cocoa solids
1 tbsp brandy
1 scant cup heavy cream
to decorate
4–8 tbsp whipped cream or
  Chantilly topping (p.216)
1 tbsp nut-free unsweetened
  cocoa powder for dusting

PREPARATION TIME 10 minutes
  plus chilling time
COOKING TIME 10 minutes
SERVES 4

1 Break up the chocolate and place in a bowl over a pot of hot water, ensuring that the bowl does not touch the water. Stir until melted.
2 Warm the brandy and cream in a saucepan until hot but not boiling. Stir into the melted chocolate until completely blended.
3 Spoon the mixture into 4 small ramekins, glass dishes, or espresso cups. Chill until firm.
4 Decorate each with 1–2 tablespoons of whipped cream or Chantilly topping (p.216) and sift the cocoa powder over the top.

SERVING SUGGESTION If you're serving these in espresso cups, decorate each with a chocolate-orange stick, or the little chocolate spoons, which are sold to stir your coffee with.

 dairy free
also egg, gluten, & nut free

Follow the recipe on the left, but use dairy-free chocolate and increase it to 2 cups (8 oz), and use ⅔ cup of soy cream alternative instead of the scant 1 cup of heavy cream. Decorate with dairy-free Chantilly topping (p.216).
◀ Pictured on previous page with dairy-free Chantilly topping.

Sweet chestnut terrine

This sumptuous, rich dessert is a smart dinner party option because it's so easy to make in advance. Serve it in thin, elegant slices in a pool of luscious vanilla-flecked cream. Many people who are allergic to nuts are able to tolerate chestnuts so if you know you can eat them, go ahead. If you can't, or are not sure, use the variation at the bottom of the page.

egg, gluten, & nut free

a little flavorless nut-free oil
1¾ cups (7 oz) nut-free
  semisweet chocolate
generous ¾ cup butter
1 cup superfine sugar
1 tbsp brandy
1 lb 10 oz cooked peeled
  chestnuts or canned chestnuts
  (drained weight)
½ cup milk

for the vanilla cream
1 cup heavy cream
2 tbsp confectioners' sugar
½ tsp vanilla extract
½ vanilla pod, split

PREPARATION TIME 20 minutes
SERVES 8–10

1 Line a 5-cup terrine dish or loaf pan with plastic wrap (trying to keep it wrinkle free) or use lightly oiled waxed paper instead of the plastic wrap.
2 Melt the chocolate in a bowl over simmering water, ensuring that the bowl does not touch the water. Add the butter, sugar, and brandy then beat until well mixed. Remove from the heat.
3 In a food processor, purée the chestnuts and the milk to a well-mixed dryish paste.
4 Add the chestnut mixture to the chocolate mixture and mix well until smooth. Pour into the mold, cover, and chill overnight until firm.
5 For the vanilla cream, gently whisk together the heavy cream, confectioners' sugar, and vanilla extract. Split the vanilla pod and scrape its seeds into the mixture. Do not overwhisk the cream—this is meant to be a pouring cream.
6 To serve, unmold the terrine and use a sharp knife that has been dipped briefly in boiling water to cut thin slices. Pour a small pool of vanilla cream around each portion.

VARIATION If chestnuts are a problem, replace them with an equal quantity of cake crumbs in a cake version that is safe for you.

dairy free
also egg, gluten, & nut free

Follow the recipe on the left, but substitute equal quantities of dairy-free spread for the butter; and soy milk for the milk in the terrine. Make sure that the chocolate is dairy-free. For the vanilla cream, use an equal quantity of soy cream alternative for the heavy cream and increase the vanilla extract to 1 teaspoon to mask the strong flavor of the soy cream.

"Rich, dense, and luxurious—an unusual treat for chocolate lovers"

Green tea ice cream

A deliciously distinctive dessert, Green tea ice cream is often served in Japanese restaurants and is increasingly popular elsewhere. This recipe uses maccha, the finely ground leaves used in Japanese tea ceremonies, but you can make a paler version with green tea leaves. Served on its own or with a drizzle of chocolate sauce, it's a stylish way to round off a meal.

gluten & nut free

2 tbsp maccha green tea
  powder
1¼ cups milk
1 vanilla pod
2 egg yolks
scant ½ cup superfine sugar
generous 1 cup heavy cream
¼ tsp salt

PREPARATION TIME 20 minutes
COOKING TIME 10 minutes plus
  freezing time
MAKES about 3 cups

1 Place the maccha green tea powder in a heatproof bowl. Heat the milk to just below boiling point and pour onto the green tea.
2 Stir the mixture to break up any lumps and strain back into the saucepan. Let infuse for 15 minutes.
3 Split the vanilla pod lengthwise and add to the pan. Heat gently, stirring the vanilla pod to release the seeds. Remove the vanilla pod, scrape out any remaining seeds, and add them to the milk, then wash and dry the pod and save for future use.
4 Place the egg yolks and the sugar in a medium-sized bowl and beat with an electric or hand whisk until the mixture is thick and pale. Bring the infused milk back to boiling point and pour it in a thin stream onto the egg yolk and sugar mixture, whisking all the time. Return the mixture to the saucepan and place on the lowest possible heat, stirring continuously as the custard thickens. Cook for 8–10 minutes, stirring, until the custard coats the back of a spoon. Do not allow to boil. The custard will be dark green at this stage.
5 Remove the custard from the heat and let cool.
6 Lightly whip the cream with the salt until just softly peaking, but not at all stiff. Fold into the cooled custard with a metal spoon.
7 Freeze in an ice cream maker following the manufacturer's instructions or pour into a freezerproof container and freeze until just firm around the edges (about 4 hours). Whisk with a fork to break up the ice crystals and freeze until firm. Remove from the freezer 5–10 minutes before serving if handmade, 20 minutes if made in an ice cream maker.
Pictured opposite ▶

dairy free
also gluten & nut free

Follow the recipe on the left, but substitute soy, rice, or oat milk for cow's milk and silken tofu or soy cream alternative (which you can whip lightly) for heavy cream.

egg free
also gluten & nut free

Follow steps 1–3 in the recipe on the left. You will need just half the quantity of superfine sugar used in the other recipes, a scant ¼ cup. Add it to the milk and stir until dissolved. Cool then chill the infused milk and whisk in 5 tablespoons of sweetened condensed milk. Proceed from step 6. The ice cream melts more quickly than the egg-based versions.

TIPS If you can't find green tea powder, infuse 4 green tea teabags in 4 tablespoons of boiling water for 15 minutes. Add both to the hot milk and infuse with the vanilla pod. Squeeze the bags to extract the maximum flavor and color then discard them. Continue as above or left.

  A quick way to make green tea ice cream is to mix 2 tablespoons of green tea powder with 1 quart store-bought vanilla ice cream.

Mango yogurt ice

Mango yogurt ice, flecked with lime zest, is a smooth and intensely fruity dessert. It doesn't take very long to make and the result is delectably refreshing and incomparably better than the store-bought variety. The scented topical fruit makes it the perfect dessert for Southeast Asian, Indian, or Mexican-inspired food, or for any meal that needs a cool, thirst-quenching finish.

 egg, gluten, & nut free

3 ripe mangoes, about
  8 oz each
generous ½ cup superfine sugar
½ cup water
zest and juice of 1 lime
4 tbsp yogurt

PREPARATION TIME 5 minutes plus
  chilling and freezing time
COOKING TIME 2 minutes
MAKES about 1 pint

1 Extract as much fruit as you can from the mangoes, using a knife to scrape the pulp from the skin and pit. Discard the skin and pit and place the pulp in a measuring cup. You should have about 1¾ cups.

2 In a small saucepan, gently heat the sugar and water and stir until the sugar is dissolved (about 2 minutes). Cool to room temperature. This makes just under 1 cup of syrup.

3 In a food processor, blend together the mango pulp, syrup, lime zest and juice, and the yogurt.

4 Place in an ice cream maker and freeze according to the manufacturer's instructions. Before serving, remove from the freezer and put in the refrigerator for 20 minutes to soften.

dairy free
  also egg, gluten, & nut free

Follow the recipe on the left, but replace the yogurt with an equal quantity of dairy-free yogurt.

TIP If you don't have an ice cream maker, use a freezeproof container, cover, and freeze for 3–4 hours or until firm around the edges. Whisk with a fork to break up the ice crystals and freeze again until firm. For a smoother ice cream, repeat the process after an hour or when ice crystals have formed again and then freeze until firm. The Coconut sorbet and Rhubarb sorbet (opposite) can be made in this way too.

"On a hot summer's day this is the nicest thing on earth"

Coconut sorbet

This deliciously creamy sorbet tastes more like a full-fledged ice cream. Quick and simple to prepare, it is special enough for any occasion and is lovely served with sliced tropical fruits.

 **dairy, egg, gluten, & nut free**

6 oz coconut powder and
   3½ cups water made up
   into thick coconut milk
   or 2 x 14 fl oz cans
   coconut milk
⅓ cup superfine sugar

1 tbsp shredded coconut
1 tbsp rum or coconut-flavored rum

PREPARATION TIME 5 minutes plus
   chilling and freezing time
MAKES about 4¼ cups

TIP It's worth using coconut powder rather than the canned variety if you possibly can because the taste and color are superior.

WATCH OUT FOR coconut allergy. It is very rare, but it is worth asking if you are giving this to people you don't know.

1 In a saucepan, combine the coconut milk with the sugar and shredded coconut. Over medium heat, stir the mixture until the sugar dissolves (about 2 minutes). Add the rum.
2 Allow the mixture to cool to room temperature and chill for at least 30 minutes. Freeze in an ice cream maker according to the manufacturer's instructions.

Rhubarb sorbet

This sorbet is a lovely delicate dusky pink color. Its unexpectedly creamy texture and tangy taste is a triumph and will convert even the most die-hard rhubarb sceptics—children included!

 **dairy, egg, gluten, & nut free**

1 cup water
juice of 1 large lemon
⅔ cup superfine sugar
1 lb fresh rhubarb
   chopped into 1-in pieces
2 tbsp corn syrup

PREPARATION TIME 15 minutes
   plus chilling and freezing time
COOKING TIME 8 minutes
MAKES about 4¼ cups

1 Place the water, lemon juice, and sugar in a saucepan. Over a low heat, stir until the sugar dissolves.
2 Add the rhubarb, bring to a boil, and simmer for 8 minutes or until the rhubarb is pulpy. Cool to room temperature.
3 Transfer the mixture to a food processor and purée until completely smooth. Stir in the corn syrup, pulsing briefly for about 25 seconds.
4 Freeze in an ice cream maker according to the manufacturer's instructions. Remove from the freezer 10 minutes before serving.

Panna cotta

This dense, creamy Italian specialty is rich and velvety and looks beautiful turned out onto a plate. It gently shimmers, wobbles, and glows in the light and the deep red cherry sauce makes a superlative contrasting accompaniment. It looks good enough for any occasion but don't just keep it for dinner parties—it is an excellent way to round off a light summer lunch, too.

egg, gluten, & nut free

vegetable oil for the molds
2 tbsp hot water
2 tsp powdered gelatin
2½ cups heavy cream
3 tbsp superfine sugar
1 vanilla pod, split lengthwise
thinly pared zest of ½ lime
for the compôte
3 cups fresh cherries, pitted
  or 1 x 14 oz can of cherries,
  drained (reserving 3 tbsp of juice)

2 tbsp black cherry conserve
3 tbsp water or juice from canned
  cherries, if using
2 tbsp confectioners' sugar
  juice of ½ lime
3 tbsp brandy
2 tsp cornstarch

PREPARATION TIME 30 minutes
  plus cooling and setting time
SERVES 4

dairy free
also egg, gluten, & nut free

Follow the recipe on the left, but use soy cream alternative instead of heavy cream.

TIP You can also use frozen cherries in this recipe. Thaw them first and prepare in the same way as fresh cherries.

1 Lightly oil 4 individual molds or ramekin dishes. Put the water in a small bowl and sprinkle the gelatin over. Let soften for 5 minutes.
2 Meanwhile, pour half the cream into a saucepan. Add the sugar, vanilla pod, and lime zest and heat gently, stirring, until the sugar has dissolved. Slowly bring almost to a boil and stir in the gelatin until completely dissolved. Remove from the heat and let cool.
3 Whip the remaining cream until softly peaked then strain in the cold, flavored cream; fold in with a metal spoon, and transfer to the molds or ramekins. Chill until set.
4 Meanwhile, make the compôte. Put the cherries in a pan with the conserve, water, or juice, confectioners' sugar, and lime juice. Heat gently, stirring until the juices run. If using fresh cherries, cook for 3 minutes only, until the cherries have softened but still hold their shape.
5 Blend the brandy with the cornstarch and stir into the cherries. Bring back to a boil, stirring all the time until slightly thickened and clear. Cook for 1 minute then remove from the heat, turn into a bowl and let cool.
6 When ready to serve, gently loosen the edges of the creams with your fingers and then turn them out onto serving plates. Spoon the cherry compôte around and on top of each cream. Serve cold.

◀ **Pictured opposite**

Crêpes

These are the light and lacy French-style pancakes as opposed to the thicker, fluffier American pancakes on page 57. Serve with a squeeze of lemon and sugar, Chantilly topping (p.216), ice cream, and chocolate or toffee sauces, or wrap them around savory fillings and top with Béchamel sauce (p.208). All versions of the crêpes freeze well—just use waxed paper or parchment paper to separate them.

 ## nut free

1 cup all-purpose flour
¼ tsp salt
2 eggs, lightly beaten
1¼ cups milk
2 tbsp butter, melted, plus
   extra for frying

PREPARATION TIME 5 minutes plus
   standing time
COOKING TIME 30 minutes
MAKES 12–15

1 Sift the flour and salt into a large bowl.
2 Make a well in the center of the flour and whisk in the eggs, gradually, drawing in the flour from the sides of the bowl.
3 Pour in the milk, whisk until the batter is smooth and free of lumps. It should now have the consistency of light cream.
4 Stir in the melted butter. Cover and let the batter stand in a cool place for at least an hour.
5 Stir the batter again in case any flour has settled at the bottom. Heat the butter for frying in a crêpe pan, or other heavy-bottomed nonstick frying pan, until hot and pour out any excess, keeping just the barest coating on the pan.
6 Use 1–2 tablespoons of batter for each crêpe. Pour in the batter and rotate the pan quickly to ensure the base of the pan is evenly coated with a thin layer.
7 Heat gently for no more than a minute, and when small bubbles appear on the surface use a spatula to flip the crêpe.
8 Slide the crêpe off the pan onto a plate and keep warm. The crêpes can be stacked and covered with foil to keep warm.

TIP Make sure you use a nonstick frying pan—this is especially important for the egg-free version. You may need to discard the first crêpe or two.
   For sweet crêpes in any version, add 2 tablespoons of superfine sugar to the batter in step 3.

 ## dairy free
also nut free

Follow the recipe on the left, but replace the milk with 1¼ cups of soy milk. Replace the melted butter with either 2 tablespoons of melted dairy-free spread, or 2 tablespoons of flavorless oil, or 2 tablespoons of coconut cream (not coconut milk since it is too thin). Use a flavorless nut-free oil, such as corn oil, for frying.

 ## egg free
also nut free

Follow the recipe on the left, but replace the eggs with 4 tablespoons of heavy cream and reduce the quantity of milk to 1 generous cup.
Pictured opposite ▶

 ## gluten free
also nut free

Follow the recipe on the left, using the following ingredients:
1¼ cups rice flour
generous 1 cup tapioca flour
¼ tsp salt
3 eggs, lightly beaten
scant 1¼ cups milk
3 tbsp melted butter, plus extra
   for frying

Brown bread

There's been a revival in bread-making at home. Maybe it's because bread machines make it easier or perhaps it's just the irresistible smell of home-baked bread. Here's a lovely, grainy, seed-studded whole-wheat bread. I started making it because there were so many "may contain traces" warnings on manufacturers' and bakery breads, but I now do it for the taste—and the smell!

 dairy, egg, & nut free

2 cups whole-wheat
  bread flour
1 cup white bread flour
½ cup rolled oats
½ cup sesame seeds
¼ cup poppy seeds
½ tsp salt
1 tbsp malt extract
2 tbsp olive oil plus a little
  extra for the loaf pan

1 tbsp instant yeast
scant 1¼ cups lukewarm water

PREPARATION TIME 5–10 minutes
  plus rising
COOKING TIME 30 minutes
MAKES 1 large loaf

1 Mix the flours with the oats, seeds, and salt in a food processor with a dough attachment or in a bowl.

2 Add the malt, oil, yeast, and water and run the machine until the mixture forms a soft (but not sticky) dough. Run the machine for another minute to knead the dough. Alternatively, mix the ingredients with a knife and then your hands to form a dough, then turn out onto a lightly floured surface and knead for 5 minutes until smooth and elastic.

3 Place in an oiled plastic bag and leave in a warm place until doubled in bulk (about 45 minutes).

4 Oil a baking sheet or 2 lb loaf pan. Knead the dough again. Either shape into a round and place on the baking sheet or shape into a rectangle and place in the pan. Cover with oiled plastic wrap and leave in a warm place for about 30 minutes or until well risen.

5 Meanwhile, preheat the oven to 425° F.

6 Remove the plastic wrap. For the round loaf, score the dough lightly in a crisscross pattern. Bake in the oven for about 30 minutes until risen, golden, and the base sounds hollow when tapped. Cool on a wire rack.

Pictured opposite ▶

WATCH OUT FOR sesame seeds, which some people can't tolerate. If this is the case, use pumpkin seeds in place of sesame seeds or omit entirely.

gluten free

The gluten-free version has a super, real bread texture and an excellent flavor. It will even slice thinly for brown bread and butter and sandwiches. See recipe overleaf.

TIP If using a bread machine, put the wet ingredients in first, then the dry, making sure the malt is nowhere near the yeast (especially if you're putting it on the timer option). Set the machine to "large rapid whole wheat" to cook in the pan, or set it to the "dough" setting, take out and continue from step 4.

Brown bread continued

 gluten free
also dairy & nut free

generous 2 cups brown rice flour
3 tbsp soy flour
1 tbsp xanthan gum
¼ cup sesame seeds
2 tbsp poppy seeds
1½ tsp salt
1 tsp lemon juice
3 tbsp nut-free flavorless
   vegetable oil, plus a little
   extra for the loaf tin
1½ tbsp molasses
1 tbsp instant yeast
1 large egg, beaten
1¾ cups lukewarm water

PREPARATION TIME 6 minutes
   plus rising
COOKING TIME 40 minutes
MAKES 1 large loaf

1 Oil a 2 lb loaf pan or a deep 8 inch round cake pan.
2 Mix the flours with the xanthan gum, seeds, and salt in a food processor (with the ordinary blade attachment) or in a bowl. Add the remaining ingredients.
3 Either run the machine until it forms a sticky dough, then run it for 1 minute to knead it, or mix everything with a wooden spoon or hand beater, beating well for 1 minute once combined.
4 Transfer to the pan and smooth the surface. Cover loosely with oiled plastic wrap and leave in a warm place until the dough reaches the top of the pan, about 30 minutes.
5 Meanwhile, preheat the oven to 400° F. Remove the plastic wrap and bake in the oven until risen, golden, and the base sounds hollow when the loaf is tipped out and tapped, about 40 minutes. Transfer to a wire rack to cool.

WATCH OUT FOR sesame seeds—some people cannot tolerate them. If so, simply increase the brown rice flour to 3 cups.

TIP You can also make this in the bread machine. Add the wet ingredients then the dry. Set the machine to "basic." This isn't suitable for cooking on the timer.

"This is really quick to make with a healthy, seedy farmhouse texture and taste"

Quick soda bread

Soda bread is the traditional Irish bread and is bread-making at its quickest; you don't have to wait for yeast to work or the loaf to rise. It makes delicious, crusty, floury bread that can be eaten straight from the oven, broken into quarters, with loads of butter and jam, and is very popular with celiac sufferers in the gluten-free form. Soda bread is best eaten on the day it is baked because it gets stale quickly.

 ## egg & nut free

2 cups all-purpose flour, plus extra for dusting
2 cups whole-wheat flour
1 tsp salt
2 tsp baking soda
2 tsp cream of tartar
1 tsp superfine sugar
3 tbsp vegetable shortening or lard

1 x 9½ fl oz carton of buttermilk
about 3 tbsp milk

PREPARATION TIME 8 minutes
COOKING TIME 50 minutes
MAKES 1 loaf

1 Preheat the oven to 375° F.
2 Sift the flours, salt, baking soda, cream of tartar, and sugar into a large bowl. Tip in any bran that remains in the sieve.
3 Using your fingertips, rub the shortening or lard into the flours until the mixture resembles breadcrumbs. Make a well in the center of the flour mixture and add the buttermilk. Stir with a round-bladed knife, adding enough milk to form a soft, but not sticky dough. You may need more or less liquid depending on the absorbency of the flours you've used. You need to work quickly now, since the rising agents will start to work once the liquid is added, and you don't want the leavening to finish before you get the dough into the oven.
4 Knead the dough very briefly on a floured surface. Do not spend more than a couple of minutes on this since overworked bread will be tough and heavy.
5 Shape into a 6 inch round, place on a greased baking sheet, and flatten slightly to 2 inch thick. Dust with flour.
6 With a knife dipped in flour, make a deep cross in the top of the bread so that it will break easily into quarters when baked.
7 Bake until well risen and brown and the base sounds hollow when tapped, about 50 minutes.
8 Place on a wire rack to cool slightly and cover with a cloth to keep the bread moist.

dairy free
also egg & nut free

Follow the recipe on the left, but use soy yogurt in place of the buttermilk. You can also use soy, oat, or rice milk, replacing 1 tablespoon of the milk with 1 tablespoon of lemon juice or cider vinegar to "sour" it. For either option, have 3 tablespoons of dairy-free milk on hand to add in to form a soft but not sticky dough.

gluten free
also nut free

Follow the recipe on the left, but substitute gluten-free all-purpose flour for the all-purpose and whole-wheat flours, or use half gluten-free all-purpose flour and half buckwheat flour. Add 2 teaspoons of xanthan gum with the flour and 1 large egg, beaten with the buttermilk.

TIP The buttermilk makes a moist, light loaf and, with the cream of tartar, provides the slightly acid environment that the baking soda needs to work. If you can't get buttermilk, use plain yogurt or the "sour milk" substitution given in the dairy-free recipe above, either with soy milk or dairy milk.

White farmhouse loaf

This is a good everyday bread for sandwiches, toast, or cutting into chunks to eat with cold meats, pâté, cheese, etc. Don't be tempted to cut it before it cools because you'll spoil its lovely soft texture. Making your own bread is worth it just for the taste, but it also means you can avoid the often dubious ingredients, plastic taste, and spongy texture of many factory-baked loaves.

🍶 ⊘ 🥜 **dairy, egg, & nut free**

5 cups bread flour plus extra for dusting
2 tsp salt
1 tbsp superfine sugar
2 tsp instant yeast
2 tbsp flavorless nut-free vegetable oil plus extra for the loaf pan
1⅓ cups lukewarm water, or as needed

PREPARATION TIME 5–10 minutes plus rising time
COOKING TIME 30 minutes
MAKES 1 large loaf

TIP You can make this in a bread machine. Put the wet ingredients in first, then the dry, making sure the sugar is nowhere near the yeast—especially if you're using the timer option. Set the machine to the "dough" setting. When risen, transfer to a loaf pan and continue from step 3.

1 Sift the flour, salt, and sugar into a food processor. Add the yeast and oil and, while running the machine, add enough of the water to form a soft but not sticky dough. Run the machine for another minute to knead it. Alternatively, mix the ingredients in a bowl with a knife, then draw together with your hands to form a dough. Turn out onto a floured surface and knead until smooth and elastic, 5 minutes.

2 Place in an oiled plastic bag and leave in a warm place until doubled in bulk, about 1 hour.

3 Oil and flour a 2 lb loaf pan. Knock back the dough, re-knead, and shape into a rectangle. Place in the pan, brush with a little water, and dust with a little flour. Cover loosely with oiled plastic wrap and leave in a warm place until the dough reaches the top of the pan, about 30 minutes.

4 Preheat the oven to 450° F. Bake the loaf in the oven for 10 minutes, then reduce the heat to 400° F and continue to bake until it has risen well above the pan, it is rich brown in color, and the base sounds hollow when the loaf is tipped out and tapped, about 20 minutes.

5 Cool on a wire rack.

gluten free
also dairy & nut free

1¾ cups gluten-free all-purpose
  flour, plus extra for
  dusting
1 tbsp xanthan gum
1¼ tsp salt
1¼ tbsp raw sugar
1 tbsp instant yeast
4 tbsp flavorless nut-free
  vegetable oil, plus extra
  for the loaf pan
1 tsp lemon juice
1 egg, beaten
1⅓ cups lukewarm water

PREPARATION TIME 5 minutes plus
  rising time
COOKING TIME 1 hour 30 minutes
MAKES 1 large loaf

1 Sift the flour, xanthan gum, salt, and sugar into a bowl. Add the
  yeast, oil, lemon juice, and beaten egg.
2 Add the water and mix to form a thick paste. Beat well with an
  electric or hand whisk for 2 minutes until smooth. Alternatively,
  mix in a food processor with the beater attachment for the same
  amount of time.
3 Transfer the dough to an oiled 2 lb loaf pan, dusted with a little
  gluten-free flour. Smooth the surface. Cover loosely with oiled
  plastic wrap. Leave in a warm place until the mixture reaches
  the top of the pan, about 30 minutes. Dust with a little gluten-
  free flour.
4 Preheat the oven to 400° F.
5 Bake in the oven until risen, richly golden in color, and the
  base sounds hollow when turned out and tapped, about 1 hour
  30 minutes.
6 Cool on a wire rack.

TIP For an egg-free and gluten-free version, you can omit the egg and
add 2 tablespoons of water, but the texture won't be quite as good.

"Crustier, lighter,
and tastier than
many store-bought
equivalents"

French-style bread

Commercially produced French bread has a very crisp crust and light texture but does get stale very quickly. This recipe is not trying to replicate French bakery breads; it has a firmer texture but slices well, has a good flavor, keeps for several days, and is ideal for freezing. Use it for filled sandwiches, baguettes, canapés, and Crostini (p.72).

dairy, egg, & nut free

a little flavorless nut-free
  vegetable oil for baking sheet
2 cups all-purpose flour
¾ tsp salt
¾ tsp superfine sugar
1 tsp instant yeast
generous ½ cup lukewarm
  water, or as needed

PREPARATION TIME 10 minutes
  plus rising time
COOKING TIME 25 minutes
MAKES 1 loaf

1 Oil a baking sheet.

2 Sift the flour with the salt and sugar into a food processor. Add the yeast. Run the machine and add enough water to form a soft but not sticky dough. Continue to run the machine for 1 minute to knead. Alternatively, mix the ingredients in a bowl with a knife, then draw together with your hands to form a dough. Turn out onto a floured surface and knead for 5 minutes until smooth and elastic.

3 Place the dough in an oiled plastic bag and leave in a warm place until doubled in bulk, about 40 minutes.

4 If using a food processor, knock back the dough and re-knead on a lightly floured surface. Shape the dough into a long stick and place on the baking sheet. Cover loosely with oiled plastic wrap and leave in a warm place to proof again until doubled in bulk, about 25 minutes.

5 Preheat the oven to 400° F. Using a sharp knife, make several slashes along the bread. Place a dish of boiling water on the bottom shelf of the oven. Cook the bread on the shelf above the dish until the bread is golden in color and the base sounds hollow when tapped, about 25 minutes. Brush the bread lightly with water and let cool on a wire rack.

SERVING SUGGESTION You can turn this bread into Crostini (p.72) or garlic bread. Cube the last stale little bits and fry them in olive oil for croutons to sprinkle on soup.

"Using perforated French bread pans makes all the difference to the crust"

gluten free

also dairy & nut free

a little vegetable oil for the
   baking sheet
generous 1¼ cups rice flour
¼ cup potato flour, plus
   extra for dusting
½ cup tapioca flour
1 tbsp xanthan gum
2 tsp superfine sugar
2 tsp salt
1 tbsp instant yeast
1 egg, separated
1 tsp lemon juice
⅔ cup lukewarm water, or as
   needed

PREPARATION TIME 8 minutes plus
   rising time
COOKING TIME 40 minutes
MAKES 1 loaf

TIP This gluten-free loaf is not
as light and airy as wheat French-
style bread but slices and toasts
really well. It's best eaten fresh
or sliced and frozen.

1 Mix the flours with the xanthan gum, sugar, and salt into a food
processor. Stir in the yeast.

2 Whisk the egg white until frothy. Add to the food processor with
the lemon juice and water.

3 Run the machine to form a soft, slightly sticky dough and
continue to run the machine for 1 minute to knead the mixture.

4 Turn onto a well-floured surface and knead until no longer
sticky. Shape into a long stick and place on an oiled baking
sheet. Cover with oiled plastic wrap and leave in a warm place
for 30 minutes or until doubled in bulk.

5 Meanwhile, preheat the oven to 400° F. Using a sharp knife,
cut slashes at intervals along the length of the bread. Place a
dish of boiling water on the lowest shelf of the oven. Brush
gently with a little of the egg yolk to glaze. Bake on the shelf
above the dish of water until golden and the base sounds
hollow when tapped, about 40 minutes. When cooked brush
lightly with water. Cool on a wire rack.

WATCH OUT FOR rice flours. Some may contain traces of nuts, so
make sure you check the label.

Focaccia

This Italian bread with its soft open texture and dimpled surface is a lovely accompaniment. Serve it plain or try the fragrant seasoned rosemary or basil variations below. It makes a great sandwich bread too. The main recipe can be baked loaflike or flat bread-style by varying the proofing time; the gluten-free version will not rise quite as high.

dairy, egg, & nut free

1¾ cups bread flour
    plus extra for dusting
2 tsp salt
1½ tbsp superfine sugar
1 tbsp instant yeast
5 tbsp olive oil plus extra for
    the cake pan
1 tsp lemon juice

1 cup lukewarm water,
    or as needed
1 tsp coarse sea salt

PREPARATION TIME 5–10 minutes
    plus rising time
COOKING TIME 30 minutes
MAKES 1 round focaccia

1 Sift the flour with the salt and sugar into a bowl or food processor.
2 Add the yeast, 3 tablespoons of the oil, the lemon juice, and water. Either mix together with a knife to form a dough then knead on a lightly floured surface for 5 minutes, or run the food processor until a dough is formed and continue to run the machine for 1 minute to knead it to a soft, slightly sticky dough.
3 Lightly oil a 9 inch cake pan and press the dough gently into the pan with wet hands. Lightly sprinkle the dough with water to keep the crust soft. Loosely cover the pan with plastic wrap and let proof in a warm place for about 30 minutes or until doubled in bulk. If you like a high loaf, let it proof a little longer.
4 Meanwhile, preheat the oven to 425° F.
5 Dust your index finger with flour then gently press it into the dough at intervals to form dimples. Lightly sprinkle with water again then drizzle with the remaining oil and sprinkle with the coarse sea salt.
6 Bake in the oven until pale golden brown in color and the base sounds hollow when tipped out and tapped (about 30 minutes). Sprinkle with water twice during cooking.
7 Transfer to a wire rack, cover with a clean damp cloth to soften the crust, and let cool.
◀ **Pictured opposite** with dairy-free cheeseless pesto (p.210).

gluten free
also dairy & nut free

Follow the recipe on the left, but substitute gluten-free all-purpose flour for the bread flour and add 1 tablespoon of xanthan gum at step 1. Add a beaten egg and increase the water to a scant 1⅓ cups. The dough will be sticky. Press it into the pan and smooth the surface with wet hands. Cook for about 45–50 minutes.

VARIATIONS For a rosemary and onion focaccia, follow either recipe, but substitute 1 teaspoon of garlic salt for the plain salt in the dough. Soak 2 thinly sliced onions in cold water for 15 minutes, drain and scatter over the dough and sprinkle with 2 teaspoons of chopped fresh rosemary before drizzling with the oil, sprinkling with coarse sea salt, and baking.

For a sun-dried tomato, olive, and fresh basil focaccia, follow either recipe, but add 2 tablespoons of chopped fresh basil to the dough. When you put the dough back in the pan, chop 4 drained pieces of sun-dried tomato in olive oil and slice 6 pitted black olives. Scatter over the surface of the dough with 6 torn basil leaves, then sprinkle with water and continue at the second half of step 3.

Southern skillet cornbread

Utterly delicious, with a crisp brown crust and golden interior, this cornbread is versatile and quick to make. Eat it on its own, with butter, with Chili con carne (p.122), flavored with sweet or savory additions, served with meals or in lunchboxes. I've singled out Southern skillet cornbread because it's naturally gluten free, but don't miss out on the four Northern cornbreads overleaf either.

gluten and nut free

1 tbsp bacon fat or dripping
generous 2 cups stone-ground
  cornmeal (white cornmeal if
  preferred)
2 tbsp superfine sugar
1 tsp baking powder
1 tsp baking soda
1 tsp salt
2 eggs, beaten
2¼ cups buttermilk

PREPARATION TIME 5 minutes
COOKING TIME 20–25 minutes
SERVES 6

1 Preheat the oven to 450° F.
2 Put the bacon fat in a large cast-iron skillet or a 9 inch baking pan and heat in the oven.
3 Mix together the cornmeal, sugar, baking powder, baking soda, and salt in a large bowl.
4 Whisk together the eggs and buttermilk and add to the cornmeal mixture. Beat until smooth.
5 Pour the batter into the hot bacon fat. Bake toward the top of the oven until the top is browned and the center springs back when gently pressed, about 20 minutes. Serve immediately cut into wedges.
Pictured opposite ▷

dairy, egg, gluten, & nut free

For these four allergen-free versions, there are Northern cornbread recipes overleaf. Sweeter and lighter than its Southern counterpart, Northern cornbread is traditionally baked in a deep pan.

SERVING SUGGESTIONS Eat Southern or Northern cornbreads on their own, with butter, or as an accompaniment to dishes such as meaty stews. Try replacing the sugar with molasses or honey (added to the wet ingredients), or add jalapeño peppers (if you can tolerate them— some people can't), Monterey Jack, cheddar or cheddar-style cheese, or sun-dried tomatoes.

Northern cornbread

 nut free

generous 1¼ cups cornmeal
1¼ cups all-purpose flour
1½ tbsp superfine sugar
2 tsp baking powder
½ tsp baking soda
½ tsp salt
2 eggs, beaten
generous ½ cup milk
generous ½ cup buttermilk
2 tbsp corn oil or 2 tbsp
  melted butter

PREPARATION TIME 10 minutes
COOKING TIME 10–12 minutes for
  muffins; 20–25 minutes for pan
SERVES 8–10

1 Preheat the oven to 450° F. Oil a 7 x 11 inch baking pan or line
a standard 12-hole muffin pan with paper muffin cups.
2 Mix the cornmeal, flour, sugar, baking powder, baking soda, and
salt in a large bowl.
3 Whisk the eggs, milk, and buttermilk together and add to the
cornmeal mixture. Beat well.
4 Stir in the oil or butter to form a thick paste.
5 Transfer to the prepared pan or paper muffin cups. Bake toward
the top of the oven until risen, golden, and firm to the touch—
about 10 minutes for the muffins and 20 minutes for the large
pan. If baked in the large pan, cut into squares. Serve hot.

TIP For the best flavor, use stone-ground yellow cornmeal in this recipe—
you can recognize it by the flecks.

 dairy free
also nut free

Replace the milk with an equal
quantity of soy milk, and the
buttermilk with an equal quantity
of soy yogurt. In step 3, stir in corn
or vegetable oil instead of melted
butter. Proceed as for the nut-free
recipe. Remember to oil the baking
pan with nondairy fat or oil. Use
dairy-free Monterey Jack or
cheddar-style cheese for variations.

egg free
also nut free

Omit the eggs. Add 2 tablespoons
of soy or potato flour to the dry
ingredients and increase the baking
powder to 1 tablespoon. Add
3 tablespoons of water and 3
tablespoons of nut-free vegetable oil
to the wet ingredients. Proceed as for
the nut-free recipe. The egg-free loaf
comes out attractively cracked on top
and the edges are slightly browner
than the nut-free recipe.

gluten free
also nut free

Prepare as for the nut-free recipe,
but substitute gluten-free all-purpose
flour for the all-purpose flour and
add 1 teaspoon of xanthan gum to
the dry ingredients. This doesn't
brown as much as the other versions.

Spiced yogurt raisin bread

This spiced loaf is similar to fruited tea breads. Using yogurt instead of milk imparts a nice fresh flavor to the bread. It tastes lovely toasted with butter for breakfast, and try it served with Fragrant poached peaches (p.151). A sliced buttered loaf makes great picnic food too, since it's portable and the flavors are strong enough to hold their own in the fresh air.

 **egg & nut free**

a little nut-free oil for the
  loaf pan
3 cups bread flour
1 tsp ground apple pie spices
½ tsp salt
½ tsp baking soda
⅓ cup soft light brown
  sugar
1 tbsp instant yeast
¼ cup butter or margarine

scant 1¼ cups plain low-fat
  yogurt
⅔ cup raisins
a little milk to glaze

PREPARATION TIME 15 minutes,
  plus rising time
COOKING TIME 40 minutes
MAKES 1 large loaf

1 Lightly oil a 2 lb loaf pan and line the base with parchment paper.
2 Sift the flour, apple pie spices, salt, and baking soda into a food processor or a bowl.
3 Add the sugar and yeast.
4 Melt the butter or margarine in a small saucepan. Stir in the yogurt and heat to warm but not hot. Add to the flour mixture.
5 If using a food processor, run the machine to form a soft, very slightly sticky dough, then run for 1 minute to knead. Turn out onto a lightly floured surface and knead in the raisins. If making by hand, add the raisins to the bowl and thoroughly mix with a wooden spoon, drawing the mixture into a ball. Turn out and knead on a lightly floured surface for 5 minutes until the dough is elastic and no longer sticky.
6 Transfer the mixture to the prepared pan. Cover loosely with oiled plastic wrap and leave in a warm place until the mixture almost reaches the top of the pan, about 1 hour.
7 Meanwhile, preheat the oven to 400° F. Lightly brush the bread with a little milk to glaze and bake in the oven until risen, richly browned, and the base sounds hollow when tipped out and tapped, about 40 minutes. Transfer to a wire rack, remove the parchment paper, and let cool.

dairy free
also egg & nut free

Prepare as for the recipe on the left, but substitute dairy-free spread for the butter or margarine and dairy-free yogurt for the cow's milk yogurt.

gluten free
also nut free

Prepare as for the recipe on the left, but substitute gluten-free all-purpose flour for the bread flour. Add 1 tablespoon of xanthan gum at step 2 and a beaten egg with the yogurt. The mixture will be quite sticky so, if using a food processor, add the raisins at the end of kneading and just run the machine by pulsing the switch once or twice to incorporate the raisins without chopping them up. You will not be able to knead it on a floured surface so spoon the dough straight into the pan. Let rise as in main recipe. Cook until risen, richly browned, and the base sounds hollow when tipped out and tapped. This will take a little longer than the other versions, 50 minutes to 1 hour.

Pizza Margherita

Pizzas are virtually a staple food now and can be tasty, nutritious, and versatile—especially if made at home. This is the classic Margherita with a simple cheese and tomato sauce topping. It's lovely with a handful of wild arugula strewn over just before serving, or you could add any extra toppings you like before baking, such as anchovies, olives, ham, mushrooms, or roasted vegetables.

 **egg & nut free**

for the dough
2 cups bread flour
½ tsp salt
1 tsp superfine sugar
1 tsp instant yeast
1 tbsp olive oil plus extra for the pizza pan
½ cup lukewarm water

for the topping
6 tbsp homemade tomato sauce or the best quality you can buy
1 tsp dried oregano

4½ oz buffalo mozzarella cheese, thinly sliced
3 large tomatoes, sliced
1 tbsp olive oil
freshly ground black pepper
a few fresh basil leaves torn into small pieces

PREPARATION TIME 10–15 minutes plus rising time
COOKING TIME 20 minutes
MAKES 1 large pizza

1 Oil a large pizza pan (about 12 inches in diameter), or a large baking sheet.

2 Put the flour in a food processor with the salt, sugar, yeast, and oil. Run the machine and add the water to form a soft but not sticky dough. Continue to run the machine for 1 minute to knead it. Alternatively, mix the ingredients together in a bowl with a knife to form a dough then turn it out onto a lightly floured surface and knead for about 5 minutes until smooth and elastic.

3 Roll out the dough so that it is about 12 inches in diameter. Transfer to the pizza pan or baking sheet and leave in a warm place to rise for at least 20 minutes.

4 Preheat the oven to 425° F.

5 Spread the tomato sauce over the dough, making sure that it doesn't quite meet the edges. Arrange the slices of cheese on top and sprinkle with oregano.

6 Top with the slices of tomato and drizzle with oil and season with pepper.

7 Bake in the oven for about 20 minutes, until crisp and golden around the edges, the cheese has melted, and everything is sizzling.

8 Add a scattering of basil leaves on top.

dairy free
also egg & nut free

Follow the recipe on the left, replacing the buffalo mozzarella with a mozzarella-style melting dairy-free cheese.

gluten free
also egg & nut free

for the dough
1 cup rice flour
¾ cup potato flour
¼ cup tapioca flour
1 tbsp xanthan gum
¼ tsp salt
1 tsp superfine sugar
1½ tsp instant yeast
1 tbsp olive oil plus extra for pan
scant 1 cup lukewarm water
cornstarch for dusting

• Oil the pizza plate or baking sheet. Mix the flours with the xanthan gum, salt, sugar, yeast, and oil in a food processor or mix by hand (see left).
• Add the water and mix to form a soft dough. Continue to run the machine for 1 minute to knead it.
• Transfer to a work surface, dusted lightly with cornstarch. Shape the dough into a ball.
• Continue as from step 3 of the main recipe, but cover the dough with oiled plastic wrap to prevent it from drying from out during rising.

◀ Pictured opposite

Piecrust

This pastry is the perfect base for fruit desserts such as Apple tart (p.149) or as a crust for savory pies like the glazed Chicken pie (p.106). Each version is delicious and has a subtly different texture and hue. If pastry makes you at all nervous, there is advice below as well as specific tips on dairy-free and gluten-free pastry making.

 ### egg & nut free

generous 2 cups all-purpose flour
  plus extra for dusting
a pinch of salt
²/₃ cup butter, chilled and cut
  into cubes
3 tbsp ice water, or as needed

PREPARATION TIME 10 minutes
  plus chilling time
SERVES 6–8

1 Sift the flour with the salt into a bowl. Using your fingertips, rub in the butter until the mixture resembles fine breadcrumbs.
2 Using a fork or knife, mix with enough cold water to form a soft but not sticky dough. Bring the pastry together completely with your hands.
3 Transfer to a lightly floured surface. Knead gently until smooth and free from cracks. Wrap the pastry tightly in plastic wrap (to prevent the edges from drying out and cracking when the pastry is rolled out) and refrigerate for 30 minutes or until firm. Use as required. It can be frozen.

TIPS The big trick to making piecrust is to keep everything as chilled as possible—cold room, cold surfaces (a marble board is ideal), cold hands, and cold liquid added to the flour and butter mix.

You can make your pastry in the food processor, if you prefer. Mix the fat into the flour mixture until just crumbly, but no more. Add the water a little at a time and only process until the mixture forms a ball. Do not overmix or the results may be leathery. The less the dough is mixed or handled the better.

For sweet piecrust, prepare as above, but add 2 tablespoons of superfine sugar with the flour.

 ### dairy free
also egg & nut free

Follow the recipe on the left, but substitute dairy-free vegetable shortening for the butter.

 ### gluten free

See overleaf for gluten-free recipe.
Pictured opposite ▶

BREADS & BAKING

Piecrust continued

gluten free
also nut free

1 cup rice flour plus
  extra for dusting
½ cup potato flour
¾ cup fine cornmeal
  (polenta)
1 heaped tsp xanthan gum
pinch of salt
⅔ cup butter, diced
1 egg, beaten with 2 tbsp cold
  water

PREPARATION TIME 10 minutes
  plus chilling time
SERVES 6–8

1 Sift the flours, cornmeal, xanthan gum, and salt into a bowl and mix well. Rub in the butter, using your fingertips, until the mixture resembles fine breadcrumbs.

2 Make a well in the center of the mixture and pour about three-quarters of the egg and water mixture into it. This should be enough to allow you to bring the ingredients loosely together with a fork. Add a few more drops if necessary to make the pastry come together. Beware of adding more liquid than you need; damp pastry may be easier to work with but it may toughen up during cooking. Draw the pastry together completely with your hands to form a ball.

3 Transfer to the work surface, lightly dusted with rice flour, and knead the dough until smooth, about 3 minutes. Shape the dough into a ball. Wrap in plastic wrap and chill for 30 minutes to rest. Use as required. It can be frozen.

TIPS For sweet gluten-free piecrust, prepare as above, but add 2 tablespoons of superfine sugar at the end of step 1.
  Pastry made with gluten-free flours gives a deliciously satisfying crumbly crust, but if you are used to regular flours you will find it a little more difficult to work with. The trick is not to cave in by adding water, but to work with a dough that has a dryish and crumbly feel to it. That is why this recipe involves using your hands, since you just don't have the same degree of control with a food processor.

WATCH OUT FOR rice flour, since it may contain traces of nuts.

Shortbread

These cookies are crumbly, delicious, and difficult to resist. If you find that they don't last long, you might like to double the quantity. As well as being an ideal snack with a cup of tea or coffee, they work well with fruit desserts. They seem to have a particular affinity to red fruit or berry compôtes and are wonderful with strawberries and cream.

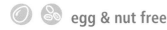 **egg & nut free**

²/₃ cup softened butter
¼ cup superfine sugar plus extra for dusting
1 cup all-purpose flour
½ cup rice flour
pinch of salt

PREPARATION TIME 25 minutes plus chilling time
COOKING TIME 25 minutes
MAKES 10

1 Beat the butter and sugar together until light and fluffy.
2 Sift the flours and salt over the butter and sugar mixture and work in with a wooden spoon until the mixture begins to form a dough.
3 Draw together with your hands to form a soft dough.
4 Knead gently on a board until the mixture forms a ball, then roll out with your hands to a sausage about 2 inches in diameter. Wrap in plastic wrap and chill for 1 hour.
5 Preheat the oven to 325° F. Line a baking sheet with parchment paper.
6 Using a sharp knife, cut the sausage into 10 slices and lay them on the baking sheet. If desired, cut with a fluted pastry cutter to give an attractive edge and remove the excess dough. You can also make them fancier by pricking the centers with a fork.
7 Bake in the oven for about 25 minutes until pale golden brown in color. Remove from the oven and sprinkle immediately with superfine sugar. Let cool for 10 minutes then transfer to a wire rack to cool completely. Store in an airtight container.

WATCH OUT FOR rice flour, since it may contain traces of nuts.

 dairy free
also egg & nut free

Follow the recipe on the left, but substitute dairy-free spread for the butter and add a few drops of vanilla extract to the mixture to enhance the flavor.

gluten free
also egg & nut free

Follow the recipe on the left, but substitute gluten-free all-purpose flour for the ordinary flour.

Raisin scones

Traditionally, scones were part of an elegant tea-time spread served with jam and whipped or clotted cream and quite possibly Earl Grey tea, too. But you really don't need to get out the best linen tablecloth to enjoy these. They take just half an hour to make, so you can eat them fresh, plain or buttered, with coffee for breakfast, or as a midmorning snack.

  ### egg & nut free

2 cups self-rising flour, plus
  extra for dusting
½ tsp baking powder
¼ tsp salt
2 tbsp superfine sugar
3 tbsp butter plus extra
  for the baking sheet
3 tbsp raisins or golden raisins
½ cup milk
2–3 tbsp cream or milk to glaze

PREPARATION TIME 20 minutes
COOKING TIME 10–12 minutes
MAKES 8–10

1 Preheat the oven to 425° F. Butter a baking sheet or line it with parchment paper.
2 Sift together into a medium-sized bowl the dry ingredients: flour, baking powder, and salt. Mix in the sugar.
3 Cut up the butter and rub it into the dry mixture until it resembles fine breadcrumbs. Add the raisins.
4 Add three-quarters of the milk and mix it in quickly with a knife. Add the remaining milk, only if it is needed to mix to a soft dough. Do not over mix since this will make the scones tough.
5 Turn out the dough onto a lightly floured surface and pat or roll out to ¾ inch thick.
6 Cut out the scones with a 2 inch floured cutter. Gather up any trimmings, roll into a ball, and cut more scones.
7 Place the scones on the baking sheet and brush the tops with the cream or milk.
8 Bake near the top of the oven for 10–12 minutes or until the scones have risen, are lightly browned on top, and the bases sound hollow when tapped. Cool on a wire rack.
Pictured opposite ▶

TIP If you like your scones with a soft crust, cover them with a clean dish towel for one minute after removing from the oven.

SERVING SUGGESTION Serve hot or cold with jam and whipped cream or a dairy-free alternative.

dairy free
also egg & nut free

Follow the recipe on the left, but replace the butter with an equal quantity of firm nondairy spread (the soft ones have too much water in them); and the milk or cream with the same quantity of soy equivalent.

gluten free
also nut free

Follow the recipe on the left, substituting the following ingredients:
4 tbsp black tea
3 tbsp raisins
2 cups gluten-free self-raising
  flour
½ tsp baking powder
¼ tsp salt
½ tsp xanthan gum
2 tbsp superfine sugar
3 tbsp butter
1 egg, lightly beaten
generous 3 tbsp milk
2–3 tbsp cream or milk to glaze

Gluten-free flours can be slightly drier and absorb more water, so make the following alterations. First soak the raisins in the black tea for at least 30 minutes. Add the xanthan gum with the dry ingredients in step 2. Drain the raisins and add to the rubbed-in mixture in step 3. Add the beaten egg before the milk in step 4.

Giant chocolate chip cookies

These thick, golden, chewy cookies, crammed full of chocolate chips, are delicious eaten warm straight from the oven. They seem to be just the right size, giant but not colossal, for children's lunch boxes and look great piled high as part of a snack-time or birthday spread. They also store well and will stay soft if kept in an airtight container.

 nut free

¾ cup butter
generous 1 cup soft light brown
  sugar
¼ cup granulated sugar
2½ cups all-purpose flour
½ tsp baking soda
½ tsp salt
1 large egg, beaten
2 tsp vanilla extract
generous 1½ cups bittersweet or
  semisweet nut-free
  chocolate chips

PREPARATION TIME 20 minutes
COOKING TIME 20 minutes
MAKES 18 giant or 24 medium
  cookies

1 Preheat the oven to 350° F. Line two baking sheets with parchment paper.
2 Melt the butter in a small saucepan and stir in the sugars, stirring until no lumps remain.
3 Sift the flour, baking soda, and salt into a mixing bowl.
4 Add the melted butter and sugars, the beaten egg, and vanilla extract and mix to a soft dough.
5 Mix in the chocolate chips.
6 With wet hands, shape the dough into 18 or 24 balls. Place well apart on the prepared baking sheets.
7 Bake for 20 minutes or until golden and well spread but still slightly soft. Remove from the oven and let cool on the baking sheets for 10 minutes then transfer to a wire rack to cool completely. Store in an airtight container.

TIP You can make the dough in advance, roll it into a log, and freeze it, ready for cutting into cookies at a later date.

 dairy free
also nut free

Follow the nut-free recipe, but replace the butter with dairy-free spread and add an extra ¼ cup of flour. Make sure the chocolate chips are dairy free.

 egg free
also nut free

Follow the nut-free recipe, but omit the egg and replace with 1 tablespoon of potato flour added in step 3, and 3 tablespoons of cream, milk, or water in step 4.

 gluten free
also nut free

Follow the nut-free recipe, but replace the flour with an equal quantity of gluten-free flour.

VARIATION Use soft dark brown sugar instead of granulated sugar to make darker, chewier cookies. This will make a wetter dough, which you will need to drop in spoonfuls onto the baking sheets.

Gingerbread

This moist and sticky, lightly spiced gingerbread is wonderfully versatile. You can serve it warm, without the icing, topped with whipped cream and a little scattered chopped crystallized ginger, or with some ginger syrup poured over it. Thickly topped with the lemony icing, it looks very festive and makes an excellent snack-time treat, as well as being a winner in lunch boxes and at school events.

 nut free

a little flavorless nut-free
  vegetable oil for baking pan
2½ cups all-purpose flour
½ tsp baking soda
½ tsp salt
1 tbsp ground ginger
2 tsp ground cinnamon
1 tsp ground allspice
generous ⅔ cup superfine sugar
½ cup butter, melted and
  cooled to room temperature
⅔ cup molasses
generous 1 cup milk
1 egg, beaten

to serve
a little stem ginger in syrup
cream
or lemon glacé icing
generous 1 cup confectioners' sugar
1½ tbsp lemon juice
1½–2 tbsp water
to decorate
candied ginger pieces (optional)

PREPARATION TIME 10 minutes
COOKING TIME 50–60 minutes
MAKES 1 slab cake

1 Preheat the oven to 350° F.
2 Oil a 7 x 11 inch shallow baking pan with the nut-free vegetable oil and line with parchment paper.
3 Sift the dry ingredients together into a bowl: flour, baking soda, salt, ginger, cinnamon, and allspice. Stir in the sugar.
4 Whisk in the remaining ingredients.
5 Add the dry ingredients to the wet ingredients and mix to combine, but do not overmix.
6 Pour the gingerbread batter into the baking tray and smooth the top with a palette knife, if necessary.
7 Bake for 50–60 minutes, until the gingerbread springs back when pressed. Cool slightly then turn out onto a plate, if serving warm, or cool on a wire rack.
8 Either serve warm with whipped cream and a little chopped stem ginger in syrup, if liked, or when cool make the icing.
9 Sift the confectioners' sugar into a bowl and add the lemon juice. Beat in enough water to form a thick, spreadable paste.
10 Spread the frosting over the gingerbread and use a butter knife dipped in warm water to smooth if desired or let it drip attractively over the sides. Decorate with crystallized ginger, if desired.

 dairy free
also nut free

Follow the nut-free recipe, but substitute the butter with an equal quantity of dairy-free spread and the milk with an equal quantity of soy, oat, or rice milk.

 egg free
also nut free

Follow the nut-free recipe, but replace the egg with 1 tablespoon of potato flour plus 3 tablespoons of water. Add the potato flour to the dry ingredients in step 3 and the water to the wet ingredients in step 4.

gluten free
also nut free

Follow the nut-free recipe, but replace the flour with an equal quantity of gluten-free flour mix or use rice flour instead—this gives a crumblier texture and a pleasant taste.

TIP If you are cutting the gingerbread into squares, do it before the icing is put on, since cutting the cake can crack the icing.

Fruity oatmeal squares

These sweet, golden squares are full of dried fruit and other good things. A great snack with a cup of tea or in a lunch box, they keep your energy levels up without ruining your appetite. The millet version is much closer to a deliciously crumbly shortbread than to a classic oatmeal square, and is a nice change whether or not you have to be gluten-free.

 ## egg & nut free

scant ½ cup butter or margarine,
    plus extra for the baking pan
2 tbsp raw sugar
2 generous tbsp light corn syrup
2 cups rolled oats
½ tsp apple pie spice
3 tbsp golden raisins
3 tbsp raisins
3 tbsp dried apricots, chopped

PREPARATION TIME 15 minutes
COOKING TIME 25 minutes
MAKES 16

1 Preheat the oven to 350° F. Butter a 7 x 11 inch baking pan.
2 Melt the butter or margarine with the sugar and syrup in
   a large saucepan.
3 Stir in all the remaining ingredients.
4 Transfer the mixture to the baking pan and press out firmly
   into the corners, using the back of a wet spoon. Bake in the
   center of the oven for about 25 minutes or until a rich golden
   brown. Check after 20 minutes to ensure the edges are not
   getting too brown.
5 Let cool slightly then cut into 16 squares. Cool completely in
   the pan then remove and store in an airtight container.

dairy free
also egg & nut free

Follow the recipe on the left, but substitute dairy-free spread for the butter or ordinary margarine.

gluten free
also egg & nut free

Follow the recipe on the left, but substitute millet or quinoa flakes for the oats.

Chocolate crinkle cookies

These are sophisticated little cookies, rolled in a generous amount of confectioners' sugar to create a snowy coating that cracks attractively and dramatically on cooking to reveal the sweet dark chocolate interior. Although intended as an adult treat they turned out to be remarkably popular with children. They are quick and easy to make and need just half an hour to chill the dough.

 ## dairy, egg, & nut free

3 tbsp granulated sugar
¾ cup self-rising flour
1 tsp baking soda
¼ cup nut-free unsweetened cocoa powder
¼ cup butter
2 tbsp light corn syrup
¼ cup confectioners' sugar for coating

PREPARATION TIME 20 minutes plus chilling time
COOKING TIME 10–12 minutes
MAKES 16 small or 8 large cookies

1 Place the sugar in a medium bowl. Sift in the flour, baking soda, and cocoa powder.
2 Add the butter and rub in with your fingers until the mixture has the consistency of breadcrumbs. Stir in the corn syrup and mix well. Draw the dough together with your hands to form a ball.
3 Divide the dough into 16 pieces for small cookies or 8 for large cookies. Chill them in the refrigerator for at least 30 minutes.
4 Preheat the oven to 350° F. Line 2 baking sheets with baking parchment.
5 Roll each piece of dough into a ball and roll in the confectioners' sugar, coating very thickly, before placing on the lined baking sheets. Place the pieces at least 1½ inches apart since they spread during baking.
6 Bake in the oven until attractively cracked on the top and still a little bit soft in the center. Check the small cookies after 10 minutes and the double-size cookies after 12 minutes.
7 Allow the cookies to firm up on the baking sheet before transferring to a wire rack to cool. Store in an airtight container.
Pictured on next page ▶

dairy free
also egg & nut free

Follow the recipe on the left, but use dairy-free spread instead of butter.

gluten free
also egg & nut free

Follow the recipe on the left, but substitute an equal quantity of gluten-free self-rising flour for the flour and ensure that the baking soda and cocoa powder are also gluten free.

TIP If you can get only all-purpose gluten-free flour, convert it to self-rising by adding 2 teaspoons of gluten-free baking powder.

Afternoon party with dairy-, egg-, and nut-free Vanilla cupcakes (p.192); nut-free Chocolate brownies (p.193); and dairy-, egg- and nut-free Chocolate crinkle cookies (p.189).

Vanilla cupcakes

Vanilla cupcakes are a childhood staple and a centerpiece at children's parties. They also figure in many children's first experiences of cooking at home or at school, which makes it a shame for those who can't join in because of food hypersensitivities. Here are versions—made easy for little hands—that make it possible for everyone to take part.

dairy, egg, & nut free

1½ cups all-purpose flour
1 tbsp baking powder
a pinch of salt
⅔ cup soft, light brown sugar
1 tsp vanilla extract
2 tbsp corn or other flavorless nut-free vegetable oil
1 tbsp white wine vinegar
1 cup water

PREPARATION TIME 15 minutes
COOKING TIME 20 minutes
MAKES 12

1 Preheat the oven to 350° F. Line 12 sections of a tartlet pan or small muffin pan with paper cupcake liners.
2 Sift the flour, baking powder, and salt into a bowl. Stir in the sugar.
3 Add the remaining ingredients and beat until you have a smooth, liquid batter.
4 Pour or ladle the batter into the cupcake liners, filling up to ⅛ in from the top of the liner. Bake in the oven for about 20 minutes or until risen and firm to touch.
5 Transfer to a wire rack to cool.
◀ **Pictured on previous page**

TIP If you are making these with children, place the batter in a pitcher for easier pouring in step 4.

SERVING SUGGESTION For a children's party, decorate the cakes with glacé icing and a cherry on top. To make the glacé icing, sift a generous 1 cup of confectioners' sugar into a bowl. Add 2–2½ tbsp of water and a few drops of food coloring, if desired, and mix to a thick, spreadable cream.

gluten free
also dairy & nut free

3 eggs
⅔ cup soft, light brown sugar
½ tsp vanilla extract
⅓ cup butter or margarine, melted
¾ cup potato flour
¾ cup soy flour
2½ tsp gluten-free baking powder

• Preheat the oven to 350° F. Line 12 sections of a tartlet pan or small muffin pan with cupcake liners.
• Break the eggs into a bowl and add the sugar. Whisk with an electric or balloon whisk until thick and pale and the mixture leaves a trail when lifted out of the mixture.
• Whisking all the time, add the melted butter or margarine in a thin trickle.
• Sift the flours and baking powder over the surface. Fold in with a metal spoon, using a figure-eight motion.
• Spoon into the cupcake liners. Bake in the oven for about 15–20 minutes, until risen and the centers spring back when lightly pressed.
• Transfer to a wire rack to cool.

Chocolate brownies

These are as brownies should be: rich, moist chocolatey squares with a distinctively cracked top. Add a handful of raisins or golden raisins to the mixture, or chopped walnuts if you can eat them. Enjoy them at snack time or at any other time! My favorite is to eat them warm, for dessert, with the very best vanilla ice cream I can buy.

 ## nut free

¾ cup all-purpose flour
1 tbsp nut-free unsweetened
   cocoa powder
good pinch of salt
1 tsp baking powder
¾ cup soft light brown sugar
¼ cup butter or margarine
2 tbsp water
scant 1 cup (3½ oz) nut-free
   semisweet chocolate
1 tsp vanilla extract
2 large eggs, beaten

PREPARATION TIME 25 minutes
COOKING TIME 20 minutes
MAKES 15

1 Preheat the oven to 350° F. Line a 7 x 11 inch baking pan with parchment paper.
2 Sift the flour, cocoa powder, salt, and baking powder into a bowl.
3 Put the sugar, butter or margarine, water, chocolate, and vanilla in a saucepan and heat gently, stirring, until melted.
4 Pour into the flour mixture, add the eggs and beat until smooth.
5 Transfer to the prepared pan and bake for about 20 minutes, until firm to the touch and slightly crusty on top.
6 Let cool for 10 minutes then mark into 15 squares. Cool completely before removing from the pan. Store in an airtight container.

◀ **Pictured on page 191**

 ## dairy free
also nut free

Follow the nut-free recipe, but make sure you use dairy-free margarine instead of the butter or ordinary margarine and dairy-free chocolate for the semisweet chocolate.

 ## egg free
also nut free

Follow the nut-free recipe to step 4 adding an extra ½ teaspoon of baking powder to the mix. At step 4, omit the eggs. Mix 2 tablespoons of potato flour and ⅔ cup water in a small saucepan. Bring to a boil until just thickened and clear, stirring all the time. Remove from the heat. Beat the potato flour and water mixture along with the melted ingredients. These egg-free brownies are even more moist and chewy than the others.

 ## gluten free
also nut free

Follow the nut-free recipe, but substitute gluten-free all-purpose flour for the ordinary flour and check that the baking powder and cocoa powder are gluten free, too.

Raspberry marshmallow crispies

Simple and inexpensive to make, these sticky cereal squares are a children's party treat—so they are just the thing whether your young guests have allergies or not. The puffed rice gives the treats an attractive honeycombed appearance. The dairy-free version is very useful for larger events because you can serve them to anyone with egg and nut allergies and gluten intolerance as well.

gluten, egg, & nut free

a little nut-free vegetable oil,
  for the baking pan
4 oz marshmallows
  (preferably pink and white)
¼ cup butter
4 tbsp raspberry jam
2½ cups puffed rice cereal

PREPARATION TIME 10 minutes
  plus chilling time
MAKES 24

1 Oil a 7 x 11 inch shallow baking pan.
2 Put the marshmallows in a large saucepan with the butter and the jam. Heat gently, stirring all the time, until everything has melted. Then boil for 1 minute, stirring throughout.
3 Stir in the cereal fairly rapidly until thoroughly coated in the sticky mixture.
4 Transfer the mixture to the prepared pan; spread out right to the corners; then press down firmly using a wet butter knife or the back of a spoon. Use a knife to mark out into 24 squares. Leave until cold then chill overnight to firm.
5 Store in an airtight container.

WATCH OUT FOR marshmallows that have been sweetened with maltodextrin or other sugars derived from barley, if you can't eat gluten. Some brands of marshmallow may contain egg. Check the puffed rice cereal label for ingredients containing dairy or gluten, if need be.

dairy free

also gluten, egg, & nut free

Follow the recipe on the left, but substitute dairy-free spread for the butter.

Lemon syrup polenta cake

A fresh-tasting gateau, golden-brown on the outside and gloriously yellow on the inside, which can be served as a dessert or at snack time. It's delicious accompanied by fresh summer fruits, blackberries, or blueberries and, if you are feeling indulgent, some dollops of Chantilly topping (p.216), too. The lemon syrup is delightfully tangy, or try the rosemary syrup for something unusual and special.

 **gluten free**

for the cake
a little nut-free oil for cake pan
²/₃ cup butter
²/₃ cup superfine sugar
2 eggs, beaten
1¼ cups ground almonds
1 tsp vanilla extract
½ cup polenta or other cornmeal
½ tsp baking powder
¼ tsp salt
grated zest and juice of 1 large lemon

for the syrup
4 tbsp lemon juice (juice of 2 lemons)
2 tbsp water
²/₃ cup confectioners' sugar

PREPARATION TIME 15 minutes
COOKING TIME 1 hour
SERVES 8–10

1 Preheat the oven to 350° F. Oil a deep 7 inch round cake pan and line it with parchment paper.
2 Beat the butter and sugar together with either an electric whisk or a wooden spoon, until soft and fluffy.
3 Add the eggs in a little at a time, whisking well after each addition.
4 Add the ground almonds and vanilla extract. Sift the polenta, baking powder, and salt over. Add the lemon zest and juice and fold everything in gently with a metal spoon.
5 Transfer the cake mixture to the prepared pan and level the surface.
6 Bake for 1 hour or until risen, golden, and firm to touch. Remove the cake from the oven.
7 To make the syrup, gently heat together the lemon juice, water, and sugar in a small saucepan, stirring, until the sugar has completely dissolved.
8 Stab the cake all over with a wooden toothpick, making the holes go almost all the way to the base. Spoon the hot syrup over the cake—there is a lot but it all soaks in.
9 Let the cake cool completely in the pan before turning out and removing the parchment paper.

dairy free
also gluten free

Follow the gluten-free recipe, but use dairy-free spread instead of butter.

egg free
also gluten free

Follow the gluten-free recipe, but substitute 4 tablespoons of sour cream plus 2 tablespoons of potato flour blended with 2 tablespoons of water for the eggs. Increase the baking powder to 1 teaspoon.

nut free
also gluten free

Follow the gluten-free recipe, but substitute gluten-free self-rising flour for the ground almonds and omit the baking powder. Use 3 eggs instead of 2 to keep the cake moist.

VARIATION An unusual variation is to use rosemary syrup. Heat together 4 tablespoons of water, 2 tablespoons of lemon juice, ¹/₃ cup of superfine sugar, and a sprig of rosemary until the sugar dissolves. Boil for 1 minute then leave to cool for 5 minutes. Strain the syrup over the cake. Decorate with fresh rosemary sprigs.

Chocolate layer cake

Ideal for celebrations and birthdays, this intensely flavored chocolate cake, layered and topped with ganache or chocolate buttercream, is universally popular. The version shown is egg, dairy, and nut-free and is particularly impressive to anyone who knows how flat and disappointing some vegan concoctions can be. The secret is to bake the cake in two pans, split each one, sandwich the layers, and cover with icing.

dairy, egg, & nut free

for the cake
3 cups all-purpose flour
1¾ cups superfine sugar
1¾ tsp baking soda
½ cup nut-free unsweetened
  cocoa powder
¼ tsp salt
2 cups unsweetened
  soy milk or water
scant ½ cup corn or other
  nut-free oil, plus extra for
  the cake pans
1½ tbsp white vinegar
1½ tsp vanilla extract

for the frosting
a double quantity of ganache (p.200)
  or 1 quantity of chocolate
  buttercream frosting (see right)
to decorate
about ⅓ cup (1½ oz) extra chocolate,
  shaved with a potato peeler, or
  a selection of fresh berries, if
  preferred

PREPARATION TIME 25 minutes
COOKING TIME 40 minutes
SERVES 10–12

1 Preheat the oven to 350° F. Oil and line the bases of two deep 8 inch, round cake pans with parchment paper.
2 Sift together into a large bowl the flour, sugar, baking soda, cocoa, and salt. In a separate bowl, mix together the liquid ingredients: the oil, vinegar, and vanilla extract, and add to the flour mixture. Stir until smooth.
3 Divide the mixture between the prepared pans, and use a palette knife or spatula to spread evenly. Bake in the oven for about 40 minutes, until risen and firm to the touch.
4 Cool in the pans for 10 minutes then turn out onto a wire rack, remove the parchment paper and let cool completely. Slice each cake in half horizontally.
5 Meanwhile, make the ganache following step 7 of the recipe on page 200. See right for chocolate buttercream variation.
6 Sandwich the cakes together using half the ganache or buttercream for the first three layers. Spread the remainder on the top and sides and rough up with a knife. Sprinkle with chocolate shavings or decorate with fresh berries.
Pictured opposite ▶

 gluten free

See overleaf for gluten-free recipe.

VARIATION For a less rich, more child-friendly frosting, make chocolate buttercream. Put ¾ cup dairy-free spread in a bowl and sift over 2⅔ cup confectioners' sugar and 6 tablespoons of unsweetened cocoa powder (nut-free, if required). Add 2 teaspoons of vanilla extract. Gradually work into the spread with a wooden spoon then beat well until smooth and fluffy.
  If you don't need to avoid dairy products, use butter or ordinary margarine, increasing the quantity to 1 cup. You may need to add 4 teaspoons of water to give the soft consistency needed for spreading.

Chocolate layer cake continued

gluten free

a little flavorless oil for cake pans
6 eggs
1½ cups superfine sugar
¾ cup butter or margarine, melted
½ tsp vanilla extract
1¾ cups soy flour
generous 1 cup potato flour

generous ½ cup gluten-free unsweetened cocoa powder
1½ tbsp gluten-free baking powder
2 tbsp milk

PREPARATION TIME 35 minutes
COOKING TIME 45 minutes
SERVES 10–12

WATCH OUT FOR intolerance to soy flour—if necessary, use gram or rice flour instead.

1 Preheat the oven to 325° F. Oil two deep 8 inch round cake pans and line the bases with parchment paper.
2 Break the eggs into a bowl and add the sugar. Place the bowl over a pan of gently simmering water and whisk with an electric whisk until thick and pale and the mixture leaves a trail when the whisk is lifted out of the mixture—this will take several minutes.
3 Remove the bowl from the pan. Gradually add the melted butter or margarine in a thin trail, whisking all the time. Whisk in the vanilla extract.
4 Sift the flours, cocoa, and baking powder over the surface. Add the milk. Gently fold in with a metal spoon, using a figure eight motion.
5 Divide the mixture between the prepared pans, and use a palette knife or spatula to spread evenly.
6 Bake in the oven for about 45 minutes, until risen and firm to the touch.
7 Cool in the pans for 10 minutes then turn out onto a wire rack, remove the parchment paper and let cool completely. Slice each cake in half horizontally.
8 Make a double quantity of ganache according to step 7 of the recipe on page 200 or make the buttercream frosting on page 196. Sandwich the cakes together using half the frosting. Spread the remainder on the top and sides and rough up with a knife. Sprinkle with chocolate shavings or decorate with fresh berries if preferred.

"If you need a super, fail-safe chocolate cake for any occasion, this is the one"

Rich fruit cake

This cake has wonderful richness and flavor and is packed with goodness. The grated apple also makes the texture extra-moist. Sprinkle it with raw sugar before baking for a lovely crunchy topping. If you want to adapt your own recipes, fruit cakes are a good place to start. Use the cooking tips in Substituting ingredients (p.48) or the versions below for inspiration.

nut free

a little nut-free vegetable oil, for the cake pan
1 dessert apple, grated, including the skin
3/4 cup softened butter or margarine
3/4 cup soft light brown sugar
3 eggs
2 cups all-purpose flour
a pinch of salt
1 1/2 tsp baking powder
1 1/2 tsp apple pie spice
1 1/3 cups mixed dried fruit
1/4 cup candied cherries, halved
1 tbsp raw sugar

PREPARATION TIME 10 minutes
COOKING TIME 1 1/2–1 3/4 hours
SERVES 8–10

1 Preheat the oven to 325° F. Oil and line a high-sided 7 inch deep cake pan with parchment paper.
2 Beat the apple with the butter or margarine and the soft brown sugar until light and fluffy.
3 Beat in the eggs, one at a time, beating well after each addition (this mixture will curdle a bit).
4 Sift the flour, salt, baking powder, and spice over the surface. Fold in with a metal spoon, then fold in the mixed dried fruit and cherries.
5 Transfer the mixture to the prepared pan and level the surface. Sprinkle with the raw sugar.
6 Bake in the oven until the cake is richly browned, firm to the touch, and a skewer inserted in the center comes out clean (1 1/2–1 3/4 hours). Let cool in the pan for 10 minutes, then turn out onto a wire rack, remove the parchment paper, and let cool completely. This cake keeps well stored in an airtight container.

TIP Fruit cakes are among the easiest of cake recipes to adapt to egg-free. Just replace each egg with 1 tablespoon of potato flour mixed with 3 tablespoons of water in your favorite fruit cake recipes.

dairy free
also nut free

Follow the nut-free recipe, but substitute dairy-free spread for the butter or margarine.

egg free
also nut free

Follow the nut-free recipe, but omit the eggs in step 3 and add 3 tablespoons of flavorless nut-free vegetable oil and 1 tablespoon of potato flour mixed with 3 tablespoons of water as an egg substitute. Increase the baking powder to 2 teaspoons and add with the other dry ingredients in step 4.

gluten free
also nut free

Follow the nut-free recipe, but for the all-purpose flour substitute an equal quantity of gluten-free flour or 1 cup brown rice flour and 1 cup soy flour and check that the baking powder is gluten free, too.

Dark chocolate torte

This rich chocolate torte, a close relation of the famous Sachertorte, is an elegant dark chocolate sponge, apricot-glazed and iced with bittersweet chocolate. A wonderfully decadent dessert for a dinner party, either on its own or with unsweetened lightly whipped or pouring cream (or nondairy alternative). Use chocolate with 70 percent cocoa solids to get the true richness or, otherwise, ordinary semisweet chocolate.

 gluten free

for the torte
1½ cups (6 oz) semisweet chocolate with 70 percent cocoa solids
½ cup unsalted butter plus a little extra for the pan
⅔ cup confectioners' sugar, sifted
scant 1½ cups ground almonds
5 eggs, separated

1 tbsp apricot conserve, strained
for the ganache
1 cup (4 oz) semisweet chocolate with 70 percent cocoa solids
½ cup heavy cream

PREPARATION TIME 45 minutes
COOKING TIME 30 minutes
SERVES 8–10

1 Preheat the oven to 375° F. Butter an 8 inch springform pan and line the base with parchment paper.
2 Break up the chocolate and place it in a bowl. Stand the bowl in a pan of simmering water and stir until the chocolate has melted. Alternatively, heat briefly in the microwave.
3 In a separate bowl, beat together the butter and confectioners' sugar until light and fluffy. Beat in the nuts, egg yolks, and chocolate.
4 Whisk the egg whites until stiff and fold in with a metal spoon.
5 Transfer to the prepared pan and smooth the surface. Bake in the oven until firm to the touch (about 30 minutes). Let cool in the pan for 10 minutes then remove the pan and transfer the torte to a wire rack to cool completely.
6 Warm the jam in a small saucepan.
7 Make the ganache. Break up the chocolate and place it in a separate pan with the cream. Heat gently, stirring all the time with a wooden spoon until thick. Let cool slightly until it is a thick, coating consistency.
8 Transfer the torte to a serving plate. Spread the top with the warmed jam. Spoon the ganache over, spreading it out with a palette knife so it coats the top and sides of the torte completely. Wipe the edge of the plate to clean up any excess chocolate. Leave to set but do not chill.

TIP I like to coat the torte on its plate since it saves disturbing it once it is finished, but if you prefer, you can coat the torte when it's on the cooling rack, then transfer it to a plate when set.

 dairy free
also gluten free

Follow the gluten-free recipe, but substitute dairy-free spread for the butter in the torte. For the ganache, increase the chocolate to 1¼ cups (5oz) and use 5 tablespoons of soy cream alternative in place of the heavy cream. Use dairy-free chocolate. If you can't tolerate soy, make a chocolate glacé icing. Melt very gently ¾ cup (3oz) chocolate with 1tbsp dairy-free spread and 3 tbsp of water. Gradually beat in 1⅓ cups sifted confectioners' sugar.

 egg free
also gluten free

Follow the gluten-free recipe, but omit the egg yolks and add 2 teaspoons of baking powder when adding the ground almonds. Whisk 3 tablespoons of potato flour with 1 teaspoon of xanthan gum and ⅔ cup water until white and softly peaking and substitute for the egg whites.

nut free
also gluten free

Follow the gluten-free recipe, but substitute 2 cups fine nut-free breadcrumbs or nut-free sponge cake crumbs for the ground almonds.

Peach-topped cheesecake

This is a lovely deli-style cheesecake with a glossy fruit topping. It is simple to make, with no cooking in the oven involved. It lends itself well to variations—change the cookie base and topping to taste. Try coconut cookies with a mango nectar topping, or a gingernut base with a berry topping. There are many combinations, just be sure to use the thick "nectar" style of juice.

 ## egg & nut free

for the base
1½ cups graham crackers
   (nut free and egg free)
scant ⅓ cup butter, melted, plus
   a little extra for the cake pan

for the filling
1 tbsp powdered gelatin
generous 1 cup peach nectar
½ cup superfine sugar
1⅔ cups cream cheese
1 vanilla pod, split
1 tbsp lemon juice
generous 1 cup heavy cream

for the peach topping
1 tbsp cornstarch
1 tbsp superfine sugar
2 tsp lemon juice
generous 1 cup peach nectar

PREPARATION TIME 20 minutes
   plus chilling time
SERVES 6–8

1 Butter an 8 inch springform cake pan and line the base with parchment paper. In a food processor, crush the graham crackers to crumbs then add the melted butter and process again briefly to combine. Press into the prepared pan and chill for 30 minutes.

2 Make the filling. Sprinkle the gelatin over 5 tablespoons of the peach nectar in a small bowl. Stir well. Let soften for 5 minutes then stand the bowl in a pan of gently simmering water and stir until dissolved completely. Stir in the remaining peach nectar. Let cool.

3 Place the sugar and cream cheese in a large bowl and beat together using an electric whisk. Split the vanilla pod lengthwise and scrape its contents into the bowl. Pour in the lemon juice, peach nectar, and gelatin mixture and whisk well to combine. Lightly whip the cream until softly peaking and fold in with a metal spoon. Spoon the filling over the graham cracker base and chill overnight, or for at least 4 hours until set.

4 Make the peach topping. Place the cornstarch and sugar in a small saucepan. Blend in the lemon juice, the nectar and stir well. Bring to a boil and boil for 1 minute, stirring constantly, until thickened and smooth. Remove immediately from the heat. Allow to cool slightly before spreading carefully over the cheesecake.

5 Chill again before serving.

dairy free
also egg & nut free

Follow the recipe on the left, but replace the butter used in the base with an equal quantity of dairy-free spread. Increase the gelatin from 1 to 1½ tablespoons. Replace the cream cheese with an equal quantity of soy cream cheese alternative and the heavy cream with an equal quantity of soy cream alternative (which will not whip as thickly as dairy cream). For a firmer cheesecake, increase the gelatin to 2 tablespoons.

gluten free
also egg & nut free

Follow the recipe on the left, but make sure that the graham crackers used in the base are gluten-free.

TIP This is not a cheesecake to leave out on a hot day—it will turn into a fruit mousse cake! Make sure you chill it well to set before serving.

Carrot cake

A luxurious carrot cake is as celebratory as any fruit cake. It is lightly spiced with nutmeg, allspice, and cinnamon and crammed full of luscious ingredients from pineapple and coconut to brown sugar and raisins. Using both puréed and raw carrots makes the cake delectably moist, and you can use pine nuts instead of the usual walnuts. It's delicious with or without its classic vanilla cream cheese topping.

nut free

for the cake
4 cups self-rising flour
2 tsp baking powder
2 tsp ground cinnamon
¼ tsp grated nutmeg
½ tsp ground allspice
1 cup soft dark brown sugar
generous 1 cup flavorless
   nut-free vegetable oil
3 eggs, lightly beaten
2 cups cooked carrots,
   cooled and mashed
1 cup grated raw carrot
1 cup pine nuts, lightly
   toasted and roughly chopped,
   if tolerated (optional)
⅔ cup golden raisins

½ cup shredded coconut,
   if tolerated
½ cup canned crushed pineapple,
   drained
finely grated zest of 1 orange

for the topping
generous 1 cup cream cheese
3 cups confectioners' sugar
generous ¾ cup unsalted butter
1 tsp vanilla extract

to decorate
finely pared zest of 1 orange
a sprinkling of ground cinnamon

PREPARATION TIME 15 minutes
COOKING TIME 1¼–1½ hours
SERVES 12

1 Preheat the oven to 350° F. Line a 9 inch springform pan with parchment paper.
2 Sift together the flour, baking powder, cinnamon, nutmeg, and allspice. Add the brown sugar and mix well.
3 Add the oil, beaten eggs, carrot purée, raw carrot, pine nuts (if used), raisins, coconut, pineapple, and orange zest. Mix well. It should be like a very thick, wet dough. Alternatively, combine all the ingredients in a food processor and mix thoroughly.
4 Spoon the mixture into the pan. Place in the oven and bake until a skewer inserted in the center comes out clean and the edges pull away from the sides of the pan, about 1¼–1½ hours.
5 Cool the cake in the pan for 15 minutes, then release the cake onto a wire rack, remove the paper, and let cool. The top may look cracked but it will be covered by the topping.
6 To make the topping, put all the ingredients into a food processor and blend until smooth, about 1 minute. Smooth over the top and sides of the cold cake. To decorate, sprinkle with orange zest and cinnamon. Chill, if necessary, to firm up the topping.

dairy free
also nut free

The cake is dairy free. For the topping (pictured opposite), use soy-based cream cheese alternative for the cream cheese and dairy-free spread for the butter. If necessary, add a little more confectioners' sugar. This version needs to be refrigerated since the topping will soften if left too long at room temperature.

egg free
also nut free

Follow the recipe on the left, but increase the baking powder to 2 tablespoons. Add the juice of the orange as well as the zest, and substitute 3 tablespoons of potato flour, mixed with 6 tablespoons of water, for the eggs.
◀ Pictured opposite
With a dairy-free topping, it is also suitable for vegans.

gluten free
also nut free

Follow the recipe on the left, but use gluten-free all-purpose flour for the self-rising flour and increase the baking powder to 3 tablespoons (make sure it is gluten free).

Fresh fruit & cream gâteau

This is a party dessert to delight friends and family—towering layers of vanilla cake, sandwiched with sweetened whipped cream, nectarines, and figs. You can use any soft, seasonal fruit—berries work particularly well. As with the Chocolate layer cake (p.196), you bake it in two pans, then split the layers, fill, layer, and top it. And yes, that is the egg-free version in the picture!

 egg & nut free

for the cake
3½ cups all-purpose flour
1¾ cups superfine sugar
1¾ tsp baking soda
¼ tsp salt
scant ½ cup flavorless nut
  free oil, plus a little extra for
  the cake pans
1½ tbsp white vinegar
2 tsp vanilla extract
2 cups milk

for the filling and topping
1⅓ cups heavy cream
2 tbsp confectioners' sugar, plus
  extra for dusting
3 large ripe peaches, pitted and
  sliced
1 ripe fig, quartered

PREPARATION TIME 35 minutes
COOKING TIME 40 minutes
SERVES 10–12

1 Preheat the oven to 350° F. Oil two deep 8 inch cake pans and line the bases with parchment paper.
2 Sift together into a large bowl the flour, sugar, baking soda, and salt. In a separate bowl mix the oil, vinegar, vanilla extract, and milk together and add to the flour mixture. Stir until smooth.
3 Divide the mixture between the prepared pans (it will be quite runny). Bake in the oven until risen and firm to the touch (about 40 minutes).
4 Cool in the pans for 10 minutes then turn out onto a wire rack, remove the parchment paper and let cool completely.
5 Make the filling and topping. Whip the cream with the confectioners' sugar until softly peaking.
6 Select about a third of the best-looking peach slices and reserve for decoration.
7 Split each cake in half horizontally. Put one piece on a serving plate. Top with a quarter of the cream then a third of the peaches not reserved for decoration. Repeat the layers then top with the last piece of cake and smother with the remaining cream. Decorate with the reserved peach slices and figs. Chill until ready to serve. Dust with a little confectioners' sugar, if liked, just before serving.
Pictured opposite ▶

 dairy free
also egg & nut free

Follow the recipe on the left, but use soy, rice, or oat milk instead of the cow's milk. For the filling and topping use 1½ quantities of dairy-free Chantilly topping (p.216) in place of the whipped cream and confectioners' sugar.

gluten free
also nut free

See overleaf for gluten-free recipe.

VARIATION Try using other fruit such as raspberries and nectarines for the filling and decoration. *Physalis* (Cape gooseberries, shown right) make a pretty garnish.

Fresh fruit & cream gâteau continued

 gluten free
also nut free

for the cake
a little flavorless nut-free oil
  for the cake pans
6 eggs
1½ cups superfine sugar
¾ cup butter or margarine,
  melted
½ tsp vanilla extract
2 cups soy flour
1½ cups potato flour
1½ tbsp gluten-free baking
  powder
2 tbsp milk

PREPARATION TIME 35 minutes
COOKING TIME 45 minutes
SERVES 10–12

1 Preheat the oven to 325° F. Oil two deep 8 inch cake pans and
  line the bases with parchment paper.
2 Break the eggs into a bowl and add the sugar. Place the bowl
  over a pan of gently simmering water and whisk with an electric
  whisk until thick and pale and the mixture leaves a trail when
  the whisk is lifted out—this will take several minutes.
3 Remove the bowl from the pan. Gradually add in the melted
  butter or margarine in a thin trail, whisking all the time. Whisk
  in the vanilla extract.
4 Sift the flours and baking powder over the surface. Add the
  milk. Gently fold in with a metal spoon, using a figure
  eight motion.
5 Divide the mixture between the prepared pans and level the
  surfaces. Bake in the oven until risen and firm to the touch
  (about 45 minutes).
6 Cool in the pans for 10 minutes then turn out onto a wire rack,
  remove the parchment paper and let cool completely.
7 Make the filling and topping as described on page 204.
  Split the cakes, sandwich them together, and decorate.
8 Chill until ready to serve. Dust with a little confectioners' sugar,
  if desired, just before serving.

Chocolate truffles

This is more one for the grown ups with its slightly sophisticated dark chocolate taste. Truffles are a delightful way to finish a meal. Serve on a pretty dish or, if you can get petit four papers (like mini- muffin liners) to put them in, so much the better. Wrapped in colored or glittery paper, truffles make excellent presents too, especially with a liqueur to suit the occasion.

egg, gluten, & nut free

2 cups (8oz) semisweet chocolate with at least 70 percent cocoa solids, nut-free and/or gluten-free, if necessary
generous ½ cup heavy cream
1 tbsp liqueur of choice such as Grand Marnier or brandy (optional)
⅓ cup confectioners' sugar, sifted
¼ cup unsweetened cocoa powder, nut-free and/or gluten-free, if necessary

PREPARATION TIME 15–20 minutes
COOKING TIME 5 minutes
MAKES 20 truffles

1 Chop the chocolate into ¼ inch pieces. Place the pieces in a heatproof bowl.
2 Heat the cream in a saucepan to just below boiling point and pour onto the chocolate pieces. Leave for 5 minutes.
3 Use an electric whisk to whisk the chocolate and cream together until there are no lumps. Whisk in the liqueur, if using, and the confectioners' sugar. Let the mixture cool then chill until it is beginning to firm.
4 Use a soup spoon to scoop out the truffle mixture. Roll the mixture in the palm of your hands into ¾ inch balls. Roll each one carefully in cocoa powder. Place on a plate or in petit four paper liners. Chill until firm.

TIP I tend to use clear liqueurs for this purpose because they have a more intense flavor than creamy ones.

dairy free
also egg, gluten, & nut free

Follow the recipe on the left, but make sure that the chocolate is dairy free. Use a soy cream alternative for the heavy cream and if you are using a liqueur make sure it is dairy free.

WATCH OUT FOR liqueurs that contain ingredients to be avoided. Avoid amaretto and nut-containing liquors for the nut-free version; grain-based liqueurs, such as whisky and vodka, if making gluten-free truffles; cream-based concoctions such as Baileys if making dairy-free truffles; and in the unlikely event you are going to put Advocaat into your chocolate truffles, please don't serve them to egg-allergics.

Béchamel sauce

The classic French béchamel sauce is a base ingredient for many recipes, from Lasagne al forno (p.136) to Moussaka (p.128), and for making savory Crêpes (p.162). It is worth taking the trouble to make it well; infusing the cloves and vegetables in the milk makes a real difference to the taste. It keeps well in the refrigerator so make double the quantity if you need to.

 **egg & nut free**

2 cups milk
1 onion, peeled, halved, and
 studded with two whole cloves
6 peppercorns
4 parsley stalks
3 tbsp butter
¼ cup all-purpose flour
2 tbsp light cream
salt and freshly ground black
 pepper

PREPARATION TIME 20 minutes
COOKING TIME 10–15 minutes
 plus 20 minutes to infuse
SERVES 4–6

1 Place the milk, clove-studded onion, peppercorns, and parsley stalks in a saucepan. Bring to a boil, simmer for 10 minutes and remove from the heat. Let infuse for 20 minutes before straining the milk back into a saucepan and discarding the vegetables.
2 Melt the butter on low heat in a separate saucepan. Add the flour. Mix well and cook for about 2 minutes taking care not to let the butter and flour mixture brown. Bring the infused milk to a simmer.
3 Keeping the flour and butter mixture on a low heat, add in the milk gradually, using a whisk to ensure there are no lumps. When all the milk has been incorporated, simmer the sauce on a very low heat for 8–10 minutes to get rid of any lingering floury taste, stirring constantly with a wooden spoon.
4 Stir in the cream. Season to taste with salt and pepper. If keeping for later, cover with a circle of wet waxed paper.

TIPS You can make a quick basic white sauce by omitting step 1 and adding a sachet of bouquet garni to the pan in step 3 before simmering the sauce. If a thinner pouring sauce is needed, add more warmed milk or stock in step 3.

 dairy free
also egg & nut free

Follow the recipe on the left, but use nondairy spread instead of the butter; soy, rice, or oat milk in place of the cow's milk; and use soy cream alternative instead of the cream.

 gluten free
also egg & nut free

Follow the recipe on the left, but use ¼ cup of a gluten-free flour mix or a half and half mix of rice flour and cornstarch.

Roast garlic tofu aïoli

I know I've included recipes for classic mayonnaise but this aïoli, safe for anyone with a nut, egg, or dairy allergy or a gluten intolerance, was just too good to leave out. Use in the same way you would a garlicky, flavorsome sauce or mayonnaise—in sandwiches, dips, on roasted vegetables, or stirred into soups. Or use the roast garlic purée on its own as a delicious topping for Crostini (p.72–73).

dairy, egg, gluten, & nut free

for the roast garlic purée
4 heads garlic
1 tsp fresh thyme (optional)
1 bay leaf (optional)
scant ¹⁄₂ cup olive oil or
  vegetable/chicken stock

for the roast garlic tofu aïoli
¹⁄₄ quantity roast garlic purée
  (see above)
1³⁄₄ cups firm silken tofu
2 tbsp light (sweet) miso paste
¹⁄₂ cup lemon juice
1–2 tbsp water or olive oil
  to thin
salt and freshly ground black
  pepper to taste

PREPARATION TIME 5 minutes plus
  1–1¹⁄₂ hours for roasting the garlic
SERVES 6–8
MAKES 2 cups

TIPS The aïoli has a slightly softer texture, with less hold to it than mayonnaise made with eggs.

If using olive oil for roasting the garlic, keep it to use as garlic-flavored oil for roasting potatoes or other vegetables.

WATCH OUT FOR bouillon cubes, which may contain traces of dairy or gluten, if you're cooking for people with severe dairy or gluten sensitivities.

1 Preheat the oven to 350° F.
2 To make the garlic purée, slice off the top ¹⁄₂ inch of the garlic heads and discard.
3 Pack the garlic heads snugly in a small ovenproof dish, scatter the thyme over and tuck in the bay leaf if using. Pour the oil or stock over.
4 Cover tightly and put in the oven.
5 Bake for 1–1¹⁄₂ hours or until the heads are soft.
6 Remove from the oven and let cool.
7 Squeeze the garlic cloves from their skins and process to a purée in a food processor. At this stage, the garlic purée can be stored, covered, in the refrigerator for up to a week.
8 To make the roast garlic tofu aïoli, process the garlic purée, tofu, miso paste, and lemon juice to mayonnaise consistency in a food processor. If necessary, use water or olive oil to thin to the desired consistency.
9 Season to taste with salt and pepper.

Mayonnaise

It seemed a good idea to give a recipe for mayonnaise, since many commercial brands contain dairy, gluten, and even nuts. Naturally, a homemade one doesn't. There's a super egg-free version too.

 **dairy, gluten, & nut free**

1 egg
1 tsp Dijon mustard
¼ tsp salt
5 tbsp olive oil
5 tbsp nut-free
   vegetable oil

1 tsp lemon juice
1 tsp white wine vinegar

PREPARATION TIME 10 minutes
MAKES generous 1 cup

1 Break the egg into a food processor. Add the mustard and salt. Run the machine briefly to mix.
2 Measure the oils in a measuring cup. With the machine running, trickle the oil in a thin, gradual stream. It will be runny at first, then will thicken. When about three-quarters of the oil is added, add the lemon juice and vinegar and then add the remaining oil in a slightly faster stream. Taste and add a little more salt, if liked.
3 Store in an airtight container in the refrigerator. Use as required.

egg free
also dairy, gluten, & nut free

2 tbsp potato flour
½ tsp xanthan gum
4 tbsp water
¼ tsp gluten-free mustard
½ cup olive oil
1 tbsp lemon juice
1 tsp white wine vinegar
½ tsp superfine sugar
salt and white pepper

Mix the potato flour, gum, and water in a food processor until white and peaking. Beat in the mustard. Now follow the recipe on the left from step 2, adding the sugar and seasoning with the lemon juice and vinegar.

Vietnamese dipping sauce

This indispensable seasoning and dipping sauce can be found on every table in Vietnam—its tangy sour-sweet flavor is addictive. Thai cuisine has a similar one, often garnished with fresh green herbs.

dairy, egg, gluten, & nut free

2 tbsp fresh lime juice
2 tbsp sugar (palm sugar if
   preferred)
4 tbsp rice vinegar
4 tbsp fish sauce
2 garlic cloves, crushed

½ red chili, seeded and finely
   chopped

PREPARATION TIME 5 minutes
MAKES about ¾ cup

1 Place all the ingredients in a food processor and process for 30–45 seconds. If a foamy head forms on top don't worry, just pour the sauce out and discard the foam.
2 Serve in small open bowls as a dipping sauce.

VARIATION To create an attractive Asian pickle, peel and julienne a carrot and ½ a daikon or mouli (white radish) and mix with the dipping sauce.

WATCH OUT FOR chilies, since some people can't tolerate them.

Pesto

The famous Genoese basil and pine nut sauce has many uses. Serve with pasta, stirred into rice salads, or in sandwiches. It works just as well without cheese.

 egg, gluten, & nut free

1 cup fresh basil leaves
$1/3$ cup pine nuts
2 garlic cloves, crushed
scant $1/4$ cup grated Parmesan
1 cup extra virgin
  olive oil
salt and pepper to season

PREPARATION TIME 10 minutes
MAKES about 2 cups

1 In a food processor, process the basil leaves, pine nuts, garlic, and Parmesan for about 30 seconds to form a rough paste.
2 Add the oil in a thin stream through the top or funnel with the food processor still running. You should have a thick paste. If it seems too dry add 1–2 tablespoons more oil. Season to taste.

dairy free
also egg, gluten, & nut free

Follow the recipe on the left, but substitute the Parmesan with an equal quantity of dairy-free cheese or omit altogether for cheeseless pesto as shown on page 172 (with focaccia).

WATCH OUT FOR pine nuts, which are classified as a seed rather than a nut. Most people allergic to tree nuts and peanuts can eat pine nuts, but check before serving to them.

Red pepper dip

This dip is based on the Syrian-Turkish specialty *Muhammara*. Some people prefer it thick and pastelike, others prefer a dipping consistency. Serve with flat breads, vegetables, or as a sauce for grilled meats.

dairy & egg free

3 red bell peppers, seeded
2 tbsp nut-free oil for roasting
1 small chili, seeded
1 slice of bread
$3/4$ cup shelled walnuts
$1/2$ clove of garlic, peeled
$1 1/2$ tbsp pomegranate molasses
2 tsp lemon juice
$1/2$–1 tsp salt

$1/2$ tsp ground cumin
5 tbsp olive oil
water to thin (optional)
1 tbsp finely chopped fresh parsley
  to garnish

PREPARATION TIME 5 minutes plus
  cooking time for peppers
SERVES 6

1 Preheat the oven to 350° F. Roast the peppers in the oil for 40 minutes, until they are soft.
2 In a food processor, blend the peppers and the oil they were roasted in with the chili, bread, walnuts, garlic, pomegranate molasses, lemon juice, salt, cumin, and olive oil until smooth.
3 Thin with water if required and garnish with parsley.

 nut free
also dairy & egg free

Follow the recipe on the left, but use lightly toasted pine nuts instead of walnuts (see warning in above recipe).

 gluten free
also dairy & egg free

Follow the recipe on the left, but use an equal quantity of gluten-free bread.

WATCH OUT FOR chilies, since some people can't tolerate them.

Asian slaw

This is coleslaw with a Southeast Asian twist. Shredded cabbage and carrot is dressed with a tangy sweet and sour sauce and garnished with mint. The Vietnamese love it with grilled or poached chicken, either as a street café snack or made at home. For canapés, try a couple of spoonfuls heaped onto Japanese rice crackers, topped with a cilantro sprig. It is pictured on page 125 with Vietnamese beef stew.

dairy, egg, gluten, & nut free

for the dressing
1 tbsp rice vinegar
2 tbsp superfine or palm sugar
3 tbsp fresh lime juice
2 garlic cloves, crushed
½ red chili, seeded,
  and finely chopped
3 tbsp fish sauce
4 tbsp flavorless nut-free oil
freshly ground black pepper
for the salad
7 oz Chinese or small hard white
  cabbage, shredded

3 oz carrots, grated or ribboned
  (with a potato peeler)
2 scallions, thinly sliced
3 tbsp chopped fresh mint leaves
cilantro sprigs to garnish (optional)

PREPARATION TIME 10 minutes
SERVES 4 as a side dish

1 In a food processor, process the rice vinegar, sugar, lime juice, garlic, chili, and fish sauce for 30 seconds or until the sugar is dissolved. Add the oil and black pepper and process briefly to combine.
2 Just before serving, combine the cabbage and carrot in a bowl, pour the dressing over and mix well. Stir in the scallions and chopped mint leaves and garnish with cilantro if using.

SERVING SUGGESTIONS For a light lunch or supper, top Asian slaw with strips of grilled chicken and sprinkle with sesame seeds (if tolerated). Serve with French bread (pp.170–171).
   Serve on rice or shrimp crackers as a predinner canapé or as a side salad with Vietnamese beef stew (p.125) or any Asian-style braised or grilled meat.

WATCH OUT FOR chili because some people can't tolerate it.

"This piquant, fresh-tasting salad is perfect for the dark days of winter"

Raita

Raita is a cooling south Asian condiment based on yogurt and is usually served alongside spicy dishes. This one has cucumber and cumin seeds and works well with grilled meats, fish, and curries.

 egg, gluten, & nut free

2 tsp cumin seeds
4-in piece cucumber, peeled
  and finely diced
1¼ cups plain or Greek-style
  yogurt
salt and freshly ground black
  pepper

PREPARATION TIME 10 minutes
SERVES 4–6

1 Toast the cumin seeds in a dry heavy-bottomed frying pan over a medium heat for about 2 minutes, until they release their fragrance. Tip out of the pan onto a plate to prevent further cooking and let cool.
2 Mix the cucumber and yogurt together in a small bowl and season with salt and pepper. Sprinkle the cumin seeds on top.

dairy free
also egg, gluten, & nut free

Follow the recipe on the left, but substitute soy yogurt alternative for the cow's milk yogurt.

SERVING SUGGESTION Serve with Tandoori fish (p.98).

Tarragon dressing

This is a simple, creamy dressing that works really well on a salad, served with chicken, fish, or vegetables. I particularly like it on a chicken and avocado salad with baby spinach leaves.

egg, gluten, & nut free

6 tbsp olive oil
1 garlic clove, crushed (optional)
2 tsp superfine sugar
finely grated zest and juice of
  1 lemon
4 tbsp light cream
3 tbsp chopped fresh tarragon

good pinch of salt
good grinding of freshly ground
  black pepper

PREPARATION TIME 10 minutes
MAKES about ¾ cup

1 Put all the ingredients in a clean, screw-topped jar.
2 Shake vigorously until thoroughly blended. Chill for at least 1 hour to allow the flavors to develop. Use as required. The dressing will keep in the refrigerator for up to 1 week.

dairy free
also egg, gluten, & nut free

Follow the recipe on the left, but substitute soy cream alternative for light cream.

Chestnut stuffing

Rich, flavorful, and traditional, creamy chestnut stuffing is perfect for a festive roast bird since it complements but doesn't overpower the meal. Chestnuts are botanically nuts, but most people with nut allergies can tolerate them. If you already know you can eat chestnuts, you can continue doing so. If you can't or are not sure, use the variation at the bottom of the recipe.

 ### egg & nut free

1 cup cooked chestnuts, peeled
¾ cup (6 oz) pork sausage
1 cup fresh white breadcrumbs
2 shallots or 1 small onion, very finely chopped
2 tbsp chopped fresh parsley
½ tsp salt
a good grating of nutmeg
freshly ground black pepper
2 tbsp butter, melted
2–3 tbsp light cream

PREPARATION TIME 10 minutes
COOKING TIME 15–20 minutes
SERVES 4–6

1 Drop the chestnuts into a food processor and finely chop (or do it by hand).
2 Mix with the remaining ingredients, adding enough cream to bind the mixture. Use to stuff the neck end of the bird. (Never put stuffing in the body cavity since it prevents air from circulating and therefore the bird from cooking. Also, the stuffing may be undercooked.) Or, for stuffing balls, roll into 12–15 walnut-sized 1-inch balls. Place on a lightly oiled baking tray and roast in the oven for 15–20 minutes, turning once.

WATCH OUT FOR chestnuts. Most people with a nut allergy can tolerate them, but if in any doubt, see the variation below.

VARIATION Chestnuts can be easily replaced with the same quantity of dried apricots or a mix of dried apricots and prunes.
   You can also make this stuffing without sausage using 2 cups of chestnuts and 2 cups of breadcrumbs. Use this version to stuff the bird rather than as stuffing balls.

 ### dairy free
also egg & nut free

Follow the recipe on the left, but substitute dairy-free spread for the butter and use soy cream alternative in place of the cream.

 ### gluten free
also egg & nut free

Follow the recipe on the left, but substitute stale (or lightly toasted) gluten-free breadcrumbs for the ordinary ones. If using with sausage, make sure the sausage is gluten-free too. Please note that this version makes a smaller quantity than the others since gluten-free bread is denser.
◀ Pictured on pages 112–113

TIP I use cooked chestnuts—either vacuum-packed or canned—for this recipe, but you could cook your own. To do so, you'll need about 1 lb of chestnuts. Slit the skin on one side of each chestnut and boil in water until tender, for about 20 minutes. Leave in the pan to cool slightly, then remove them from the pan, one at a time, and peel off the shell and inner skin.

Vegetable gravy

This is for when you'd like some luscious gravy but until you've roasted or grilled the meat, you don't have any juices to make it with. If you don't want a last-minute rush, it can be easier to make some in advance. The browned vegetables and seasonings gives this gravy plenty of depth and flavor and it's vegetarian-friendly too.

dairy, egg, gluten, & nut free

1 tbsp flavorless nut-free
  vegetable oil
1 onion, chopped
1 carrot, chopped
1 celery stick, chopped
1 tsp soft dark brown sugar
1 bay leaf
1 tsp mustard powder
1 tsp Worcestershire sauce
2 cups vegetable stock,
  made with vegetable cooking
  water, or plain water

2 tsp vegetable stock powder
1–2 tbsp cornstarch
1–2 tbsp water
salt and freshly ground black pepper

PREPARATION TIME 15 minutes
COOKING TIME 11 minutes
SERVES 4

1 Heat the oil in a saucepan. Add the vegetables and fry, stirring, until lightly golden, 3 minutes.
2 Add the sugar and continue to fry the mixture over medium heat, stirring all the time, for 5 minutes, until richly browned. Take care not to let it burn.
3 Add the bay leaf, mustard powder, and Worcestershire sauce and stir in the stock or water and stock powder. Bring to a boil, stirring. Reduce the heat and simmer gently until the vegetables are really soft, about 10 minutes.
4 For smooth, glossy gravy, strain the liquid then return it to the rinsed-out saucepan. Blend the cornstarch with the water and stir into the liquid (use the smaller quantities for thinner gravy, the larger ones for thicker gravy). Bring to a boil and boil for 1 minute, stirring. Season to taste.

WATCH OUT FOR Worcestershire sauce and mustard since they can contain gluten. Make sure you use a gluten-free version, if necessary. Also, check that your stock is gluten free and/or dairy free, as need be.

SAUCES, DRESSINGS, & ACCOMPANIMENTS

Chantilly topping

Chantilly is cream that has been whipped and sweetened and flavored with vanilla. Below is a delicious problem-solving version for dairy avoiders to use wherever a recipe calls for whipped cream.

🍶 🥚 🌾 🥜 dairy, egg, gluten, and nut free

2 tsp powdered gelatin
2 tsp water
1 cup soy alternative to light cream
2 tbsp confectioners' sugar, sifted
1 tsp vanilla extract

PREPARATION TIME 10 minutes plus chilling time
MAKES generous 1 cup

1 Sprinkle the gelatin over the water in a small heatproof bowl. Let soften for 5 minutes. Stand the bowl in a pan of gently simmering water and stir until dissolved completely.
2 Whip the soy cream in a food mixer or with an electric or hand whisk to incorporate air and thickness.
3 Whisk in the sugar then the gelatin and the vanilla extract and chill for about 40 minutes, until just set. Whisk again just before using to fluff up the topping.
Pictured opposite ▶

VARIATION The standard, dairy-based Chantilly cream is also egg, gluten, and nut free. Whip 1 cup of heavy cream. As it starts to thicken, add 1–2 tablespoons of sifted confectioners' sugar and ½ teaspoon of vanilla extract and whisk again to incorporate.

TIP For a vanilla bean-flecked topping, split ¼ of a vanilla pod, scrape the contents into the topping, and mix.

Cashew cream

This is another tasty and useful cream for topping fresh fruit and desserts or to stir into soups for added richness. It is the consistency of thick heavy cream but is dairy free.

🍶 🥚 🌾 dairy, egg, & gluten free

for the cashew cream
½ cup unsalted cashews
½ cup water
for sweet cashew cream
½ tsp vanilla extract
¼ tsp maple syrup

PREPARATION TIME 5 minutes
MAKES about ¾ cup

1 In a food processor blend the cashews and half the water to a thick paste (about 2 minutes), stopping and scraping down the sides as necessary.
2 Slowly add the remaining water through the funnel or top and blend until smooth (about 2 minutes). To make sweet cashew cream, blend in the vanilla extract and maple syrup.

nut free
also dairy, egg, & gluten free

It would be impossible to make a nut-free cashew cream. Use ordinary heavy cream, soy cream substitute, or Chantilly topping (see above).

TIP Thin with a little extra water if a thinner cream is required.

Resources

SUPPORT ORGANIZATIONS

Allergy & Asthma Network Mothers of Asthmatics (AANMA)
Tel: (800) 878-4403
www.aanma.org
A national nonprofit network of families whose goal is to overcome, not cope, with allergies and asthma. AANMA produces practical and livable alternatives with a magazine, e-news updates, toll-free help, and community awareness programs.

American Academy of Allergy Asthma & Immunology
Tel: (414) 272-6071
info@aaaai.org
www.aaaai.org
The largest professional medical specialty organization in the US representing allergists, immunologists, and other health professionals. AAAAI also provides resources for patients and health-care professionals.

The American Dietetic Association
Tel: (800) 877-1600
www.eatright.org
The largest US organization of food and nutrition professionals.

Anaphylaxis Canada
Tel: (416) 785-5666
www.anaphylaxis.org
Answers questions about life-threatening allergic reactions and provides support groups for those at risk of anaphylaxis in Canada.

The Asthma and Allergy Foundation of America (AAFA)
Tel: 800-727-8462
info@aafa.org
www.aafa.org
AAFA, a nonprofit organization, provides practical information, community-based services, and support through a national network of chapters and support groups.

Canadian Allergy, Asthma and Immunology Foundation
Tel: (613) 730-6272
www.allergyfoundation.ca
Offers information about various allergies, including those related to food.

Canadian Celiac Association
Tel: (800) 363-7296
www.celiac.ca
Provides services and support for persons suffering from gluten intolerance.

Canadian Diabetes Association
Tel: (800) 226-8464
www.diabetes.ca
The website offers nutrition guides, meal plans and tips for healthy eating, and information on diabetes prevention and management, all concerns that are relevant to people on restricted diets due to serious food allergies.

Celiac Disease Foundation
Tel: (818) 990-2354
cdf@celiac.org
www.celiac.org
CDF provides support, information, and assistance to people affected by celiac disease and dermatitis herpetiformis. The foundation also increases awareness among the general public and works closely with health-care professionals.

Dietitians of Canada
Tel: (416) 596-0857
www.dietitians.ca
This association is committed to promoting health through food and nutrition.

Food Allergies in the Real World
www.faanteen.org
Part of the Food Allergy & Anaphylaxis Network (FAAN), this website is designed for young adults who want to take a more active role in managing their food allergies.

The Food Allergy & Anaphylaxis Network (FAAN)
Tel: (800) 929-4040
faan@foodallergy.org
www.foodallergy.org
FAAN, a nonprofit organization, raises public awareness and provides advocacy and education to advance research on behalf of all those affected by food allergies and anaphylaxis.

Food Allergy News For Kids
www.fankids.org
Part of the Food Allergy & Anaphylaxis Network (FAAN), this website contains food allergy news for kids.

USEFUL FOOD SUPPLIERS

Amy's Kitchen
Tel: (707) 578-7270
www.amyskitchen.com
An online company that sells organic, dairy-free, frozen entrees.

Amazon.com
Through their partners, Amazon.com sells most of the popular brands of soy milk and rice milk products.

Asian Food Grocer
Tel: (888) 482-2742
info@asianfoodgrocer.com
www.asianfoodgrocer.com
This is an excellent online site for Japanese and other Asian ingredients including miso, short-grain rices, nori, and soft and firm tofu.

Authentic Foods
Tel: (310) 366-7612
sales@authenticfoods.com
www.authenticfoods.com
Makers of natural, preservative-free and gluten-free foods, Authentic Foods is an online resource with local stores in many states as well.

Gluten-free Pantry
Tel: (800) 291-8386
pantry@glutenfree.com
www.glutenfree.com
This website caters to people with celiac disease, wheat and gluten intolerance, and wheat allergies. Products available online include breads, cookies, pastas, cooking and baking ingredients, condiments, sauces, and cereals.

Rosewood
Tel: (734) 665-2222
rosewood@chartermi.net
www.mi-way.com
Online site for various flavors of tofu cheeses including cheddar, mozzarella, and Monterey Jack.

Tofutti
Tel: (908) 272-2400
info@tofutti.com
www.tofutti.com
Dairy-free products with a wide range of tofu-based products including soy-based nondairy ice cream, nondairy cream cheese, and nondairy sour cream. Good for recipes such as aïoli (p.209).

The Vegan Store
Tel: (800) 340-1200
info@veganstore.com
www.veganstore.com
An online provider of dairy alternatives including nondairy cheeses, nondairy butter, soy milk, egg alternatives, heavy cream substitute, silken tofu, and baking supplies.

Whole Foods Market
Locations throughout the US and Canada
www.wholefoodsmarket.com
With locations in most states and in Canada, this grocery store is an excellent source for gluten-free products as well as dairy substitutes and nut-free foods. Whole Foods Market does not take online orders.

BOOKS

Let's Eat Out: Your Passport to Living Gluten and Allergy Free. Kim Koeller and Robert La France. R&R Publishing.
www.allergyfreepassport.com
Good book for celiacs and its associated website is a great source of links and information.

Understanding and Managing Your Child's Food Allergies
Scott H. Sicherer, MD
John Hopkins Press
This book helps parents learn how to recognize emergency situations, understand allergy test results, and how to protect children at home and away.

Index

Page numbers in *italics* indicate illustrations.

A

additives, food 17–18
aïoli, Roast garlic tofu aïoli 209
allergies *see* food allergies; specific allergens (eg eggs)
anaphylaxis 15, 18, 19
anchovies
  Tapenade 73
  Vitello tonnato 120
antigens 15
apples
  Apple crumble 146
  Apple tart *148*, 149
  Cinnamon, raisin, & apple muffins *61*, 62
  Duck with apples & celeriac 115
  apricots
  Apricot and mango smoothie *20*, 59, *60*
  Fragrant poached peaches variation 151
arugula, Pasta with arugula *140*, 141
Asian salsa verde 99
Asian slaw 212
atopy 16
avocados
  California hand-roll temaki sushi *34*, 74, *75*
  Guacamole 77
  Salsa 70
  Seven-layer dip *82*, 83

B

Bacon & onion quiche 84
Banana oatie smoothie *20*, 59, *60*
Basmati & wild rice pilaf 144
beans
  Chili con carne 122, *123*
  Lemony green beans 102
  Seven-layer dip *82*, 83
Béchamel sauce 208
beef
  Chili con carne 122, *123*
  Lasagne al forno 136–8, *137*
  Meatloaf 121
  Polenta pasticciata 136
  Ragu Bolognese 117
  Vietnamese beef stew 124, *125*
beets, Braised 102
Blini with smoked salmon 76
blood tests 16
Blueberry muffins *61*, 63
bok choy, Noodles in hot ginger broth *34*, 142, *143*
Bolognese sauce *see* Ragu Bolognese
Braised beets 102
brands & manufacturers 37–9
bread
  Brown 164–6, *165*
  Crostini & toppings72–3

flours 43, 49
Focaccia *172*, 173
French-style 170–1
gluten-free mixes 43, 45, 49
Indian flat breads 35
Northern cornbread 176
pizza dough 179
Quick soda 167
Southern skillet cornbread *21*, 174, *175*
Spiced yogurt raisin bread 177
White farmhouse loaf 168–9
see also Croissants; Chocolate croissants
breakfasts 45, 47, 49, 52–67
Brown bread 164–6, *165*
brownies, Chocolate *17*, *191*, 193
bulgur wheat, Tabbouleh 91
buttercream, Chocolate 196
butternut squash, Leek & butternut squash soup 86, *87*

C

cabbage, Asian slaw 212
cakes 45, 46
  Carrot *101*, 203
  Chocolate brownies *17*, *191*, 193
  Chocolate layer 196–8, *197*
  Cupcakes *17*, *190*, 192
  Dark chocolate torte 200
  Fresh fruit & cream gâteau 204–6, *205*
  Gingerbread 187
  icing 196, 203
  Lemon syrup polenta 195
  Peach-topped cheesecake 201
  Rich fruit 199
  Rosemary syrup polenta 195
California hand-roll temaki sushi *34*, 74, *75*
calves' liver, Fegato alla Veneziana 116
Canadian Food Inspection Agency (CFIA) 38
Carrot cake *101*, 203
Cashew cream 216
celeriac, Duck with apples & celeriac 115
celiac disease 14, 20–1
  see also gluten
Chantilly topping 216, *217*
cheese 47, 48
  Moussaka 128, *129*
  Pizza Margherita *178*, 179
  Seven-layer dip *82*, 83
  see also cream cheese
cheesecake, Peach-topped 201
Cherry compôte *160*, 161
chestnuts
  Chestnut stuffing *113*, 214
  Sweet chestnut terrine 155
chicken
  Chicken drumsticks *78*, 79
  Chicken fajitas 77
  Chicken, olive, & chickpea stew 108
  Chicken pie 106, *107*
  Chicken roasted in olive oil *113*, 114

Lemon thyme grilled chicken 109
  Thai green chicken curry *19*, *110*, 111
chicken livers, Ragu Bolognese 117
chickpeas, Chicken, olive, & chickpea stew 108
children, food allergies 8, 16, 18, 19, 21, 26–8
Chili con carne 122, *123*
Chili dipping sauce 103
Chinese food 34
Chinese-style spare ribs 126
chocolate
  Chocolate brownies *17*, *191*, 193
  Chocolate buttercream icing 196
  Chocolate crinkle cookies *17*, 189, *191*
  Chocolate croissants *64*, 65–6
  Petits pots au chocolat *152-3*, 1
Chocolate croissants *64*, 65–6
Chocolate layer cake 196–8, *197*
  Chocolate truffles 207
  Dark chocolate torte 200
  Giant chocolate chip cookies 186 54
Cinnamon, raisin, & apple muffins *61*, 62
Classic shepherd's pie 130
classical food allergies 14–16
Coconut sorbet 159
compôte, Cherry *160*, 161
cookies 45
  Chocolate crinkle cookies *17*, 189, *191*
  Fruity oatmeal squares 188
  Giant chocolate chip cookies 186
  Raspberry marshmallow crispies 194
  Shortbread cookies 183
corn & cornmeal 43
  Grilled corn on the cob *78*, 79
  Noodles in hot ginger broth *34*, 142, *143*
  Northern cornbread 176
  Southern skillet cornbread *21*, 174, *175*
  Tortillas 68, *69*
  see also polenta
Corned beef hash 58
costs & prices 39
coulis, Raspberry 59
Couscous 33, *134*, 135
cream cheese 48
  Herb dip 71
  icing 203
  Peach-topped cheesecake 201
Crêpes 162, *163*
crinkle cookies, Chocolate *17*, 189, *191*
crispies, Raspberry marshmallow 194
Crispy squid *88*, 89
Croissants 54–5
  Chocolate croissants *64*, 65–6
cross contamination 29, 38, 39
cross reactivity 17–18, 19
Crostini & toppings 72–3
crumble, Plum crumble & variations 146, *147*

cucumber
   Cucumber & wakame salad 91
   Middle Eastern salad 92, *93*
   Raita 213
cupcakes, Vanilla *17, 190*, 192
curries *19, 110*, 111, 131
cytotoxic blood tests 16

D
dairy 9, 17, 19–20, 42
   pantry & substitutions 43, 46–7,
      47, 48
   worldwide cuisines 32, 33, 34, 35
Dark chocolate torte 200
desensitization 16
desserts 16, 47, 49, 146-63
diagnosis & tests 15–16, 17
dietary alert cards 31
dipping sauces 103, 210
dips 71, *82*, 83, 211
dressings 91, 209, 210, 212, 213
Duck with apples & celeriac 115
dumplings, Shrimp 103

E
eating out 29, 30, 32–5
eggplant
   Eggplant & mushroom crostini
      72
   Moussaka 128, *129*
eggs 9, 18, 42
   Bacon & onion quiche 84
   Kedgeree 67
   pantry & substitutions 43, *46*,
      46, 49
   worldwide cuisines 32, 33, 34, 35
emotions 22
epinephrine pen 15, 31
essential checklist 25
etiquette 24–5

F
fajitas, Chicken 77
farmhouse loaf, White 168–9
Fegato alla Veneziana 116
fennel, Roast pork with fennel 127
fish 18, 43
   California hand-roll temaki sushi *34*,
      74, *75*
   Fish pie 96, *97*
   Haddock & spinach pasta bake 139
   Kedgeree 67
   Marinated swordfish 99
   Miso marinated salmon *100*, 101
   Potato-crusted halibut 102
   Tandoori fish 98
   Tapenade 73
   Vitello tonnato 120
   see also seafood; smoked salmon
flours 43, 49
Focaccia *172*, 173

food additives 17–18
Food Allergen Labeling and Consumer
   Protection Act (FALCPA) 38
food allergies 14–17, 22–5
   anaphylaxis 15, 18, 19
   author's experiences 8, 10, 22–3, 30
   away from home 29–35
   children 8, 16, 18, 19, 21, 26–8
   classical ("true") 14–16
   cross reactivity 17–18, 19
   emotional & practical support 22–3, 31
   symptoms & reactions 15, 18, 19,
      20, 21
   see also specific allergens (eg, eggs);
      specific topics (eg, tests)
food challenges 16, 17
food histories & diaries 15, 16, 17
food intolerances 14, 17–18, 19-20, 21,
   24–5
food labeling 9, 38–9
food shopping 36–7
food substitutes 43, 48–9
Fragrant poached peaches 151
French food 35
French-style bread 170–1
Fresh fruit & cream gâteau 204–6, *205*
Fresh spring rolls 90
fruit cake, Rich 199
Fruity oatmeal squares 188

G
gâteau, Fresh fruit & cream 204–6, *205*
Gazpacho 85
Giant chocolate chip cookies 186
Gingerbread 187
gluten 9, 40
   celiac disease 14, 20–1
   pantry & substitutions 43, *44*,
      45, 49
   worldwide cuisines 32, 33,
      34, 35
granola, Honey 52, *53*
Gratin gallois 94
gravies 132, 215
Green tea ice cream 156, *157*
Gremolata 118
Grilled polenta 81
Guacamole 77

H
haddock *see* smoked haddock
halibut, Potato-crusted 102
hash, Corned beef hash & variations 58
Health Canada 38
Herb dip 71
   Herb dip with roasted peppers tortillas
      68
histamine 15, 18
Hoisin sauce 126
Honey granola 52, *53*
Honeyed Welsh lamb 132, *133*

I
ice creams 156, *157*, 158
icing 196, 203
idiopathic food intolerances 18
IgE (RAST) test 16
immune system responses 14–16
immunotherapy 16
Indian food 34–5
intolerances, food 14, 17–18, 19–20, 21,
   24-5
Italian food 32

J
Japanese food 33, 219

K
Kedgeree 67

L
labels, food 9, 38–9
lactose intolerance 19–20
   see also dairy
lamb
   Classic shepherd's pie 130
   Honeyed Welsh lamb 132, *133*
   Lamb tagine *33, 134*, 135
   Moussaka 128, *129*
   Spinach & yogurt lamb curry 131
Lasagne al forno 136–8, *137*
latex allergy 38
leeks
   Chicken pie 106, *107*
   Gratin gallois 94
   Leek & butternut squash soup 86, *87*
Lemon syrup polenta cake 195
Lemon thyme grilled chicken 109
Lemony green beans 102
lentils
   Kedgeree 67
   Scallops & shrimp with lentils *104*, 105
liver, Fegato alla Veneziana 116
lupin 38

M
maccha, Green tea ice cream 156, *157*
management plans 28
mango
   Apricot & mango smoothie *20*, 59, *60*
   Mango yogurt ice 158
manufacturers & brands 37–9
Marinated swordfish 99
Mayonnaise 210
   Roast garlic tofu aïoli 209
Meatloaf 121
MedicAlert® bracelet 15, 31
Melon, grape, & pear smoothie *20*, 59, *60*
Mexican food 32–3
Middle Eastern salad 92, *93*
milk allergy 19
   see also dairy
milks, dairy-free 20, 43, 46, 48

Miso marinated salmon *100*, 101
Mixed berry smoothie *20*, 59, *60*
mollusks 17, 38
Moussaka 128, *129*
Muffins *61*, 62–3
mushrooms
    Chicken pie 106, *107*
    Eggplant & mushroom crostini 72
    Noodles in hot ginger broth *34*, 142, *143*

N
Noodles in hot ginger broth *34*, 142, *143*
Northern cornbread 176
nuts 9, 16, 18-19, 40-1
    pantry & substitutions 43, 47,
      48
    worldwide cuisines 32, 33, 34, 35

O
oatmeal squares, Fruity 188
olives
    Chicken, olive, & chickpea stew 108
    Seven-layer dip *82*, 83
    Sun-dried tomato, olive & fresh basil
      focaccia 173
    Tapenade 73
onions
    Bacon & onion quiche 84
    Fegato alla Veneziana 116
    Rosemary & onion focaccia 173
Osso buco 118, *119*

P
packaged food 39
Pain au chocolat *see* Chocolate croissants
Pancakes *19, 56,* 57
Panna cotta *160,* 161
pantries *44,* 45–7, *46, 47*
pasta 32, 45, 46, 49
    Couscous *33, 134,* 135
    Haddock & spinach pasta bake 139
    Lasagne al forno 136–8, *137*
    Noodles in hot ginger broth *34*, 142,
      143
    pasta dough 138
    Pasta with arugula *140,* 141
    Ragu Bolognese 117
piecrust & piecrust dishes 45
    Apple tart *148,* 149
    Bacon & onion quiche 84
    Chicken pie 106, *107*
    Piecrust 180–2, *181*
    Sweet piecrust 180
    patch tests 16
Peach-topped cheesecake 201
peaches
    Fragrant poached peaches 151
    Fresh fruit & cream gâteau 204–6, *205*
peanuts 16, 18–19, 31, 34, 40, 41, 47, 48
pears, Melon, grape, & pear smoothie
    20, 59, *60*

peppers
    Chicken fajitas 77
    Chili con carne 122, *123*
    Herb dip with roasted peppers
      tortillas 68
    Pepper, zucchini, & sun-dried tomato
      crostini 73
    Red pepper dip 211
    Seven-layer dip *82*, 83
    Thai green chicken curry *19, 110,* 111
Pesto 211
Petits pots au chocolat *152–3,* 154
Piecrust 180–2, *181*
pies
    Chicken 106, *107*
    Classic shepherd's 130
    Fish 96, *97*
    Moussaka 128, *129*
pilaf, Basmati & wild rice 144
pine nuts (pine kernels) 10, 17, 43, 47, 48
pizza 32, 45, 49
    Pizza Margherita *178,* 179
plums
    Fragrant poached peaches variation 151
    Plum crumble 146, *147*
polenta
    Grilled polenta 81
    Lemon syrup polenta cake 195
    Polenta pasticciata 136
    see also corn & cornmeal
pork
    Chinese-style spare ribs 126
    Fresh spring rolls 90
    Meatloaf 121
    Roast pork with fennel 127
    Vitello tonnato variation 120
potatoes
    Classic shepherd's pie 130
    Corned beef hash 58
    Fish pie 96, *97*
    Gratin gallois 94
    Hash browns 58
    Potato-crusted halibut 102
    Red flannel hash 58
    Roast potatoes with garlic & sea salt
      95, *112*
prevention research 16
prices & costs 39
probiotics 16

Q
quiche, Bacon & onion 84
Quick soda bread 167
quinoa
    Saffron quinoa couscous 135
    Tabbouleh variation 91

R
Ragu Bolognese 117
    Lasagne al forno 136–8, *137*
    Polenta pasticciata 136

raisin bread, Spiced yogurt 177
Raisin scones 184, *185*
Raita 213
    Tandoori fish 98
Raspberry coulis 59
Raspberry marshmallow crispies 194
RAST (IgE) test 16
reactions & symptoms 15, 18, 19, 20,
    21, 28
recipe styles & adaptations 10–11, 18, 43,
    48–9
red flannel hash 58
Red pepper dip 211
rhubarb
    Rhubarb crumble 146
    Rhubarb sorbet 159
rice
    Basmati & wild rice pilaf 144
    California hand-roll temaki sushi *34,*
      74, *75*
    Kedgeree 67
    Rice pudding 150
    Risotto alla Milanese 145
Rich fruit cake 199
Risotto alla Milanese 145
roast chicken *113,* 114
Roast garlic tofu aïoli 209
Roast honeyed Welsh lamb 132, *133*
Roast pork with fennel 127
Roast potatoes with garlic & sea salt
    95, *112*
Rosemary & onion focaccia 173
Rosemary syrup polenta cake 195

S
Saffron quinoa couscous 135
salads
    Asian slaw 212
    Cucumber & wakame 91
    dressings 91, 209, 210, 212, 213
    Middle Eastern 92, *93*
    Tabbouleh 91
salmon, Miso marinated salmon
    100, 101
salsas 70, 99
sauces
    Béchamel 208
    Bolognese *see* Ragu Bolognese
    dipping 103, 210
    dressings 91, 209, 210, 212, 213
    gravies 132, 215
    Hoisin 126
    Pesto 211
    Ragu Bolognese 117
    Vanilla cream 155
sausages & sausage meat
    Chestnut stuffing *113,* 214
    Meatloaf 121
    Soy-honey glazed sausages
      80
scallion curls 103

scallops
  Kedgeree 67
  Scallops & shrimp with lentils
    104, 105
schools 26–8
scones, Raisin 184, *185*
seafood 17, 18
  Crispy squid *88*, 89
  see also fish; mollusks; shrimp;
    scallops
seaweed
  California hand-roll temaki sushi *34*,
    74, *75*
  Cucumber & wakame salad 91
seeds 9, 17, 43, 47, 48
sensitization 15
sesame seeds 9, 17, 43, 47, 48
Seven-layer dip *82*, 83
shepherd's pie, Classic 130
shopping, food 36–9
Shortbread 183
shrimp
  California hand-roll temaki sushi *34*,
    74, *75*
  Fish pie 96, *97*
  Fresh spring rolls 90
  Scallops & shrimp with lentils *104*,
    105
  Shrimp dumplings 103
skin prick tests 16, 17
smoked haddock
  Fish pie 96, *97*
  Haddock & spinach pasta bake 139
  Kedgeree 67
smoked salmon
  Blini with smoked salmon 76
  Smoked salmon with crème frâiche
    tortillas 68
Smoothies *20*, 59, *60*
soda bread, Quick 167
sorbets 159
soups *34*, 85–6, *87*, 142, *143*
Southeast Asian food 34
Southern skillet cornbread *21*, 174,
  175
Soy-honey glazed sausages 80
soy 9, 18, 43, 46, 48
spare ribs, Chinese-style 126
special occasions 30
Spiced yogurt raisin bread 177
spinach
  Haddock & spinach pasta bake 139
  Spinach & yogurt lamb curry 131
spring rolls, Fresh 90
squash, Leek & butternut squash soup
  86, *87*
squid, Crispy *88*, 89
stuffing, Chestnut *113*, 214
substitute foods 43, 48–9
Sun-dried tomato, olive & fresh basil
  focaccia 173

supermarkets 36, 39
sushi 33
  California hand-roll temaki sushi *34*,
    74, *75*
Sweet chestnut terrine 155
Sweet piecrust 180
swordfish, Marinated 99
symptoms & reactions 15, 18, 19, 20,
  21, 28

T
Tabbouleh 91
tagine, Lamb *33*, *134*, 135
Tandoori fish 98
Tapenade 73
Tarragon dressing 213
temaki sushi, California hand-roll temaki
  sushi *34*, 74, *75*
terrine, Sweet chestnut 155
tests & diagnosis 15–16, 17
Thai green chicken curry *19*, *110*, 111
tofu 43, 49
  Herb dip 71
  Kedgeree 67
  Roast garlic tofu aïoli 209
tofutti
  Herb dip 68
  Smoked salmon with crème frâiche
    tortillas 68
tomatoes
  Chicken fajitas 77
  Chili con carne 122, *123*
  Gazpacho 85
  Lasagne al forno 136–8, *137*
  Middle Eastern salad 92, *93*
  Osso buco 118, *119*
  Pepper, zucchini, & sun-dried tomato
    crostini 73
  Pizza Margherita *178*, 179
  Polenta pasticciata 136
  Ragu Bolognese 117
  Seven-layer dip *82*, 83
  Sun-dried tomato, olive & fresh basil
    focaccia 173
  Tomato & sweet basil crostini 72
torte, Dark chocolate 200
tortillas 32, 49
  Chicken fajitas 77
  Tortillas 68, *69*
  Tortilla chips 70
traveling 31–5
tree nuts *see* nuts
"true" (classical) food allergies 14–16
truffles, Chocolate 207
tuna, Vitello tonnato 120

U
US Food and Drug Administration
  (FDA) 38
V
Vanilla cream 155

Vanilla cupcakes *17*, *190*, 192
veal
  Osso buco 118, *119*
  Vitello tonnato 120
Vegetable gravy 215
Vietnamese beef stew 124, *125*
Vietnamese dipping sauce 210
Vitello tonnato 120

W
wakame, Cucumber & wakame salad 91
wheat allergies & intolerances 21
  see also gluten
White farmhouse loaf 168–9
wild rice, Basmati & wild rice pilaf 144

X
xanthan gum 43, 45, 49

Y
yogurt 46, 48
  Herb dip 71
  Mango yogurt ice 158
  Raita 213
  Spiced yogurt raisin bread 177

Z
zucchini, Pepper, zucchini, & sun-dried
  tomato crostini 73

Acknowledgments

To my family: allergic Archie, nonallergic Ben, and generally intolerant Guy, my mother Lily who is the reason I know how to cook, and my mother-in-law Mollie for taking the trouble to find things that Archie can eat. My thanks to Lucy for being the most intelligent and inquisitive cook I know, to Michelle and Tony for keeping the ship afloat, to the Prof for Italian accents and children's stories, and to the Kit Cat girls for a good time.

I'm grateful to Dr. Adam Fox for bringing his medical expertise to this book, to the allergy team at St. Mary's Hospital, to Westminster Community Children's Nursing Team, and to Mrs. Hampton and Connaught House School for taking such good care of Archie. I'd like to acknowledge the Anaphylaxis Campaign for their indefatigable work on behalf of people with serious allergies, and, of course, Allergy UK for their support for this book. My thanks also to Dr. Lesley Regan for introducing me to Maggie Pearlstine.

With much gratitude to Mary-Clare Jerram for commissioning this book, to Esther Ripley for editing it with calm and grace, to all the team at DK, in particular Penny Warren, Marianne Markham, Anne Fisher, Vicky Read, and Helen Murray, and to Carolyn Humphries, in appreciation of the knowledge and skills she has brought to bear on this project. Finally, a great deal of credit is due to the team who made the photographs and food in this book look so beautiful; my thanks to art director Luis Peral, photographer Kate Whitaker, prop stylist Chloe Brown, and food stylist Sarah Tildesley.

Alice Sherwood

Publisher's acknowledgments
DK Publishing would like to thank Carolyn Humphries for testing the recipes and giving invaluable advice; Chloe Brown for prop styling; Sue Bosanko for the index; Katie Hardwicke for proofreading; Angela Baynham and Zia Allaway for editorial assistance; and Jack Fisher and Stevie Hope for being our models (p.27).

Picture credits:
The publisher would like to thank the following for their kind permission to reproduce their photographs: Corbis: 28, and 15 (used on tint boxes throughout Chapter 1).